Performance By Design: Sociotechnical Systems in North America

The Prentice Hall Series on Human Resource Development

❧ ❧

R. WAYNE PACE, EDITOR

PACE, SMITH, AND MILLS *Human Resource Development: The Field*

OTTE AND HUTCHESON *Helping Employees Manage Careers*

MARQUARDT AND ENGEL *Global Human Resource Development*

Performance By Design: Sociotechnical Systems in North America

JAMES C. TAYLOR, PH.D.
DAVID F. FELTEN

PRENTICE HALL, Englewood Cliffs, New Jersey 07632

Library of Congress Cataloging-in-Publication Data

Taylor, James C.
    Performance by design : sociotechnical systems in North America /
by James C. Taylor and David F. Felten.
        p.   cm. -- (Prentice Hall series on human resource
development)
    Includes bibliographical references and index.
    ISBN 0-13-656497-6
    1. Organizational change--North America.   2. Organizational
behavior--North America.   3. Industrial management--North America.
4. Industrial sociology--North America.   I. Felten, David F.
. II. Title.   III. Series.
HD58.8.T39   1993
658--dc20   92-19141
                                                           CIP

Acquisition Editor: Alison Reeves
Production Editor: Lisa Kinne
Copy Editor: Brenda Melissaratos
Cover Designer: Karen Marsilio
Prepress Buyer: Trudy Pisciotti
Manufacturing Buyer: Patrice Fraccio
Editorial Assistant: Diane Peirano
Production Assistant: Renee Pelletier

 © 1993 by Prentice-Hall, Inc.
A Simon & Schuster Company
Englewood Cliffs, New Jersey 07632

Printed in the United States of America
10 9 8 7 6 5 4 3 2 1

ISBN 0-13-656497-6

Prentice-Hall International (UK) Limited, *London*
Prentice-Hall of Australia Pty. Limited, *Sydney*
Prentice-Hall Canada Inc., *Toronto*
Prentice-Hall Hispanoamericana, S.A., *Mexico*
Prentice-Hall of India Private Limited, *New Delhi*
Prentice-Hall of Japan, Inc., *Tokyo*
Simon & Schuster Asia Pte. Ltd., *Singapore*
Editora Prentice-Hall do Brasil, Ltda., *Rio de Janeiro*

To Albert Cherns . . .
Who taught but also learned.

Contents

About the Authors

James C. Taylor has served on the research staff of the University of Michigan and on the faculty of the University of California, Los Angeles. He is one of the founding members of UCLA's Center for the Quality of Working Life. Jim is currently Adjunct Professor at the University of Southern California's Institute of Safety and Systems Management, and divides his time between teaching, research and consulting. He has lectured widely in Great Britain, Italy, Scandinavia, India, Mexico, Canada, and the USA. His three previous books are *Technology and Planned Organizational Change, The Survey of Organizations* (with D.G. Bowers), and *Design of Jobs* (with L.E. Davis). Other publications include numerous articles on these and related topics.

David F. Felten has worked as a fulltime consultant for over fifteen years with major Fortune 500 companies. His expertise includes STS design and implementation, gainsharing and skill-based pay systems, member selection and development efforts, developing joint union/ management partnerships, teambuilding, and team skill development. Dave has authored a wide variety of developmental materials for STS design and redesign efforts throughout North America and Europe. He has established several North American "Networks" for organizational executives responsible for change. Prior to becoming a consultant, Dave served as Director of Human Resources Development for Clark Equipment Company and as Employee Relations Manager for the Westinghouse Electric Company.

Both Jim and Dave are founding members of **STS International**, an organization of sociotechnical systems design consultants. Their combined consulting experience covers the spectrum from basic manufacturing to high tech, from health care to government services. Projects have been completed in North America, Europe, and the Far East. Their STS work-design efforts have included such companies as Donnelly, The Travelers, Amoco, Masonite, Chevron, CPC International, Hoechst Celanese, Exxon and ABB Power.

Preface

This book is about successful organizational change — change through the use of a purposeful, product-oriented vision shared by all members. It stresses four pillars of sociotechnical methodology: systems, power, product, and purpose. It presents this view supported by many examples of its use in North American organizations since 1980. It was written to help manage the complexity of modern organizational change. As businesses cut layers and levels of management, it is essential that organizational redesign activities take into account the relationships between technology and people. Managing these relationships will lead to greater business effectiveness and competitive advantage.

The *systems* approach demands thinking in wholes and about dynamic interrelationships. Any organization can be considered a sociotechnical system (STS) if it is seen as a bounded, purposeful enterprise in a recognizable external environment that contains transformation (technical system) and people working together over time (social system). The scientific management model of F. W. Taylor, on the other hand, focuses only on management plans, tools/equipment, and worker tasks — it is at best fragmented and not holistic. The earlier factory models of Adam Smith and Charles Babbage focused only on the machinery itself.

The preindustrial "craftsman" model of an even earlier era can be described as focusing on the product of work (e.g., chinaware, knitted lace, or wooden kegs). Those products were largely simple enough to be held within the human scale of a single craftsman or the products were special enough (a cathedral, sailing ship, or a piece of fine jewelry) to be the product of a single brilliant craftsman or several in a guild. In our more complex age it is imperative to provide more of the craftsman's (or expert's) knowledge to the average worker, and information is the key. Sociotechnical systems understanding provides a way for people throughout today's systems to understand these work systems and their roles in them. Information is *power*, and people working together can access information better and faster than people operating alone. This allows the whole to become greater than the sum of its parts.

The sociotechnical system's methodological focus on the throughput, *product*, and purpose represents a significant departure from the earlier concepts and management methods. The application of "unit operations" as state changes in the production throughput, and of "technical variances" as deviations in that throughput during the "normal" process, are powerful tools in this methodology. Without the benefit of the sociotechnical systems paradigm, "what gets done" to a product often gets described, instead of "what happens" to it. This recognition of the technical system analysis as fundamentally different from earlier models was (and is) slow to come to many of the practitioners trying to apply STS. The concept of unit operation is central to technical system methodology. But without that focus on throughput, the "unit operation" term has been, and still often is, incorrectly applied to functional departments or to machines or to skill clusters, instead of to state changes in the throughput. Unit operations have often been mistakenly applied to steps in a manufacturing or industrial process where state change does not occur—the quality inspection step is a typical example of a function in which there is no change in throughput. Inspection merely assures that the throughput has been converted or transformed as intended!

Similarly, the central concept of technical variances is often misapplied. Without that focus on the system's mission or *purpose*, the term "variance" has been incorrectly associated with "problems" and, worse yet, with human activities gone awry or other calamities unrelated to normal variations in the throughput.

These kinds of misuses of the technical system methodology simply reinforce the unfortunate notion that STS is nothing more than industrial engineering dressed up in behavioral science trappings. As such, it is usually ineffective and set aside as simply elaborate and time-

consuming. Such fundamental misapplication of the concepts as originally conceived and presented reinforce how difficult it is for social
science to recognize a new paradigm, and how easy it is for people to
think that they see what others do when they don't. This inability to see
the underlying power of the technical system methodology has created
unnecessary debate about STS practice and confusion among those who
try to describe the underlying methodology. People trying to modify the
classical approach in the application of STS to complex knowledge work
have been stymied in their attempts, in part, because this confusion
between task and product focus has not been resolved. Most of the
writings on this topic continue to perpetuate the Scientific Management
focus on tasks and activities. Until the produce-*versus*-task debate has
been actively joined and resolved, new attempts to apply STS methodology for nonroutine systems will be unsuccessful because of confusion
and ambiguity with respect to the methodology.

We hope that in writing this book, and in clarifying the issues, that
significant progress can be made toward improving and enhancing the
effectiveness of North American organizations while improving the
satisfaction and dignity of their employees. In Europe and Australia STS
has reemerged as a subject of active interest, and it is moving ahead in
different but complimentary paths from those of North American organizations. In this book we will not be discussing the experience or
development of STS outside of North America, but the interested reader
can review these trends in the sample references listed at the end of this
preface (cf. Eijnatten, 1991; Emery & Emery, 1989; Gustavsen, 1989;
Neumann, 1991).

This volume (and sociotechnical systems practice in the larger
sense) has been aided substantially by the North American companies
and other organizations in which the methodology has been developed.
Those of us who have participated in the development and those who
benefit from it owe a deep debt of gratitude to those companies, their
management, employees, and trade unions.

At times in our careers the assistance of particular persons has been
of crucial importance to help us see a new concept, or help to develop a
practice, or to improve a method that we describe here. Our list—but
by no means an exhaustive one—must include Bob Asadorian, Albert
Cherns, Tom Christensen, Lou Davis, Rich van Horn, Bonnie Johnson,
and Brian Tucker.

In addition, many persons have provided us encouragement to
write this book and offered us support by reading sections of the manu-

script. Among those who provided us with such help and excellent suggestions include Allen Bishop, Tom Christensen, Rik Frost, Cindy Lee, Jay Romans, Josh Smith, and Bert Weller.

Wayne Pace, our series editor, provided continual encouragement and guidance, as well as sage advice and suggestions that have improved the manuscript immensely.

Our wives—to whom we owe much—Ellen Jo Baron offered significant and exceptional editorial suggestions on the entire manuscript, and Vickie Felten prepared the bibliography, rendered the manuscript into a document for our publisher, and performed other indispensable activities in getting this volume ready. Their assistance is truly appreciated.

Despite all this help we, of course, remain entirely responsible for mistakes or inaccuracies that may remain.

James C. Taylor, Pacific Palisades, California
David F. Felten, Burlington, North Carolina

REFERENCES

EIJNATTEN, F. M. VAN., *From Autonomous Work Group to Democratic Dialogue and Integral Organization Renewal: 40 Years of Development and Expansion of the Socio-Technical Systems Design Paradigm.* Eindhoven: University of Technology, Monograph BDK/T&A007, 1991.

EMERY, F. E., & M. EMERY., "Participative Design: Work and Community Life, Parts 1–3." In M. Emery (ed.), *Participative Design for Participative Democracy.* Canberra: Australian National University, Centre for Continuing Education, 1989.

GUSTAVSEN, B., *Creative Broad Change in Working, the LOM Programme.* Toronto: Ontario Quality of Working Life Center, 1989.

NEUMANN, J., "Sociotechnical Systems as Template: Dilemmas in Changing Organisations for 'High Performance' and 'Teamwork.'" *Tavistock Institute of Human Relations 1990 Review.* London: TIHR, 1991.

CHAPTER 1

ไ ไ

"What Are Sociotechnical Systems?"

INTRODUCTION: STS AS METHODOLOGY

The sociotechnical system (STS) is a philosophy and it is a method. As a philosophy it supports the value of empowerment as well as the systemic focus on product and customer. As a method STS helps provide custom solutions for performance by design. This combination of philosophy and method is methodology—an informed approach to organizational improvement.

ไ Organizations as STS

All organizations are sociotechnical systems. Every organization contains a technical subsystem to produce the core output and a social subsystem to coordinate activities among people to assure the flexibility and long-term survival of the enterprise. Some organizations are self-conscious, purposeful sociotechnical systems, as defined by their members—and they are successful. Other organizations have members with a systems consciousness who are trying to improve organizational performance by designing or redesigning their structure and processes to promote adaptive behavior in pursuit of purpose.

1

> **ANY ORGANIZATION IS A SOCIOTECHNICAL SYSTEM!**
>
> Despite that bold statement, any trucking firm, insurance office, government agency, peanut-butter factory, or chemical plant can be variously effective and successful. That success depends on whether the organization is an *appropriately designed* sociotechnical system. A chemical plant, for instance, can be comprised of all the "best pieces" of hardware, software, and "liveware," yet still not be effective because those pieces were not chosen, shaped, and designed to work together for a common and conscious purpose. Yet in a plant just like that, employee and management involvement with sociotechnical systems methodology produced "performance by design." A little later in this chapter that plant will be described in greater detail.

Other organizations ignore their systems characteristics and instead are seen by their employees as mechanistic or machine like. Those organizations that are successful with machine-style models of command and control typically are not required to be adaptive or flexible, and they survive only as long as their environments remain placid or reactive. There are also organizations, managed as machines, that are not successful and whose members do not understand why—this last type is in its last days unless its identity is changed and appropriate structures and processes are designed and implemented.

The Four Basic Principles of STS

- Organizations can be "purposive" (i.e., have the appearance of having purpose, but no one is sure what it is) or "purposeful" (i.e., have a purpose that is known to employees) and the latter is superior.
- Focus on system "product," or output, represents a radical and effective change from the historical (and still present) North American work design focus on activities or behaviors.
- North American managers and labor leaders recognize the chaos in their environments, and are beginning to understand that "tried and true" mechanistic organizational models are no longer appropriate.

- The best organizational design intentions are helpless in achieving their ends if people throughout the organization are disinterested in, or distracted from, participation in this essential task.

What STS Is Not, and Why

- It is not fixed, rigid, or standardized. STS begins with purpose, environment, product, and people. These things will be different for every system. STS does provide a structure to approach performance by design, but the steps in the process should be taken as guidelines rather than unyielding requirements.
- It is not a standard solution, such as "autonomous groups." This does not mean that teamwork is not important in STS—it is essential. Cooperation and coordination among people in the same system are indispensable replacements for internal competitiveness and independence, but the form of groups or teamwork is not fixed in advance.
- STS is not a problem-driven approach to organizational improvement. Although all organizations have problems, they are often difficult to define. Usually by the time problems are identified, they are yesterday's. Today's problems are far more difficult to articulate, and tomorrow's problems are unknowable. To design for purpose, on the other hand, looks to operating in a "normal" not problematic mode, and in doing so typically eliminates the source of many problems and reduces the effects of most others. The system then has time to cope with the problems that do occur.
- It does not pursue *the* standard goal of "quality of working life." STS is a way of improving organizational effectiveness through involving the best that people have to offer—their creativity and their ability to communicate.
- STS does not take the standard focus of "job design." Although it will provide people with different jobs, STS is intended to provide different work systems where the product is delivered more effectively. When an appropriate *work system* is designed, many jobs will carry joint responsibilities, overlapping skills, and close coordination in order to deliver the product they share.
- STS does not embrace the standard scope confined to one group or department at the margin of the enterprise. It addresses the issues of a "whole system," and is underused when applied to one work unit or "corner of the shop." Defining system boundaries, however, is a human choice, and what constitutes a whole system varies from one STS application to another. For instance, the maintenance department in a particular oil refinery is often a poor choice to conduct an STS design, but in another company the financial department might be very appropriate as the target for change.
- It does not require the standard guidance of a "Socio-tech specialist." STS can be, and has been, guided by internal consultants; and redesign for continuous improvement is carried out by system members (workers and managers together) given adequate knowledge and advice from others with STS experience. The experienced STS consultant's role in design is to

guide people in the STS analysis to design their system for purpose and performance.

- STS does not define the standard technical system as mere artifacts such as furniture, buildings, or machines. The definition of "technical system" used in this book is based on the stages and phases of the product (or "it") as it passes through the purposeful, productive system.

- The STS approach does not define the standard technical variance matrix as mere inventory of the present. This powerful tool will be defined, in this book, as a methodology to understand and guide the performance of complex knowledge systems where many important issues cannot be predicted, and to help to frequently update and improve ongoing systems.

⅋ *The Process of STS*

Sociotechnical systems understanding of any particular enterprise comes from applying a series of steps in which various systems aspects of the organization are examined. These steps are illustrated in Figure 1.1, which provides a "roadmap" of the STS process from the discovery step through the implementation of the new work system.

There are seven major steps in four phases to achieve a successful sociotechnical system. The four phases are delimited in Figure 1.1 by dashed horizontal lines between them, and the seven steps are shown as shaded boxes. Within each step, the most important means of accomplishment are listed. The *discovery* phase is also the first step; it is followed by the second phase of systems "understanding." This understanding is accomplished through the second, third, and fourth steps of *system scan, technical analysis,* and *social analysis,* respectively. The third phase accomplishes system design through the fifth and sixth steps of *joint optimization* and *provisional design.* The fourth phase, and seventh step, is *implementation* of the design, which returns again to the beginning of the process.

The "discovery" of the first phase is the *recognition of the sociotechnical systems paradigm.* That realization comes via appreciation of this unique and powerful means provided by the focus on customer/product/purpose, combined with a holistic systems view and the joint optimization of social and technical subsystems within it. This STS viewpoint avoids the scientific management fallacy of assuming that a focus on subdividing and simplifying work make it "idiot-proof" (Alic, 1990). These conceptual differences are not trivial.

How does "discovery" take place? For some people the STS paradigm is presented to them in a college or university course, a management training program, or a professional or trade association workshop

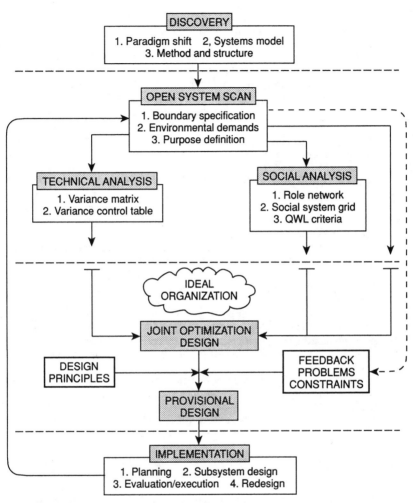

FIGURE 1.1
The Process of STS

or presentation. For others, the paradigm is recognized and understood through discussion with others who have experienced STS organizational changes firsthand, or by way of a tour through one of the STS-designed plants or offices that welcome visitors. The STS paradigm, the "discovery" step, and an example of how STS has been applied in a typical case are described more fully later in this chapter.

Why Is STS of Interest?

1. *Effective performance.* Where STS has been used in North America to design for purpose it has improved relevant performance an average of 15% and the distribution is skewed to the higher side (Pasmore et al., 1982)

2. *National interests in global economy.* Industries in the United States, Canada, and Mexico must learn to succeed "their way" in the international marketplace. To do so requires understanding how to work together so that we can compete abroad. It does not mean searching for models in other cultures and countries.

3. *Chaotic environments.* As originally conceived (Ackoff & Emery, 1972; Emery & Trist, 1965) a turbulent environment was said to include both complexity and dynamic characteristics. A variety of factors make an environment dynamic—unpredictable shifts in economy, unexpected changes in customer demand or competitor supply, rapid changes in technologies, in government support, or in labor markets. The element of complexity is varied, containing information from a multitude of sources and of varying degrees of randomness. However, most people *in* organizations recognize or experience only a limited degree of such turbulence. As a consequence we have rarely applied STS in response to turbulence.

   Since Emery and Trist's 1965 milestone article the world has moved one more step. The notion of "chaos" has added another dimension to turbulence—that of the importance of initial conditions to the form of final results (the so-called butterfly effect, Gleick, 1987), and of our inability to predict these nonrandom events. Ironically, this added uncertainty of chaos has caused people in organizations to recognize and appreciate their environments.

   This chaotic world makes understanding our organizations and institutions more important than ever. The shift away from machinelike bureaucracies toward self-organizing systems requires shifts in our "thought worlds." The ability to understand and anticipate these shifts greatly increases our ability to respond. However, during the past 80 years of scientific management, a strong set of patterns or trends has developed about how we view organizational life. These patterns or sets of rules have served us well in a fairly stable environment but can blind us from alternatives required to survive in today's global world. By better understanding the way these patterns or trends have shifted, we can better anticipate the future.

4. *Flexible organizational response to chaos* is a major reason to consider STS methodology. In international competition, a flexible organizational response is greatly enhanced by organizational understanding of flexible industry or institutional response. If we see our system as part of a regional or national effort to compete, then the elements in performance by design are different than if each organization sees itself as a closed system.

5. *Putting complex systems into human scale.* Participation in learning to understand (analysis), discovering what to change (design), and in organizing to succeed (implementation) is *empowerment*. Anything less is not likely to be as effective.

STS is important in part because it provides a structure and a purpose around which to exercise power and control at the workplace. With STS, all members (managers, support professionals, and workers alike) share a common language of work—a language based on changes in their primary product or output of the enterprise. This common language makes participation possible and rational—everybody is focused on the same product and customer. With STS, shifting power and widespread control make more sense and tie directly to participation and system success.

6. *Empowered work force.* STS is first of all understanding our work world in a new way. Being able to use this understanding to "wrap our minds around" the whole work system enables, or empowers, us to make changes to the work system consistent with that new understanding.

FOUR KEYS TO EMPOWERMENT:

Information, Knowledge, Skills, and Control.
These build on one another.
Stress is greatest when information is high, but control is low.

THE ROLE OF EMPOWERMENT

A Definition of Empowerment. The exercise of joint responsibility by both management and nonmanagement people (Pace et al., 1991). This joint responsibility requires all members to be both leaders and followers in order to shift between these roles. The power to lead others is based on skill, knowledge, and experience for the matter at hand. Power transfers from one person to another as the situation changes. Having control in any given circumstance can refer to influence over objects, or over people, and it can be held by many or by few. In empowered organizations, control shifts from the control by the hierarchy to control of the product by all.

Successful Empowerment. Empowerment that clearly leads to achievement in organizational performance and in quality of working life—requires that three conditions be met:

First, that power at the workplace be vested in the persons doing the job. In short-term tasks dealing with the core technology or with the main product of the enterprise, these are the workers. In longer term tasks and strategic matters, these are managers. In support functions, these are the skilled craftspeople or professionals responsible for required internal services. In all three cases, these people must be assured that the power for decision-making is theirs and that the others in the organization are supportive and interested in assessing the eventual outcome effect of those decisions.

Second, empowerment requires putting complex systems into human scale. In other words, creating an understanding of the work world in a way that all members of the organization can grasp. Being able to "wrap their minds around" the whole work system enables, or further empowers, people in organizations to make changes to the work system consistent with that new understanding.

Third, empowerment requires participation among all members in learning to understand (action research or study), discovering what to change (design), and in organizing to succeed (implementation). This is empowerment. Anything less is not likely to be as effective.

Power, Control, and Influence

"Employee Empowerment" may be a misnomer if we focus only on the nonmanagement members of the organization as the empowered employees. Taken this way empowerment sounds like something employees do if we give it to them, or we invite them to, or if the rules are somehow relaxed. Empowerment is none of these things—it requires a fundamental change in management assumptions and management actions, as well as a change in responsibility taken by nonmanagement employees.

In actuality, empowerment is the exercise of joint responsibility by both management and nonmanagement people. On one side, management grants to employee groups powers that they have never had. This may be the control over short-term decision making: to spend money to satisfy a customer, to stop a machine and correct a run-out, or to call a meeting to discuss a member's behavior. This power may also be the authority to decide their own employee benefits, or to earn as much as they can—commensurate with their contribution to the gains or profits of the enterprise. Finally, this power may involve participation in long-term investment decisions: the design of a new plant or office in which they will work as members, or the decision to create or deliver a new product or service.

On the other side, employees accept authority to make decisions related to their work, as it is directed toward a shared vision of the purpose of the enterprise. This joint responsibility requires all members to be both leaders and followers in order to shift between these roles. But why complicate things by talking about shifting between roles? Because empowerment is an exercise in leadership—which is both leading and being led. This requires more people being involved in both.

Empowerment culture lies on a scale of intensity from totally traditional to totally empowered. Finding real organizations at either extreme of that scale is unlikely. Most North American companies fall somewhere in the middle.

EMPOWERMENT CULTURE IS A CONTINUUM:

"Totally Traditional"‡———‡———‡"Totally Empowered"

In companies on the more traditional side of this middle range, the version of "empowered" behavior may take on the appearance of a reaction to an event that is rare or unimportant. In such a setting, the counterculture is allowed to believe: "It is better to explain later for a decision made at the right time than to seek approval for it in advance." This allowance is based on the assumption that opportunities for empowered decisions are unlikely and that decisions can usually (and should be) made by management. Management doesn't want to know that members are making decisions without checking first. If employees do and it doesn't work out, "There'll be a lot of explaining to do!" If, on the other hand, an important opportunity is seized and the decision is a success, then management will beam happily—if they hear about it. Employees in more traditional organizations have been acting in a counterculture for many years. They often take the appropriate and effective action rather than follow the rules to get the job done. This behavior can be recognized at times of labor relations discord as a kind of passive aggression in which employees withdraw their appropriate behavior, and "work by the book," or show a "malicious obedience" to rules irrespective of the consequence.

In companies where the culture has truly shifted toward empowerment, a proactive stance is taken. Unanticipated events are expected at any time. In this setting, empowered members are encouraged to make decisions when the time is right and to meet with others as soon as possible thereafter to discuss the implications. What happens is that managers and workers alike soon discover that opportunities to make "powerful" decisions are more numerous than they had thought. Their workdays are filled with assessing opportunities to improve performance, making decisions and implementing them, evaluating the results in the short term and long term as well, and rewarding and supporting themselves for the success achieved. Nonmanagement employees exercise this power primarily at the production floor, transaction center, or customer interface to maintain and improve the delivery of product or service. Managers exercise this power primarily at the executive suite to assure that the continually enhanced product continues to find a ready market, that appropriate technology is available to assure cost-effective and high-quality deliverables, and that the overall purpose of the enterprise remains in focus. In other words, management gets out of the way so that subordinates can be responsible for the output. This frees up management to assure that the product is "right" for the company's overall purpose, and "right" in the longer-term context of economy, technology, marketplace, and political environment.

For both management and workers, control shifts from the control of people to the control of product. Workers and managers are both leaders and led within their own level, depending on the task to be done. There is also ample cross-over between the levels. When workers enter decisions about longer-term aspects of the product, or are involved in deciding about the larger context, they cross over into the management arena. Conversely, when managers join subordinates in decisions about the product or production process itself, they too cross over. This should be commonplace in the empowered organization because the boundaries between short or long term, and small or large context, are necessarily blurred.

❧ *Empowerment and Understanding*

Empowerment, or delegating the responsibility, the power, and the control to employees and encouraging them to make decisions, demands that they understand the subject of those decisions. This understanding must *extend beyond* those subjects to their larger context as well. This delegation *is* empowerment, and it is only as effective as the quality and extent of *shared understanding* among all members of the organization. The challenge for organizations in the 1990s is to exploit new knowledge and information from the many new occupational specialties and technologies, and to share an understanding of their common base among employees throughout the system. We call this an understanding and control of product. It obviously requires a clear identification of customers as well. Often internal relationships and dependencies are crucial to understanding the final customer, and these people or roles or departments, which are dependent upon a system's output, are sometimes called "internal customers." As we will develop in Chapter 2, the notion of internal customers is not as appropriate in sociotechnical systems as is the concept of "partners" in serving the "real customers."

In fact, in service systems it is not enough to identify one's customers. Customers should be prioritized, and the most important ones for the business are provided even better service than the rest. A motto for such a system becomes "Satisfy all customers, and delight the key ones."

Sociotechnical systems understanding provides the detail *and* the "big picture" across functional, hierarchical, and occupational specialties. STS provides a way that all members of an organization can wrap their minds (and their hearts and souls too) around the enterprise. They can understand where it's going, why it's that way, and what the importance of *their* role in the enterprise is. STS not only meets the challenge of exploiting new information and knowledge, but it provides a way of focusing it for flexibility and rapid adaptation. STS is a structured, teachable, and participative method for designing organizations for their purpose and product. It provides a method for attaining meaningful and successful empowerment. Without information, knowledge, and skill, understanding how to control and decide is impossible.

❧ *Empowerment and Participation*

The value of participation has been established for decades. In the earliest studies in participation, it was shown as a technique to help management implement a decision they had already made (Coch & French, 1948). Since then, STS has become a method to be used with employees and managers alike to understand their own work system in a new way, and then to redesign its structure, its jobs and work design, its technology, and sometimes its physical space (Taylor, 1986).

STS thus provides a focus for participation in the major decisions as well as in their implementation. This differs from management fads such as "job enrichment" or "quality circles" or "management by objectives," which provide a clearly structured solution for implementation. Involving nonmanagement employees in fad programs asks them to implement the solution, but does not invite them to question the need for it to begin with or to decide on the response to that need. Such participation is often seen by managers as risky. The closer an organization is to the traditional end of the empowerment continuum, the riskier such employee participation becomes. The real benefit of participation is the effect of synergy upon the quality of the output. Mature teams that effectively deal with their differing views are far more competent than newly formed teams, or individuals. None of us is brighter or more intelligent than "all of us" are.

STS requires management (and, where it involves them, trade union leaders as well) to deal with this risk. Participation is a necessary risk if we wish to develop the kind of understanding required for employees to truly "wrap their hearts and souls and minds around" the purpose of the enterprise and their role in it.

WHY IT'S SO DIFFICULT—SCIENTIFIC MANAGEMENT AND ITS PARADIGMS

Earlier in this chapter, the four phases of the STS process were introduced. The first phase, called "discovery," was described as the recognition and appreciation of purposeful systems, and of the joint optimization of social and technical subsystems within the whole. The discovery phase provides a summary contrast between the machine view of organizations, which we associate with the scientific management approach to organization design, and the purposeful system view which is the subject of this book.

1. *The Purpose/Product Paradigm Shift.* It seems ridiculously simple that a focus on the control of "product" of work *instead* of the control of activities or actions of people at work is an important shift in thought worlds, but it is. This shift has proved difficult for managers, engineers, and social scientists because work organizations and people in them are so firmly grounded in what is being replaced. It still seems more comfortable to describe our work lives as action—what we "do"—and not as "product," or what results from that action.

2. *Chaos Thinking, and the Scientific Paradigm.* Since 1980, chaos thinking in physics (Gleick, 1987) has continued to cut away at the positivist linear and deterministic tenets of Newton's physics. This "paradigm shift" in scientific thinking continues the challenge by Einstein's "relativity" and Heisenberg's "uncertainty" to scientific thought (Kuhn, 1970). Engineering advances in biotechnology and computers have further strengthened the connection between chaos and adaptive systems response in turbulent environments—enabling us to consider, as the "real world," systems that

are not random, but not predictable, that never quite find a steady state (systems that almost repeat themselves but never quite succeed).

3. *Organizational Paradigms.* The lists in Table 1.1 describe the shift from the machine model to the systems model of organization.

TABLE 1.1

"Discovery": The Paradigm Shift from Machine
Thinking to Systems Thinking

The Changing Organization	
From:	*To:*
Purposive	Purposeful
Focus on tasks	Focus on product
Quantity	Quality
Closed	Open
Tall—many levels	Flat—few levels
Short term	Focused balance
The Changing Role of Management	
From:	*To:*
Risk taking avoided	Innovation encouraged
Directive	Participative
Control of people	Enabling control of product
Inform if need to know	Inform if want to know
Commitment to boss	Commitment to purpose
Competitive	Collaborative
The Changing Role of Unions	
From:	*To:*
Protecting	Empowering
Opposition	Active involvement
Resistance	Innovation
Reactive	Proactive
Separation	Partnership
What's in it for us	What's best for the whole
Adversarial	Collaborative
The Changing Role of Employees	
From:	*To:*
Dependent	Empowered
Passive	Assertive
Childlike	Mature
Cynical	Optimistic
Competitive	Cooperative
Distrustful	Trusting
Ignorant	Informed
Unskilled	Skilled
Assumed lazy	Motivated

4. *Union/Management Paradigms.* Whenever there are unions present, their active and visible involvement is essential from the beginning. That requires both management and union leadership to explore their paradigms and, through open discussion, build together their shared and common understanding of what is required to build a "true partnership."

"Discovering" and Applying the STS Approach: A Case Illustration

The following case illustrates the first step, "discovery," and briefly addresses the following three phases of the sociotechnical process. These steps and phases were introduced in Figure 1.1, which provides a "roadmap" of the STS process from the discovery step of the paradigm through the implementation of the new work system. The reader is encouraged to refer to Figure 1.1 while reviewing this case.

❦ *The Setting for Redesign*

A chemical plant in the midwestern United States was considering redesign after only a year of operation (Taylor & Christensen, 1990). Although it had set out to use innovative design elements from the beginning, many, if not most, of its 240 members were frustrated with the progress they had made toward their ideal. It was clear that the plant's design had been assembled from the best elements and ideas of other plant designs, but without a systematic regard for the whole. The "state-of-the-art" technical system and physical plant had been designed by a contractor specializing in that type of plant. The plant's social system had been copied from elements of several organizations the original start-up team had seen during visits to other companies.

Phase 1: "Discovering" and Deciding (September–March). The plant manager, new to the site that summer, had attended a public STS workshop where he "discovered" that it was possible to realize the STS paradigm in his plant. The plant manager reasoned that it wasn't enough for *him* to be convinced that STS would turn the plant into a satisfying and effective place, but he would need those above and below him to share his enthusiasm.

Over the course of three months, successive groups of employees (eventually the entire plant's work force) attended an STS workshop, based on the recommendations of the previous attendees. The plant manager's boss and his boss' boss, as well as several staff managers from corporate headquarters, also attended the workshops.

Phase 2: Getting Organized (April–August). A management STS steering committee was formed to undertake the initial systems scan, to seek volunteers from throughout the plant to staff a temporary STS design team, and to support and encourage the active involvement of all employees in a new design. Once that STS team was formed, it also conducted a systems scan and the two groups discussed and combined their joint findings.

The design team, with steering committee support, continued the STS process as portrayed in Figure 1.1. The team publicized their work and met often with the other plant members to review the results. The second and third steps of Phase 2, technical system and social system understanding, were completed over the following four months and were summarized for wider distribution in the company. By August the STS team was ready to generate a new design for the plant.

Phase 3: Designing the System (September–November). After completion of its analysis, the analysis/design team produced their "ideal design," using a process which required both individual creativity and group synergy. The design team then tested their emerging design for how well it provided for a "joint optimum" involving the people and the technical process. They did this by testing how well the new design would control key technical variances and achieve production objectives, how well it would cause or enable necessary cooperation and coordination among people, and how well it would provide important qualities of working life for its members. Certain features of the new plant design were changed to accommodate for their understanding of the plant as a sociotechnical system, and in response to comments and reactions the team received from co-workers and members of corporate staff. In doing this, the design team also assured itself that they had designed for the purpose of the plant and for the performance they desired, and (not unimportantly) that the new design was practical, realistic, and efficient.

Phase 4 and Beyond: Implementing the Design and Operating in the New System. During the following year, the plant continued operation under the old design while some 18 task forces (or "tiger teams") that eventually included everyone in the plant, planned, confirmed, and implemented the elements of the new design. Although the process was energizing, it was not always smooth and many old ideas and strong egos required adjustment.

As these kinds of projects go, the overall process went quickly. Eighteen months later the plant was able to announce that dramatic performance improvements and cost reductions were directly attributable to their sociotechnical system design (Taylor & Christensen, 1991).

CONCLUSION

This chapter has only introduced you to sociotechnical systems as a method and philosophy. It requires a commitment to designing organizations using what can be known about the purposes, contexts, technical processes, and social interactions of the work system. Applying sociotechnical systems also requires those using it to appreciate their work world in a new way—to realize a paradigm shift from the old machine models, the deterministic and positivist tenets of physical science, to the adaptive, fluid, living models of biology, general systems and chaos thinking. Sociotechnical systems require the participation of system members and in that involvement provides both the content of, and the reasons for, empowerment.

To succeed using STS, it takes commitment and support to actively and visibly get involved, to explore, to let go and lend real support, to enable and encourage growth and development. STS also requires faith in the process—a basic belief in the underlying principles and trust that the transition to the new system can be survived.

REFERENCES

ACKOFF, R. L., & F. E. EMERY. *On Purposeful Systems.* Chicago:Aldine-Atherton, 1972.

ALIC, J. A. "Who Designs Work?" *Technology in Society,* 12, 1990, 301–317.

COCH, L., & J. R. P. FRENCH, JR. "Overcoming Resistance to Change." *Human Relations,* 1, 1948, 512–532.

EMERY, F., & E. TRIST. "The Causal Texture of Organizational Environments." *Human Relations,* 18, 1965, 21–31.

GLEICK, J. *Chaos: Making a New Science.* New York: Viking, 1987.

KUHN, T. S. *The Structure of Scientific Revolutions.* Chicago: University of Chicago Press, 1970. (Originally published 1962).

PACE, R. W., P. C. SMITH, & G. E. MILLS. *Human resource development.* Englewood Cliffs, NJ: Prentice Hall, 1991.

PASMORE, W., C. FRANCIS, J. HALDMAN, & A. SHANI. "Sociotechnical Systems: A North American Reflection on Empirical Studies of the Seventies." *Human Relations*, 35, 1982, 1179–1204.

TAYLOR, J. C. "Long-Term Sociotechnical Change in a Computer Operations Department. *Journal of Applied Behavioral Science*, 22(3), 1986, 303–313.

TAYLOR, J. C., & T. D. CHRISTENSEN. "Employee Guided Design and Implementation in a Chemical Plant." In H. L. Meadow & M. J. Sirgy (eds.), *Proceedings of the Quality of Life/Marketing Conference*. Blacksburg: Virginia Polytechnic Institute & State University, 1990, 540–547.

TAYLOR, J. C., & T. D. CHRISTENSEN. *A High Involvement Redesign*. South Bend, IN: STS Publishing, 1991.

CHAPTER 2

ॐ ॐ

How Did We Get Here? Twenty-five Years of Sociotechnical Systems in North America

INTRODUCTION: NORTH AMERICAN INSTITUTIONS AND STS

This chapter illustrates major North American efforts (U.S., Mexican, and Canadian) in STS organization improvement. These illustrations provide a baseline for comparison with experiences elsewhere in the world.

The historical overview of STS in North America, 1967–92, is organized as follows:

1. Industrial practice in STS
2. Government and private foundation support for STS
3. The academic basis of STS theory and practice in North America
4. Private practitioners and STS

ॐ Industrial Practice of STS

Some of the earliest interest in STS in North America started with the 1968 design project at the Aluminum Company of Canada's (Alcan) continuous process ingot casting facility in Arvida, Quebec. Alcan co-sponsored the first UCLA "STS short course" in 1968. The company

18

subsequently used STS in several redesign efforts in Quebec and British Columbia. Although most of the projects were continuous process operations, several dealt with equipment repair and materials handling.

The other North American pioneer in STS was Proctor & Gamble (P&G). Its experience was very directed and very constant. "Open systems planning" (OSP) was used to train managers and engineers in systems concepts and to help them design new continuous process consumer products plants. This sequence was repeated many times between 1968 and 1980. The company has historically treated its OSP/STS strategy as proprietary and used it as a competitive advantage. For this reason, the company has been apparently unwilling to publish the results of its efforts.

In 1980, after a dozen years of being removed from public view, P&G began sending participants to public STS workshops. About this same time, other P&G employees, some of them STS consultants and trainers, left the employment during a period of organizational downsizing. Sparse but consistent data from these sources and others suggested that P&G was changing its strategy from building new STS plants to redesigning existing plants using what had been learned over the preceding dozen years. A current P&G practitioner has published a useful review of systems methodologies that provides some added insight into P&G use of OSP and STS (Hanna, 1988).

General Foods (GF) had an early success in new plant design with the 1971 continuous process pet food plant in Topeka, Kansas. Unfortunately, the actions of the parent company suggested uncertainty in dealing with a plant that was profitable and had high morale but that also required a different style of work organization (Ketchum, 1982). For 17 years the plant continued to best its older conventional sister plant and to perpetuate itself as different in the GF family. Some managers were unwilling to transfer there because they feared it could mean the end of their careers. After the first two plant managers had left the company, few in management could articulate the reason for the design or why it worked. It was seen by some in the company as a "failure," despite its high performance on all counts. It was apparently too alien for a conservative culture in the company. In 1986 the GF grapevine said that the plant had been closed, but this was actually a year before it was purchased (operating as a robust producer) by Quaker Oats. The plant's planners looked like they knew what to do if the experiment had failed, but not so clear about what to do if it succeeded. GF has recently returned to STS ideas to design new plants in Texas and

Iowa. The present corporate strategy for diffusion of STS-based results is unknown.

Other continuous process industries in North America have been prolific in their application of STS. These include papermaking, glass-making, chemicals (e.g., Davis & Sullivan, 1980), and petroleum refining. In addition to P&G and GF, woodpulping and food processing have also been popular targets for other companies' applications of STS methods.

Applying STS in the public sector requires added attention to the support of upper and middle management. Government organizations have attempted STS interventions since early in the 1970s. The Social Security Administration, the Immigration and Naturalization Service, and the Federal Aviation Administration all engaged the UCLA Center for Quality of Working Life (CQWL) during that time. In the 1980s, the U.S. Army and the Internal Revenue Service (IRS) mounted STS projects with Case Western, Harvard, and UCLA. These projects all foundered in implementation after successful analysis activities. They illustrate how STS analysis and employee participation alone are not enough, and how the vested interests of the bureaucratic establishment must be closely involved.

Beginning in the mid-1970s the Canadian federal government voiced an interest in QWL. Several successful projects within Labour Canada (the Canadian Department of Labor) were reported at that time. Renewed interest at Labour Canada surfaced again in the late 1980s (Kolodny, 1987). The middle and upper management of that agency were (and are) committed to the values of STS for the Canadian work force as well as for their own organization. As a result, their redesign activities have added energy to succeed.

General Motors (GM) began a commitment to STS in design of new plants shortly before the oil crisis of 1973. They had learned much from the Swedish Volvo and SAAB experiences and were willing to begin experimenting. The severe restrictions of the oil crisis slowed but did not stop STS application. GM began to forge a cooperative agreement between themselves and the United Auto Workers (UAW) union to improve quality of working life. GM's first use of STS in design of plants began with visionary general managers at Packard Electric and Delco Remy divisions. Several small STS-based plants that manufactured batteries, wiring harnesses, and alternators were opened in the middle 1970s. Several other GM component divisions followed with new plants and redesigns. In 1980 Buick and Oldsmobile began the first joint

UAW/GM STS plant designs with Factory 81 and the Delta Engine plant. The Buick 3800 engine plant and a Pontiac engine plant followed. These early plants were quite successful and were strongly supported by the shop floor and local unions. Some STS principles have become a part of most new plant designs and redesigns at GM. Support for STS came from the more progressive divisions and plant managers. The Saturn Project was a hybrid STS/Toyota Production System approach with much attention paid to designing technology, organization, and people factors simultaneously for best fit. Toyota Production System principles currently appear to be dominant at GM. When GM began its interest in STS in 1973, Ford Motor Company seemed to be suspicious of any new management ideas. By 1980, however, Ford had changed remarkably. Ford managers, workers, and staff specialists attended the 1981 Toronto STS/QWL conference in large numbers. Soon after, they undertook the STS redesign of an aging plant in California and slightly later began the new design of several plants in Mexico. These were not experiments to be evaluated in terms of success or failure. These Ford plants were learning experiences, often in collaboration with the UAW, in an overall strategy guided by the new CEO, Donald Petersen. By the early 1980s Petersen had a high and visible commitment to increased employee involvement and to high product quality. If changing management values and organizational structure were required to get there, Ford would do it. Ford has continued to develop its redesign approach to pursue these goals. At this point it is difficult to know what sort of STS thinking or method has spread throughout the company. Enterprises like Ford and GM are immense; 10 or 20 years may not be enough time to diffuse new management thinking. Both companies have progressed, but the difference between them seems to be GM's interest in experiment versus Ford's "just do it."

STS is extending more rapidly now. Part of the credit must be given to annual meetings like the "Ecology of Work" conferences where employees and managers who have lived with changes to new forms of work organizations tell their story to an audience of others with similar experiences or who are preparing to change their own systems.

Another vehicle for diffusion of STS in industry has been the several managers' networks that have emerged over the past 15 years. The original network was the creation of Lyman Ketchum, the first manager of the GF Topeka plant. He began a network for managers involved in or embarking on STS organization shortly after leaving GF around 1975. For nearly a decade his networks were sufficient for the North

American interest in such matters. In the early 1980s the Texas Tech networks added to the capacity and have continued to flourish. Other fully subscribed STS networks founded by the Work in America Institute and TSO, Incorporated, in 1988 further demonstrate the appeal of this forum for managers preparing for organizational change.

The "new" steel industry in the United States has relied on STS ideas for design guidance. Inland Steel employed STS principles in its new joint venture with Nippon Steel. In 1988 LTV steel began to build a joint labor-management system with the United Steelworkers Union and to redesign plants. They, too, rely on STS thinking and analysis methods. Smaller steel operations have also applied the STS approach to the design of new systems in the Midwest and Far West.

Several high-tech electronics companies have also applied STS thinking in the design or redesign of manufacturing plants (Taylor & Asadorian, 1985). Digital Equipment Company (DEC), Tektronix, and Zilog (a subsidiary of Exxon) have all successfully designed new electronics and manufacturing plants since 1980. Hewlett Packard has recently undertaken a serious redesign effort in several of its mature manufacturing plants.

Health-care organizations have long been interested in STS applications. Chisholm and Ziegenfuss (1986) reviewed the body of knowledge in this area and found little consistent application across sites.

STS Practice in Nonroutine Work Settings. The first application of STS to engineering work began about 1982 (Taylor, Gustavson & Carter, 1986). Interest in STS for professional work increased in the late 1980's. Professional work is knowledge work, usually applied in a nonroutine technical system. It has been referred to as non-routine work or non-linear work. Adapting STS methods to accommodate to these differences from more traditional work settings will be the topic of Chapter 11.

GOVERNMENT INSTITUTE AND PRIVATE FOUNDATION SUPPORT FOR STS

❧ *U.S. Institutions*

Two institutions to pursue QWL issues were created as a result of a 1972 conference sponsored by the Ford Foundation. The UCLA Center for Quality of Working Life, founded in 1972, was the first publicly funded state center for STS and QWL. In addition to the UCLA CQWL, the Work in America Institute (WIA) was also given support by the Ford Foundation. WIA was founded in 1975, not to provide consulting assistance or action research, but to foster labor-management cooperation in organizational change and to conduct research related to national policy issues and decisions in QWL. WIA has succeeded at this mission and has enlarged upon it. It has expanded its interest in STS and currently supports the STS managers' networks mentioned above.

It wasn't long after the two original centers began that other state centers followed. In the mid-1970s centers appeared in Ohio, Indiana, Maryland, Massachusetts, Michigan, Pennsylvania, Washington State, and Iowa. They received some state funding, and all were dedicated to the improvement of QWL. Many were involved in promoting better labor-management relations. Some of them encouraged the application of STS; many did not. In 1978 the National Center for Productivity and QWL was created, but, as a symbol of a one-term president, it was short-lived. Out of it, however, the American Productivity Center (APC) was founded in Houston, Texas. The APC has become a premier private institution in the United States, broadly engaged in training sessions, conferences, consulting, research, and interested in STS thinking.

In time, most of the state centers followed the national center in diminished activity. A few, such as the Pennsylvania center, remain vital. Those state centers that exist today have a practical applications or clearinghouse mission and profess at least some interest in STS. They include the two in Texas already mentioned, Indiana's Center for Quality and Productivity Improvement, the Works Council of North-east Ohio, two in California (at the Universities of Southern California [Center for Effective Organizations], and at Sonoma State [Center for Studies on Human Dignity in Organizations]); New York has two (an academic center at Cornell as well as the WIA). The missions of these institutions vary, and the connections between them are tenuous at present.

In 1988 DEC and the Society of Manufacturing Engineers (SME) sponsored an STS research network that included scholars, practitioners, and users. This forum, called the STS Roundtable, has continued to evolve with considerable response from the consulting community and a concurrent shift toward an interest in issues of practice and theory.

¿ *Canadian Institutions*

Canada also had a very prominent QWL/STS center in the province of Ontario. Many studies were funded and reports published by the Ontario Centre over a 10-year period. This center was closely tied to the politics of provincial government and to trade union support. The election of new provincial officials and new national trade union leaders in the late 1980s brought about its sudden termination in 1988. Currently the Canadian Council of Working Life sponsors a Canadian "Ecology of Work" conference that is organized along the same lines and by the same people as its older U.S. counterpart. Both of these conferences feature STS in many of the presentations and workshops.

¿ *STS and Quality Management*

Institutions usually support "movements," and we would be remiss to conclude this section on institutions without mentioning "managing for quality." The revival of U.S. manufacturing interest in quality dates back to the early 1970s when the Japanese applications of Americans Deming and Juran began receiving publicity here. That work emphasized the use of statistics for understanding flaws or errors, as well as having employees meet in "quality circles" to discuss improving quality. Both the focus on quality "levers" and the use of employee "discussions" were consistent with STS methods and intentions, although the quality management methods were never a substitute for the larger system view rendered by STS. Total quality management (TQM) was introduced in the late 1980s by the U.S. Defense Department as a template for management in the acquisition of military contracts by vendors and manufacturers. The TQM template contains two elements: statistical process control and large-scale employee participation. It has not taken long for the recently emergent TQM institutes to embrace STS as a methodology for realizing the best effects of the template. STS panels, presenters, and workshops have appeared recently on TQM programs, and some joint STS-TQM workshops have begun to be offered by some STS trainers. There are as yet no published cases illustrating the effectiveness of the STS-TQM combination.

The application of STS can enhance the potential of TQM in several ways. First, STS provides the vital ability to distinguish those aspects on which to collect statistical data for charting. Statistical process control (SPC) training (a central feature in the TQM template) usually advises the learner to apply a logical approach called Pareto analysis, or the 80/20 rule, which relies on the identification of a short list of items (the 20%) that account for the highest value problems (the 80%). The result is often a hasty and ill-informed "skimming" of serious problems that may leave more interrelated and obscure issues undiscovered. Ironically, many organizations using SPC chart more variables than employees can appreciate all at once, and the result is to dilute the significance of the important variables in favor of more trivial ones. STS technical variance analysis (described in Chapter 4) provides a way to carefully reveal the small set of truly important variables to chart using SPC techniques.

Second, STS provides a rationale to restructure an organization for greater effectiveness and higher quality of working life. STS emphasizes the product that is delivered to and enjoyed by the enterprise's primary customer. Many TQM programs urge managers and employees to identify numerous customers, many of whom are inside the enterprise — "internal customers." Although it is important to pay attention to others "downstream" in the production process, identifying them as "customers" leaves unquestioned the boundaries between them. These boundaries between departments and functions define the provincialism and closed-mindedness of functional "stove-pipes." The STS focus on product and external customer defines those producing the product as "partners" in the process, reducing the need for internal boundaries and permitting consideration of consolidation and changes in organizational structure.

Third, TQM is undertaken by training, leadership, and participation alone. STS requires these as well, but its main effect is, through understanding, to inform managers and employees about effective changes in structure, technology, physical space, jobs, and procedures. With appropriate changes in these aspects, an enterprise can truly make the most of a seriously supported TQM program.

Over the past 25 years, STS has been developed as a methodology in North America. This emphasis was originally on improving quality of working life. Gradually it has shifted to provide a methodological paradigm for emphasizing organizational effectiveness that includes QWL, TQM, and productivity through empowering members with information. Over its 25 years, STS has expanded to embrace dimensional manufacturing work, transaction processing work, service work, nonroutine work, and professional work, all within an increasingly chaotic environment. Currently there are more than 115 active STS designs or redesigns operating in the United States, of which around 25% (or one-fourth) are clearly not continuous process technologies. Continuous process industries still predominate in STS applications, but the number and proportion of application to other work systems are increasing. Most U.S. STS training courses teach technical variance analysis. Most private practitioners attempt to use that variance analysis, and many are now using a product/purpose focus. A broader understanding is emerging as academics debate and practitioners apply. The North American experience began with pure method and application on one hand, and theory on the other. It is evolving toward a methodology and toward understanding the purposeful, output- and customer-oriented paradigm. The journey is well started, but it is not completed. With the current U.S. success of STS in professional work, it is within reach to apply STS methodology to management systems as well.

ACADEMIC BASES OF STS THEORY AND PRACTICE IN NORTH AMERICA

Since 1967, North American universities have produced an evolving methodology of STS practice. The original emphasis was on expanding the range of application and of producing case studies and comparative literature surveys.

But long before it was practiced here, STS was known among U.S. academics as an intriguing idea as well as by an interesting case from a British coal mine (e.g., Katz & Kahn, 1966; Schein, 1965). A few Americans, such as Louis Davis and Will McWhinney, had worked with Eric Trist and others and had written about STS prior to the time that the ideas moved to the United States (and UCLA) in 1967 with Trist.

UCLA, 1967-1987

After spending a period abroad as a visiting professor at the University of Birmingham, England, Louis Davis returned to the University of California, Berkeley. He had worked closely with Eric Trist, Fred Emery, Albert Cherns, and others associated with the Tavistock Institute's Human Relations Centre. Upon his return, Davis moved from the Berkeley campus and convinced Trist to join him at the UCLA Graduate School of Management. A group of faculty at the School of Management including McWhinney, James Clark, and others had already invited Trist to at least visit if not join the faculty there. Trist arrived in 1967 and, with enthusiastic support from many faculty and students, forged a study program bridging the organizational behavior and behavioral science groups in that school. Over the next three years a vigorous program for teaching and application emerged at UCLA. A four-course STS curriculum was developed to blend with the existing course offerings in organizational studies. Graduate students interested in the STS "stream" were engaged in action research projects by the faculty. One unconventional product of that program was an 80 class-hour, two-week academic-style "short course" on STS developed by Trist and the UCLA faculty for two application clients, P&G and Alcan. The short course provided the theory and background of STS to managers and behavioral science practitioners from these two companies.

By 1970 several students had finished the academic program at UCLA and went on to faculty positions at Case Western Reserve, Pennsylvania State, and the University of Montreal, while others joined P&G and TRW. Several faculty, most notably Trist himself, left for other universities. Others (former employees of the early UCLA/STS client systems, as well as UCLA faculty and students) left to form consulting alliances.

Albert Cherns visited UCLA from Loughborough University of Technology as a visiting professor from 1972 to 1976, during which he worked closely with Davis and the staff of the UCLA Center for Quality of Working Life. The influence of Cherns' collaboration built on the earlier North America experience. Most of what happened subsequently in North America can be traced to these fortuitous foundations and subsequent diffusion of the principles developed during those early years. A few examples follow:

1. "Open Systems Planning" was developed at UCLA about 1970 (notably by McWhinney and Clark) in concert with P&G (in particular with Charles Krone). It provided a method for understanding organizations as purposeful systems in an environmental context (Jayaram, 1976). The influence of this method is still felt in organizational development (OD) practice and new plant design in continuous process (long-linked) industries.
2. "Technical variance analysis," both method and methodology, continued to be developed and applied at UCLA from its Tavistock beginnings. Just as open systems planning provided an applications window to the turbulent environment, so technical systems understanding provided for a paradigm shift in the design of service systems as well as production organizations (e.g., Taylor, 1986). Technical analysis methodology was responsible for the popularity of STS applications in participative redesign in a wide variety of industries.
3. "Social systems analysis" was developed at UCLA with the stimulus and encouragement of Albert Cherns. Just as technical analysis provided a new paradigm, the social analysis focused on cooperation and coordination to enhance the application of the technical system methodology.

4. In June 1972 Davis and his colleagues at UCLA organized an international invitational meeting on Quality of Working Life. The meeting was funded by the Ford Foundation and held at Arden House in Harriman, New York. Among the products of this meeting were: (a) a two-volume proceedings (Davis & Cherns 1975), in which several chapters addressed STS to improve QWL; (b) the creation of two institutions to pursue QWL issues; and (c) increased visibility for both STS and QWL in North America.

5. UCLA's Center for Quality of Working Life, created as a result of the 1972 Arden House conference (with support from the Ford Foundation and the State of California), became the initial institutional forum for the application of STS to social and individual well-being as well as productivity. Under Davis' direction this center developed a number of STS innovations. Among them were (a) action research projects in government organizations; (b) surveys of international STS experience and of work design practices (Taylor, 1977; Taylor, Landy, Levine, & Kamath, 1973); and (c) the STS "short course" for managers and practitioners was adapted as an annual public offering. The CQWL STS course was further developed by the staff for presentation in Canada, where it was offered annually for nearly a decade. Both the UCLA and Canadian STS short courses changed from a presentation of theory and history only to an application/appreciation of the methodology in real-world settings as well. Gradually, STS faculty retired or moved, carrying their energy and interest in continuing STS studies to other places. With the arrival of a new dean in 1982, the UCLA Graduate School of Management shifted from an organizational studies focus to a macroeconomics and finance focus. By the mid-1980s (after nearly 20 years), the UCLA STS program had diminished in faculty and students; the new leadership of the CQWL dropped its STS focus.

University of Pennsylvania, 1970-1980

Trist's 1970 move from UCLA to the University of Pennsylvania expanded his scope of influence and his action research. Located near "coal country," Trist and new colleagues found an opportunity to revisit his original underground mining experiences and STS application (Trist, Susman, & Brown, 1977). The Rushton coal mine study permitted North Americans to see STS applied by its best-known exponent in its most famous industrial setting. Trist was also to put his mark on large-scale systems change by engaging the city of Jamestown, New York, in a redesign project of lasting influence (Trist, 1986). Such an effort was to be repeated later in the community of Sudbury, Ontario. His students were actively engaged in the fieldwork in these cities and their constituent organizations, and a number of interesting papers resulted (cf. Trist, 1986). Trist's classes, seminars, and tutorials continued to inspire and energize his students, who in turn went on to faculty positions at Pennsylvania, Harvard, and elsewhere. During this period,

Fred Emery (Australia) visited Trist at Pennsylvania several times and worked with Russell Ackoff to further develop the notions of purposeful systems (Ackoff & Emery, 1972). In 1980 Trist left Pennsylvania for a post at York University in Toronto.

ᵓ *Pennsylvania State University, 1970–1992*

Gerald Susman, one of the early graduates from the UCLA STS stream, joined the faculty at Pennsylvania State University Park campus. Susman collaborated with Trist and others at the University of Pennsylvania, Pennsylvania State, and Carnegie Tech in the Rushton coal mine study. His continued interest in STS theory resulted in the 1976 publication of *Autonomy at Work*. By founding the Center for Managing Technology and Organizational Change, Susman maintained a role in STS thinking and retained STS visibility at the University Park campus.

The Pennsylvania State Harrisburg campus has continued and expanded the university's STS teaching and research involvement. Rupert Chisholm and his colleagues in the Pennsylvania State Harrisburg CQWL have been active in studying STS applications in health-care organizations and other government service systems.

ᵓ *Case Western Reserve University, 1970–1992*

Thomas Cummings, another of the early graduates from the UCLA STS stream, joined the faculty at Case Western Reserve University. There he and others actively pursued action research in STS redesign and undertook literature surveys of effective change. A number of his students went on to teaching and consulting careers in STS.

William Pasmore joined the Case Western faculty in 1976. He came from Purdue University, where he had worked with Trist in STS application at General Foods. He was instrumental in the development of an extensive literature search to list and evaluate specific STS change projects (Pasmore, Francis, Haldeman, & Shani, 1982). His books dealing with STS (Pasmore, 1988; Pasmore & Sherwood, 1978) are important reference works. He continued to develop the STS study course at Case Western during the 1980s and has currently expanded it into a vigorous program in the study and design of professional work systems. This last effort has also been the source of a series of recent workshops on STS in the information age.

❧ Texas Tech University, 1980-1992

Barry Macy joined the faculty at Texas Tech in the late 1970s. Macy had been involved earlier with case evaluation at the Bolivar Tennessee plant of Harman International, a redesign based on STS principles guided by Michael Maccoby and Einar Thorsrud. Texas Tech has continued to promote student development and case evaluation. The Texas Center for Productivity and QWL was founded by Macy shortly after his arrival at Texas Tech and has continued an active program of research, communication, and diffusion. The center's STS managers' network has grown continuously since its inception in 1979 and provides an important forum for managers to share their experiences and their concerns. The Texas center has developed an impressive list of case studies and opportunities for plant tours of STS-based organizations.

❧ Harvard University, 1970-1985

Richard Walton was one of the first U.S. academics to engage in the design of new forms of organization. His design work in the early 1970s included the General Foods plant in Topeka, Kansas, and the Cummins Engine plant in Jamestown, New York. Both of these plants have been subsequently described as applications of sociotechnical systems methodology (e.g., Ketchum, 1975), and their managers have gone on to use STS in the design and redesign of other work systems (e.g., Ketchum, 1982). In the late 1970s Calvin Pava (a student of Trist's) joined the Harvard faculty and shortly thereafter published his important critique of earlier STS methods and approach (Pava, 1983). Apart from these landmark contributions by Walton and Pava, academics at Harvard have not pursued studies of STS thinking or practice.

❧ Canadian Universities, 1975-1981

Few Canadian STS scholars were known outside the country prior to the Arden House conference in 1972. Several Canadian graduates of the UCLA STS program returned to Quebec during the early 1970s, which increased the base of academics interested in STS. A rapid increase in interest about STS and QWL brought many students from Canada to the UCLA short course. During the period 1975-76, policymakers, managers, and practitioners from the Canadian Department of

Labour, as well as faculty from several Canadian universities including Toronto, Montreal, McGill, and British Columbia, attended the courses. In 1978 Eric Trist began dividing his time between Pennsylvania and Toronto's York University.

❦ *University of Toronto, 1978-1992.*

It wasn't long thereafter that Harvey Kolodny, and his students at the University of Toronto, began publication of STS change studies. The late 1970s were a period of intense Canadian activity in work improvement and design in general, and STS in particular, that culminated in the open international conference "QWL in the 80's" held in Toronto in 1981. The conference was organized by Kolodny and other academics from Toronto and Montreal together with Hans van Beinum of the Ontario Province Centre for Quality of Working Life. Over 2,000 people attended the conference—nearly half of whom were Canadians. Like Arden House, the Toronto conference produced an important book (Kolodny & van Beinum, 1983), and increased visibility for the topic. Once again, much of the conference addressed STS as a way to improve quality of working life.

The University of Toronto remains an active center of STS interest. Kolodny has continued to develop STS theory and practice and has been instrumental in the education of a number of STS scholars and practitioners. He has assured continuity of public STS training programs in Canada through a series of courses at the University of Toronto that continue to the present. STS-based programs at the University of Montreal, McGill, and other universities around Canada have largely disappeared.

❦ *Other Universities*

Will McWhinney and Frank Friedlander, both long involved in the study and practice of organizational change, have joined the faculty of Fielding Institute at the main campus in Santa Barbara, California. Since that time a growing number of Fielding graduates have undertaken research in various aspects of sociotechnical systems. Loyola University in Chicago began an STS teaching and research program in 1990.

STS AND PRIVATE PRACTITIONERS

Most STS academics have been involved in consulting to private clients and many continue to do so on a regular basis. Most private consulting in STS projects, however, is done by practitioners who began their careers inside organizations. Charles Krone (formerly P&G) and Lyman Ketchum (formerly General Foods) are among the best known and have been active for the past 25 years. Major corporations involved in STS projects include Alcan, Clark Equipment, Exxon, GM, Mead Paper, Shell Canada, and Weyerhaeuser, to name a few. Organization-based practitioners often began with involvement in an STS project as human resources development (HRD) Specialist or OD representative or manager. Since 1980, a number of former P&G practitioners entered private practice, apparently as a consequence of a downsizing and shift in corporate strategy away from the continued increase in new plant construction.

Most consultants practice as individuals or in small consortia. Few major management consulting firms have experts in STS practice. The American Productivity Center in Houston has employed skilled STS consultants over the past 10 years and has recently marketed its version of design for purposeful systems. Most consultants hold advanced degrees, usually in psychology or management. Many of the consultants with P&G experience have engineering backgrounds.

There are periodic public meetings that deal with STS organized by the OD network and by "Ecology of Work." These conferences, directed primarily toward private consultants or the internal OD practitioners, have included STS topics since about 1980.

A number of public STS workshops are offered by private consultants. STS workshops are regularly offered by the following private firms: Alexander, Scott & Associates (Tavares, Florida); American Productivity Center (Houston, Texas); Block-Petrella-Weisbord (Philadelphia); Cotter & Associates (North Hollywood); Organizational Consultants (San Francisco); STS Organizational Consultants (Montreal); STS International (Burlington, North Carolina); and the Synapse Group (Portland, Maine).

CONCLUSION

STS has contributed to organizational effectiveness in North America for over two decades. This impact has been steady, and the effects on productivity, quality, cost, and satisfaction are considerable. STS has been applied to a great many industries. Its major successes have been in process industries and manufacturing. Its application to service systems and professional and knowledge work has also proved effective and will continue to do so, especially in the private sector.

The long-time institutional and academic support for STS assures its continued development and application. The STS approach has aided the application of many popular management remedies such as job enrichment, management by objectives, and quality circles, to name but a few—and it has survived. STS provides a holistic approach, an emphasis on purpose and product, and an advocacy for people and their values. Its systemic focus and attention to structural and technical change assure the continued development of STS.

REFERENCES

ACKOFF, R. L., & F. E. EMERY. *On Purposeful Systems.* Chicago: Aldine-Atherton, 1972.

CHISHOLM, R. F., & J. T. ZIEGENFUSS. "A Review of Applications of the Sociotechnical Systems Approach to Health Care Organizations." *Journal of Applied Behavioral Science,* 22(3), 1986, 315–328.

DAVIS, L. E., A. B. CHERNS & ASSOCIATES. *The Quality of Working Life.* (Vols. 1, 2). New York: Free Press, 1975.

DAVIS, L. E., & C. S. SULLIVAN. "A Labour-Management Contract and Quality of Working Life." *Journal of Occupational Behavior,* 1, 1980, 29–41.

HANNA, D. P. *Designing Organizations for High Performance.* Reading, MA: Addison-Wesley, 1988.

JAYARAM, G. K. "Open System Planning." In W. G. Bennis, K. D. Benne, R. Chin, & K. E. Covey (eds.), *The Planning of Change* (3rd ed.). New York: Holt, Rinehart & Winston, 1976.

KATZ, D. R., & R. L. KAHN. *The Social Psychology of Organizations.* New York: Wiley, 1966.

KETCHUM, L. D. "A Case Study of Diffusion." In L. E. Davis & A. B. Cherns (eds.), *The Quality of Working Life.* Vol. 2. New York: Free Press, 1975.

KETCHUM, L. D. "How to Start and Sustain a Work Redesign Project." *National Productivity Review,* 1, 1982, 75–86.

KOLODNY, H. "Canadian Experience in Innovative Approaches to High Commitment Work Systems." In R. Schuler & S. Dolan (eds.), *Canadian Readings in Personnel and Human Resources Management.* Anaheim, CA. West Publications, 1987.

KOLODNY, H., & H. VAN BEINUM (eds.). *The Quality of Working Life in the 1980s.* New York: Praeger, 1983.

PASMORE, W. A. *Designing Effective Organizations.* New York: Wiley, 1988.

PASMORE, W., C. FRANCIS, J. HALDEMAN, & A. SHANI. "Sociotechnical Systems: A North American Reflection on Empirical Studies of the Seventies."*Human Relations,* 35(12), 1982, 1179–1204.

PASMORE, W. A., & J. J. SHERWOOD (eds.). *Sociotechnical systems: A Sourcebook.* San Diego: University Associates, 1978.

PAVA, C. *Managing New Office Technology.* New York: Free Press, 1983.

SCHEIN, E. H. *Organizational Psychology.* Englewood Cliffs, NJ: Prentice-Hall, 1965.

SUSMAN, G. I. *Autonomy at Work: A Socio-Technical Analysis Perspective.* New York: Praeger, 1976.

TAYLOR, J. C. "Experiments in Work System Design: Economic and Human Results." *Personnel Review,* 6(2&3), 1977.

TAYLOR, J. C. "Long-Term Sociotechnical Change in a Computer Operations Department." *Journal of Applied Behavioral Science,* 22(3), 1986, 303–313.

TAYLOR, J. C., J. LANDY, M. LEVINE, & D. R. KAMATH. *Quality of Working Life: An Annotated Bibliography, 1957–1972.* (Prepared under a contract from the Manpower Administration, U.S. Department of Labor, Published by the Center for Organizational Studies, Graduate School of Management, UCLA). 1973. NTIS Document No. PB218380.

TAYLOR, J. C., & R. A. ASADORIAN. "The Implementation of Excellence: Socio-Technical Management." *Industrial Management,* 27(4), 1985, 5–15.

TAYLOR, J. C.; P. W. GUSTAVSON, & W. S. CARTER, "Integrating the Social and Technical Systems of Organizations." In D. D. Davis (ed.) *Managing Technological Innovation.* San Francisco: Jossey-Bass, 1986.

TRIST, E. L. "Quality of Working Life and Community Development: Some Reflections on the Jamestown Experience." *Journal of Applied Behavioral Science,* 22(3), 1986, 223–239.

TRIST, E. L., G. SUSMAN, & G. BROWN, "An Experiment in Autonomous Working in an American Underground Coal Mine." *Human Relations,* 30, 1977, 201–236.

## CHAPTER 3

Designing for Purpose: Understanding the Business We're In

"What then is an organization? It is a unique kind of system. It is a system which has a purpose of its own, which consists of parts that have purposes of their own, and is itself part of a larger system which has purposes of its own. Thus, a corporation has purposes, it has parts with purposes, and it is part of an economy of society which has purposes."

(Ackoff, 1972)

BACKGROUND TO THE PRACTICE

A high-commitment, high-performance organization is the result of its members successfully undertaking three tasks. The first is understanding and supporting the purpose of the enterprise. The second is developing the competence to work together to control the product or output during its production process. The third is understanding and appropriately responding to the changing environment surrounding the enterprise.

By being personally involved in this process, members of an organization learn how they contribute to organizational excellence by understanding the role they play in the purposeful sociotechnical work systems that comprise the larger, complex, enterprise. Members learn to appreciate the relationship between their purposeful work systems and the organizations of which they are members. They thereby learn to act together in appropriate ways to promote the *survival* as well as the *success* of the enterprise. It's the process of involvement that builds this critical new understanding.

Purposeful work systems must be defined in such a way that their essential product or output is emphasized, rather than the formal reporting relationships or job descriptions of the organization itself, if others are to understand the system. This definition requires input-output (or throughput) boundary setting, which allows a meaningful portion of an organization to be examined in a unique way. This unique perspective, or focus on the system output, permits the arrangement and orientation of various work systems to jointly pursue the overall purpose of the larger enterprise. Understanding work system boundaries in this way is a powerful tool for revealing and fostering new ways of designing and managing organizations. It is a central concept in sociotechnical systems theory and practice.

> **SCANNING is the process of defining boundaries. It is key to understanding the purpose, the process, and the environment of any system.**

The STS analysis and design process we describe in this book consists of seven clearly defined steps in four phases:

1. Discovering purposeful, product-focused systems thinking.
2. Understanding the *whole system*—scanning the organization in systems terms.
3. Understanding how to make *it* happen in a unique market niche—the technical system analysis.
4. Understanding how to make it happen—the social system analysis.
5. Understanding how it all comes together—ideal design and joint optimization.
6. Provisional design—understanding how to make it relevant and realistic.
7. Understanding how to make it succeed—implementation and continuous improvement.

This chapter describes the details of collecting data for "scanning," the second step listed above. The occasional highlighted statements are intended to help in the practice of sociotechnical systems understanding.

The STS approach to organizational design and management has established itself as a powerful aid in achieving high-commitment, high-performance organizations. STS is based on a systemic analysis of the technical system and of the accompanying patterns of human interaction in an organization. "Scanning" is a process of defining one's workplace and organization in system terms. The scan document resulting from the process describes the organization in systems terms. Figure 3.1 presents graphically the model of any purposeful system. The scan process converts such an image of one's *specific* work system into a word picture or narrative description.

THE SYSTEM SCAN

Any organization, or part of an organization, or parts of more than one organization, can be considered a sociotechnical system *if* that

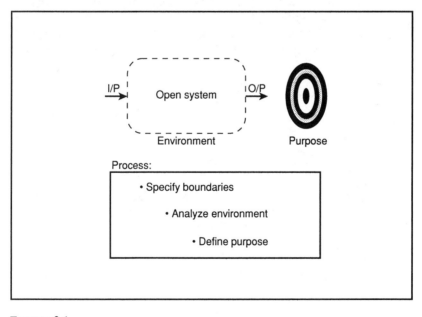

FIGURE 3.1
Open System Scan: Purpose: To Define the Organization in Systems Terms

system contains a purposeful transformation process (a technical system) and people working together over time in some stable relationships (a social system). A purposeful sociotechnical work system can be considered part of a larger organization (from which it is analytically separated) if its mission and philosophy are aligned with, and contribute to, those of the larger body. The scan is an overview of the system to be examined—its purpose (technical mission and social philosophy), its boundaries, inputs and products, its people, its relationship to its environments—and the "presenting" or immediate problem, if any.

The scanning process allows the users to agree on the general dimensions of the organization and the inputs and outputs of the technical system. The system as "scanned" is seen as a bounded region in space and time in which inputs are converted or transformed into outputs or products—a system that has certain relationships with its environment and that has certain requirements to be met. This boundary-setting procedure is as important for an office or service unit as it is in a plant or factory where the product of the transformation is more tangible. The scanning procedure is the crucial first phase in the analysis process, as it is the step in which work system boundaries are initially (but not irrevocably) defined.

Table 3.1 presents a checklist of the essential items to be covered in a sociotechnical systems scan. The following sections describe each of the items on that list.

TABLE 3.1
SCAN: A Systems Overview

- Purpose (Mission and philosophy)
- Objectives (Technical, economic, and social)
- System output (Product or deliverable)
- System input (The thing transformed)
- Philosophy
- Boundaries
  - Throughput
  - Territorial
  - Social
  - Time
- Environment
- Presenting problems

ᚼ *Purpose*

Purpose includes both the business mission of the system and its philosophy of human values. Any enterprise is composed of four interactive and interdependent elements (Davis, 1982). These elements are revealed as four identities: a transforming medium, an economic entity, a minisociety, and a gathering of individuals. As a purposeful system, an enterprise is first and foremost a transforming agency—converting certain inputs into desirable outputs. Second, every enterprise is an economic entity—acting in a marketplace to produce profits, income, or other valuable resources. The third element of any enterprise is that of a "minisociety"—developing and maintaining the norms of member behavior. Finally, every enterprise is a collection of individuals who come together with other people for their own purposes—to achieve the personal goals and objectives unique to themselves. Thus, we can say that any enterprise is at once a production system, a system for fiscal gain, a social system, and a system for individual satisfaction or quality of working life (QWL). Figure 3.2 depicts the enterprise as these four elements, and it also shows how the deliverables from each element join together to form the purpose of the system. In the pursuit of expected product and financial objectives, a "mission" is created and confirmed for that specific system. From the development of social norms and the desire to achieve a high quality of working life comes a "philosophy of human values" for that unique system. But the purpose does more than

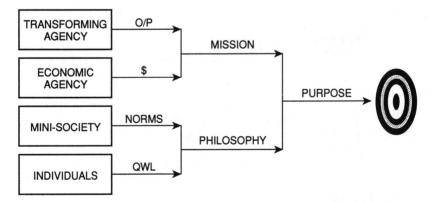

FIGURE 3.2
Defining a Purposeful System

reflect the outcomes of the system. It provides the energy and forward-looking vision of the enterprise and thus can shape the outputs as well.

Mission. Table 3.2 contains a list of essential characteristics of a system mission. Although identification of the mission is among the most important tasks of the system scan, it may take the user several "tries" before a satisfactory (in terms of the listed characteristics) statement is at hand. Despite what the current and historical business of the enterprise has been, the system scan provides the users with the opportunity to draft a statement of core business that is brief, memorable, energizing, yet still consistent with the distinctive competencies that the enterprise has developed in the past.

An example of a distinctive competency from a manufacturing plant is the past record (and therefore capability) to maintain very low scrap and waste levels. This competence is extraordinary or distinctive, and it would be consistent with a mission statement that emphasizes high quality (because low waste is a sign that the plant "did work right the first time"), and also consistent with mission statements that focus on low cost, low price, or high profit (because low scrap and waste indicates that operations are efficient, and/or material costs are modest).

It is important that the mission can be seen by present and future employees as "special," but also possible to achieve based on realistic expectations and actual performance from the past. It is crucial to remember that in this chaotic, turbulent world the mission must be viewed as a living document, continuously open to change.

TABLE 3.2
Criteria for Mission
The Business We're In

1. Simple, easy to remember
2. Describes "distinctive competence"
3. Singular: One aspect emphasized
4. "Unattainable," but can be pursued
5. Specific enough to see it being pursued
6. Relevant, realistic
7. One sentence reflecting product, distinction, customer

Objectives

The stated *technical objectives* that can relate to this mission are such things as yearly production to standard and average annual quality rates to target. It is through these measurable, attainable objectives that the mission can be pursued. Goals and objectives are different in terms of their time horizons, and both are important ways of realizing the mission. "Goals" are relatively short-term expectations of technical system performance—typically stated as daily, weekly, or monthly measures. Examples of quality goals for a manufacturing facility include expected *daily* scrap rates, *weekly* hours spent in rework compared to budget, or *monthly* averages of defects per 100 units of output compared with standard. Objectives are longer-term statements of the same expectations and others that lend themselves to longer time horizons. Examples of objectives, drawing from the same manufacturing illustration, are *quarterly* or annual statistics on scrap rates, rework time, or defect rates to standard. In addition, if long-term reliability of product is central to the quality mission as stated, then warranty returns compared with forecast, as well as measures of the longer-term, out-of-warranty reliability, could be included as technical system objectives as well.

Social objectives are also created (or confirmed) as links between the desired social norms and quality of working life of the system and the philosophy statement expressing the system's human values. These social objectives will be discussed in greater depth in following chapters.

While a well-stated objective must not be impossible to achieve, it

---

CRITERIA FOR GOALS AND OBJECTIVES

- **Can be accomplished**
- **Each is a single specific end result**
- **Accomplished by a specific date, or within a specific time**
  Long-term = Objectives
  Short-term = Goals
- **A maximum "return" in dollars, hours, etc.**
- **Consistent with the Purpose.**
  Technical Goals and Objectives consistent with Mission.
  Social Goals and Objectives consistent with Philosophy.

should have enough stretch to capture the energy and creativity of system members. An objective does not include "how" to achieve the desired end result. That needs to be left up to those assigned that responsibility and to the training methods that prove effective.

Commitment and support for the goals and objectives within the social system are crucial and should be understood by those who must contribute time and resources to their accomplishment. This web of relationships is often wider than merely those who create the performance targets. The social system includes those in other departments who must support and/or approve the goals and objectives if they are to be meaningful to the purpose and performance of the larger enterprise. Commitment to the goals and objectives is also a requirement for anyone who is actively involved in the development, elaboration, or execution of the action plans to achieve the goals and objectives.

System Output

The product or output identified for this analysis should be (but may at first not necessarily be) consistent with the technical mission. The output should be described in terms of its characteristics: physical dimensions, appearance, finish, cost and time to produce, expected life, maintainability, point in its life cycle, price and profit, major competitors in the marketplace, and its distinctive advantages over them. Any other characteristics intrinsic to the product by reason of company mission (e.g., after-sales service or product guarantees) or industry (e.g., taste and aroma of food products) must also be listed.

System Input

The input for this analysis should be *only* that which is actually transformed or converted into the product or output identified above. Like the output, inputs are described by their characteristics. Input characteristics include vendor/supplier, cost, quality in various significant dimensions, availability, perishability, as well as other considerations relevant by specific product and/or industry.

Philosophy

A philosophy is a statement of principles and human values enacted or espoused by management and employees. Table 3.3 contains a list of criteria for a usable organizational philosophy statement. In many orga-

TABLE 3.3
Criteria for Philosophy
Our Values about People

1. Limited number of tight statements
2. Can be tested against behavior
3. Willing to publish
4. Useful as design criteria
5. No unrealistic expectations

nizations the statement of human principles and values guiding the management of the enterprise is often not stated clearly or considered very believable by people at lower management ranks or at the shop floor. Conversations with management may reveal very little in the way of values, but sometimes a query about values is answered with the explanation that the company has mottos or slogans such as "People are our most important asset." Such utterances may reflect conscious and active behaviors, but they more often merely record history of the company or values from its past.

As the scan begins, one's best guess about the philosophy for a system is captured in existing *social objectives* stated in terms of human behavior and performance toward achieving them. Examples of social objectives are quarterly or annual levels of absenteeism, turnover, the level or number of labor grievances, and personnel accidents and injuries—each in terms of its respective rates and targets. Despite what the current and historical values of the enterprise have been, the system scan provides the users with the opportunity to draft a statement of philosophy that is consistent with the values of present and future employees, as well as being an improvement upon, and/or departure from, the present enacted values of the enterprise. Often, employees of traditionally designed organizations find that the structure drives a value system contrary to what they, its individual members, really value and believe. Table 3.4, a questionnaire on organizational values, is designed to reveal this discrepancy between the traditional machine-age model and the open sociotechnical systems model.

❧ Boundaries

Given the above, it is essential to identify the system's boundaries or the limits of responsibilities of the organization. There are four types of boundaries that need to be defined.

Table 3.4

Key Values Underlying Organizational Models

This questionnaire represents nine values that have developed around Frederick Taylor's (1911) ideas of scientific management. Contrasted to these are nine values articulated by Eric Trist (1981) for a sociotechnical systems model.

Directions: Taking one item at a time, circle the dot on the scale that best represents the current state of the organization today, as seen in practice as opposed to espoused. Next, place a box around the dot on the same scale that represents the attainable level the organization is capable of reaching in actual practice.

Machine Model	*STS Systems Model*
1. Optimize Technology	Joint optimization
•............•...................•..................•...............•	
2. People as extensions	People as complementary
•............•...................•..................•...........•	
3. People as expendable	People as resources
•............•...................•..................•...........•	
4. Maximum task breakdown	Optimum task grouping
•............•...................•..................•...........•	
5. External control	Internal control
•............•...................•..................•...........•	
6. Tall, autocratic organization	Flat, participative organization
•............•...................•..................•...........•	
7. Competitive, gamesmanship (win/lose)	Collaboration, collegiality (win/win)
•............•...................•..................•...........•	
8. Alienation	Commitment
•............•...................•..................•...........•	
9. Safe and protective	Spontaneity and growth
•............•...................•..................•...........•	

The Throughput Boundary. This boundary is essential to a sociotechnical system. It is located at one end by the entry of the input (where input stops belonging to the supplier and starts belonging to the system) and at the other end by the point of export of finished output to users or customers (that point where the product or deliverable stops belonging to the system and starts belonging to the user or customer).

The throughput boundary is not the only boundary of the system, but it aids in identifying and establishing other boundaries that are useful for understanding and describing an organization as a purposeful system.

> The throughput boundary is the major boundary of a purposeful system. It defines the system in terms of the product.

The Territorial Boundary. The boundary of a purposeful system can be defined by its territory or by the physical space occupied or used for the product conversion. It helps our mental picture of a system to understand whether it occupies a single, continuous space or whether it is spread or scattered in small areas over a larger territory. An example of the former is a single plant or factory manufacturing a physical product—its territorial boundaries may begin and end at the factory walls or the fence around its parking lot. The U.S. air traffic control system, however, may include the "territory" surrounding the FAA control centers in various U.S. cities plus the "territory" in the sky surrounding the individual aircraft within range of the center's radar and radios. It may be important for members of the system to know and understand that their obligations and responsibilities go beyond the physical space that they themselves occupy.

The Social (or "People") Boundary. The boundary of a purposeful system can also be defined by the people directly involved in the creation, production, or transformation of the input into the output. Specifications here include the number of people, what roles or titles they hold, and to what formal organizations they report. In the case of the manufacturing plant, the people involved may include only the production employees in that plant plus their immediate supervisors, production control employees, and material services employees dealing directly with the throughput to the plant. In the case of the air traffic control system, the people would include not only the FAA controllers themselves, and possibly their immediate supervisors, but the flight crews in the aircraft to whom their messages and direction are intended.

The Time Boundary. A purposeful system can also be defined by whatever aspects of time form relevant boundaries, given the system's mission. In the case of a manufacturing factory, the critical time boundary may be annual (if it is measured primarily to a yearly target) or seasonal (if its product is outdoor furniture or snowmobiles), or the critical time boundary may be weekly (if the plant closes down from

Friday to Monday). The critical time boundary may even be defined by work shifts, if the plant is an "around-the-clock" continuous process operation. The time boundaries in the air traffic control example are more easily thought of as a combination of boundaries between work-shifts *plus* the time envelope (a matter of a few minutes normally) around each individual aircraft from the time it comes into radar and/or radio contact with a traffic control center until it is confirmed to be landed or out of territorial range.

Once the various boundaries have been identified, the limits of the system's environment are also specified by default—the environment is what lies outside the boundaries. The user's task is to identify the most relevant and important aspects of that overall environment.

᪥ *Environment*

The search for goodness of fit between system and environment begins with the identification of the major trends going on around the system and selecting those most relevant to the preferred organizational future (e.g., focus on product quality, customer satisfaction, competition in world economy). With these trends in mind, it is important to continue assessing and scanning the specific system's most relevant environments by listing the important environmental stakeholders for the system. For example, the various markets in which the enterprise has commerce provide a good first step in thinking of institutional stakeholders. Government, customers, competitors, home office, the holding company, the local community, and trade unions are all possible stakeholders outside the boundaries of the system. Some practitioners like to include employees as stakeholders, but those employees are clearly inside and part of the purposeful system itself. All employees are included in the social systems defined and discussed in Chapter 6.

Once a satisfactory list of environments and stakeholders is assembled, the system and its environment are compared in terms of expectations of the stakeholders of the system and the expectations of the stakeholders by the system. Table 3.5 presents an illustration of such a comparison of expectations for a U.S. military aircraft overhaul depot.

When these expectations conflict there may be reasons for changing the system, its purpose, product, boundaries, or environments. Where the comparison yields ambiguity rather than conflict, there is an invitation to more closely or clearly specify the individual and joint expectations between system and stakeholder. Conflicts and ambiguities also become an excellent opportunity to identify what the system can be-

TABLE 3.5
Environmental Elements
Army Helicopter Overhaul Facility

They Are Saying to the System		The System is Saying to Them
Give us information	**News media**	Be fair and supportive
Comply	**Local (city, county) regulations**	Be less resistant to change
Give us good helicopters	**Army**	We will support you
Abide by the contract	**Unions**	Provide good representation and we will work with you
Take our people	**State Employment Commission**	We will hire qualified people Help us meet EEO guidelines
Clean up your act	**OSHA inspectors**	Don't shut us down
Provide good jobs	**Local community**	Support us
Meet our standards	**TSARCOM**	Support us
Control costs	**DESCOM**	Give us more people, money, workload
Maintain readiness	**DARCOM**	We will do our part
Gotcha!	**GAO auditors**	We can justify it!
Understand our demands We will support you	**Other shops and divisions in the depot**	Meet your schedules and support us
Give us good training	**Army reserve units**	We will train you
Tell us your requirements and we will help you	**Civilian personnel office**	We are not happy with you— you are not supporting us
We will help you when we can	**Contracted services**	Meet your obligations
Give us your business Give us more lead time	**Vendors**	Reduce lead time Give it to us sooner

Continued

TABLE 3.5
Environmental Elements
Army Helicopter Overhaul Facility Continued

They Are Saying to the System		*The System is Saying to Them*
Follow our directives Do it our way	**EEO**	Don't overreact
Hire us but pay competitively	**Available labor force**	Check us out
Tell us what you want changed	**TSARCOM engineers**	We need timely deviations
Don't mess with the pigeons	**SPCA**	Understand they cost us money
Don't overlook our interests	**Community organizations**	We're involved
Use our services Follow our directions	**Metallurgical oil analysis labs**	Keep up the good work

come (a vision of organizational future), and what can be pursued (item 4 in Table 3.2). Where there is agreement and/or symmetry between system and stakeholder, the environmental part of the scan can be considered (at least) temporarily congruent.

❧ *Presenting Problems*

This part of the scan can describe what challenges and opportunities face the system as well as what threatens it. The "presenting problems" are visible when the STS process begins. They are not identified in order to seek a direct solution for them, but to recognize an energy or "appetite" for system change and the probable direction that change will take. With presenting problems, people in the system describe their need for change.

The STS process "map" presented as Figure 1.1 in Chapter 1 can be used to visualize the relationship between presenting problems and systems understanding and, in turn, the relationship between presenting problems and design. Figure 1.1 shows this relationship as a deferral of problem-solution until after the preliminary system design is completed.

At that time the list of presenting problems is reassessed to see which, if any, of the sources of items on the list cannot be addressed, or have not been addressed by the design. If any problems remain that will not be eliminated (or substantially reduced) by the design, then they can be resolved as an aspect of the "provisional design" shown as the last design action in Figure 1.1.

CONCLUSION

System scanning is a process by which the members of an organization understand their enterprise in systems terms. The essentials of system scan emphasize purpose, product, boundaries and environment, and their interdependencies. There are other items on the scan "checklist" that are essential as well, and they have been described above. These include setting or confirming objectives that are consistent with both the product and the purpose of the enterprise, and the "presenting problems," that provide an indication of the organization's energy for change and improvement. They help define the need for change.

The scan is not completed when top management finishes responding to the list of items in Table 3.1. Others in the system must be able to understand and confirm the mission statement, the philosophy, the output, the input, and the rest. It is inevitable that, during the process of cascading from the top, the conclusions drawn in the scan's initial drafting will be questioned, challenged, and changed. This process of involving others and beginning to empower people lower in the hierarchy contains hazards—it will not go smoothly, but it is necessary. The more people are involved, and the more they see the effort as an authentic opportunity to shape the common view of the enterprise, the more they will sincerely question those initial efforts. If, on the other hand, management tries to effect change in haste, these employees will see little or no chance to comment or respond. In some cases they may distance themselves from the process entirely.

Typically (in our experience with organizational "redesigns") a "management-only" scan will soon be followed with a parallel effort by a group of employees from various groups and levels from throughout the company. Usually called a "design team," this group will not only perform the scan, they will also complete the technical and social analyses described in later chapters. This second scan perspective will often be different from the first—to some degree. Working through these differences will usually result in a more balanced view of the sociotechnical system, and will often provide for a clearer, more appropriate scan for further dissemination.

Once the results of the scan have been disseminated and discussed throughout the organization, the process is still not complete. The STS analysis process is iterative and the elements interdependent: That is, as later steps in the process are undertaken, all previous results can be (and often are) called into question. It is not infrequent that a mission statement, objectives, or the definition of the product itself will be modified as the technical analysis gets under way. Likewise, the human values, the definition of relevant environments, or social objectives will be called into question, and occasionally modified, as the social analysis is taken on.

The scan process is at once the guideline to begin the sociotechnical design, and it is often the most reviewed and revised aspect of the "systems" understanding as the process continues.

The scan process creates a "living document" describing a living system — the sociotechnical organization.

REFERENCES

ACKOFF, R. L. "The Second Industrial Revolution." Speech delivered to For-
dyce House University of Pennsylvania, April 20, 1972. p. 26.
DAVIS, L. E. "Organization design." In G. Salvendy (ed.), *Handbook of industrial engineering.* New York: Wiley, Interscience, 1982.
TAYLOR, F. W. *The Principles of Scientific Management.* New York: Harper,
1911.
TRIST, E. L. "The evolution of socio-technical systems: A conceptual framework and an action research program." Ontario Quality of Working Life
Centre, Issues in the Quality of Working Life Occasional Paper, no. 2, June
1981.

CHAPTER 4

ช ช

Designing for Product/Service: Understanding How to Make " IT" Happen

"Technology is like genetic material—it carries with it the code of the society that conceived it."

(Source Unknown)

INTRODUCTION

If you want to understand the technical system, keep your eye on the product. This is a radical point of view. It seems ridiculously simple that a focus on the product of work *instead* of on the activities or actions of people at work would amount to an important paradigm shift, but it is. This shift has proven difficult for managers, engineers, and social scientists because they are often quite firmly grounded in the old world-view. It seems to them more comfortable to describe their work as action—what they "do"—rather than "product," or the purpose and outcome of their action.

This chapter deals with the need to focus on the product and the "product-in-becoming." This product focus is a fundamental insight guiding sociotechnical analysis and design.

ช The System Scan

As we discussed in Chapter 3, any organization can be considered a sociotechnical system (STS) if it is seen as a bounded, purposeful enter-

51

prise in a recognizable external environment, containing product transformation (technical system) and people working together over time to
bring about that transformation (social system). Among other things,
the scan involves identifying the system's technical mission, its core
outputs and inputs, and their boundaries. Only when these elements of
the scan have been defined can the technical analysis make sense.

⅋ *The Technical System Analysis*

The technical system analysis employs a methodology for understanding and then designing the product-creation or "transformation"
process.

This chapter shows how technical system methodology is used in
actual organizations, how it provides a stimulus to action, and how it
generates insights that too much precision might exclude.

Chapter 11 will show how the methodology is used for handling the
unique challenge of knowledge work and how the methodology could be
used in the wider range of professional and management settings.

A METHODOLOGY FOR UNDERSTANDING

Let's clarify what is meant by "methodology." Borrowing from a
definition by Peter Checkland (1981, pp. 161–162), "methodology"
does not mean "method." The outcome of developing a methodology
"is not *a method* but a set of *principles of method* which in any particular situation have to be reduced to a method uniquely suitable to that
particular situation."

Checkland takes methodology to be intermediate in status between
a philosophy and a technique or method. "A methodology will lack the
precision of a [method or] technique but will be a firmer guide to action
than a philosophy. Where a technique tells you 'how' and a philosophy
tells you 'what,' a methodology will contain elements of both 'what' and
'how.'"

STS technical analysis is a methodology, not just a method. The
importance of this distinction should become increasingly clear as we
proceed. To begin with, Checkland says a methodology always has these
four characteristics: It should be capable of being *used* in actual problem
situations; it should not be vague — it should provide a greater spur to
action than a general everyday philosophy; it should not be precise, like

a technique, but should be open to insights that precision might exclude; it also should be open to new developments in "systems science" that could be included in the methodology and used in a particular situation, as appropriate.

STS technical analysis methodology meets all four of these criteria. It also has some unique features all its own.

The *purpose* of technical systems methodology, as described in this chapter, for example, is intended to aid understanding. It is easy for people to learn and to use, easy to understand, and it provides an easily understood graphic display of the throughput conversion process for review by any interested party.

As stated above, the second purpose of the methodology is to focus on the product-in-becoming and to reduce attention on tools or human activity. The methodology avoids blaming people and concentrates instead on the need for control of the throughput, wherever and however that can best be achieved.

Finally, the purpose of the methodology is also to help people identify the most important aspects of the transformation process, those that will lead to a new design that best fulfills the mission of the enterprise.

These most important aspects of the transformation process are called "key variances." In making peanut butter on a commercial scale, it is *important* for the nuts to be roasted "just right." Too much variance from the factory's standard could affect the product's taste and lead consumers to try other brands. It is not only important, but *essential* that raw nuts received not be contaminated by a poisonous fungus. Any "variance" from zero fungus would be calamitous for the factory and maybe for its parent company. Both "degree of roast" and "amount of fungus" are key variances in the *product throughput*. More about variances and key variances follows later. For now it's enough to say that the concept of variance analysis lies at the heart of the new paradigm.

❧ Technical System Paradigm: Product as Purpose

Although the foundations of a paradigmatic revolution were laid with the development of key variance analysis from 1964 to 1967 (Davis & Engelstad, 1966; Engelstad, 1972) it was not until the early 1980s that it began to be publicly recognized as a radical departure from Scientific Management, in which the focus is on the tasks and activities of workers. This new focus on the product, and not the task, allows employees to get outside of narrowly predetermined job classifications, broadening their roles and enabling them to identify and perform whatever tasks and activities they see needing to be done to further the purpose of the system. When employees take these tasks and activities out of the technical system and put them conceptually into the social system, where they belong, they can start making the paradigm shift required. By putting the people over *there*, employees can more clearly see the product, right *here* in front of them. This shift in viewpoint differentiates subjects and objects, a very important step toward psychological maturity (cf. Erikson, 1963).

For a long time, our society has allowed technology to define and drive people, as opposed to creating workplaces wherein people drive technology in pursuit of the mission. To meet the mission, people require an overview or "big picture" of the product-in-becoming. Technical systems analysis gives them that overview and it helps empower them to manage their work for outcomes, instead of just doing the tasks to which they were assigned. It makes them more responsible, and more responsive, to what needs to get done. This allows the needs of the product to drive the tasks and activities as opposed to narrowly defined job descriptions and classifications.

Technical system, the part of the sociotechnical system encompassing product creation and delivery, differs from "technology." Technology is a more limiting concept, a component of the entire technical system.

For our purposes, *technology* is comprised of the tools, the work rules, the information (such as technical drawings and job specifications), machines and equipment, and other artifacts that are used to convert the system's input into its product. For these technological objects, the emphasis is on what they will "do" to the input *when it is made available.*

But *input* is not always available. In the case of machines, it is easy to visualize "doing" (activity) without result—picture a garbage disposal running in an empty sink, grinding and roaring uselessly. Likewise, human operators may obey all work rules, but without product to work on, they are doing only the "task" of waiting. The Maytag repairman (of television commercials) waits endlessly for something to repair.

Things don't work by themselves; *people* do. When workers are seen as part of the technology, they often have to be started, stopped, and "operated" from above. When they're understood to be part of the social system instead, they can operate the technology cooperatively using their own knowledge and initiative. They're not mindless objects anymore. They know how the transformation process works; they know what the key variances are; they know to keep those variances under control and thereby to meet the mission that keeps the whole enterprise afloat.

Here's the paradox, focus on the product and the people live.

ǂ *Input Plus Technology = "IT"*

The importance of outputs and inputs was introduced in Chapter 3. Careful definition of technical system inputs and outputs is also important because they define the *beginning and end of the throughput inside the system*—the primary focus of technical system analysis. Input-throughput-output is the familiar image of the product flow in systems thinking, and it refers to the core of the technical or producing aspect of every sociotechnical system.

The technical system is *not* defined as a collection of technology (machinery, equipment, tools, or hardware), nor is it seen as a collection of tasks (work orders, instructions, job definitions, or other human activities). In order to define the technical system in a way that is at once truly useful in developing improved organizations, and that is most relevant to the purpose of the enterprise, a different combination of elements comprising the conversion process is demanded.

The first essential element in the technical system is input ("I"), or that which is to be converted into output. The other essential element is the technology ("T"), which converts the input into the required output. The two elements require each other—input waiting to be converted is just an inert pile, while technology waiting for input is simply idle equipment and work rules.

Together I + T become a dynamic system in which input becomes output which pursues the purpose (mission) of the organization. That combination becomes embodied as throughput, or product-in-becoming, and is abbreviated "IT" (and rhymes with fit). "IT" becomes the internal focus of the purposeful sociotechnical system, the one thing that all members have in common, the language of work that they all share.

Input is a necessary element in the technical system, as is the technology, but each requires the other in order to be sufficient as a technical system. In this combination the technical system can be seen as the transformation of the input's potential to the resulting output—in other words "potential-in, product-out." Peanuts-in, peanut butter-out sounds simple, but for a commercial food processor, this contains many complexities and pitfalls. The technical system methodology describes a dynamic process. It requires the activities of people and equipment and the presence of adequate information about input to process, but it goes beyond these and defines the conversion of the product (or "IT") in pursuit of the purpose of the enterprise. Understanding the technical system as a dynamic conversion process that may (and usually does) extend beyond the human scale or horizons of the typical member/employee of an organization is a unique contribution of the sociotechnical system approach to work design.

Earlier models of work organization focused either on tasks alone or on the technology. One of the last North American auto plants to be designed to maximize the technology was the General Motors plant in Lordstown, Ohio. In this 1966 plant the assembly-line technology was streamlined, the work cycle time shortened, and the concern for human communication, cooperation and creativity was eliminated (*Newsweek*, 1972). The resulting worker focus couldn't possibly be on the car itself, although the employees themselves mourned the fact that they couldn't take the time to assure quality in production. The focus was on meeting the unforgiving schedule of 101.6 Chevrolet Vegas per hour (one every 38 seconds) through the assembly line (United States Senate, 1972, pp. 10–19).

Later analyses of the global auto industry concluded that successful auto plants are focused on cars (the "IT") with specific characteristics, ones that all employees can understand. For instance, in Toyota's case the most important feature of a car is reliability—quality of the car is represented in the precise definition of "starting every morning, and not leaving its owner stranded" (Womack, Jones, & Roos, 1990, p. 64). In the joint GM/Toyota New United Manufacturing, Inc. (NUMMI) plant in Fremont, California, which produced Chevrolet Novas in 1984–88, that focus on product was manifest as well. As a point for comparison, the line speed in the GM/Toyota NUMMI plant during 1986–88 was 53–80 Novas per hour (a flexible range from 45 seconds, to 68 seconds per car). NUMMI workers were, further, permitted to stop the line if they saw a problem.

Unit Operations — The Changes in State IT Goes Through During Technical Transformation. During the early 1960s, engineers Louis Davis, from the United States, and Per Engelstad, from Norway, began work with Emery, Trist, and the others at the British Tavistock Institute to help design experiments using STS to improve labor relations and organizational effectiveness in Norway. Working with a troubled Norwegian papermill, the extended Tavistock team created a method whereby pulp plant operators could understand their technical operations well enough to rotate through their plant and control the pulp for various initial conditions. Chief among the concepts introduced into the technical analysis, as an enhancement of operator understanding, was the notion of "unit operations" (Davis & Engelstad, 1966; Emery, 1966). The concept of unit operations had originated with A. D. Little for the design of chemical process plants (A. D. Little, Inc., 1965), but never had it been used in sociotechnical system design. As originally used in chemical engineering, unit operations described state changes in a chemical substance as it passed from earlier forms to later ones in a transformation process. A generic model of unit operations is diagrammed in Figure 4.1.

Throughput: The Conversion of Input into Output. Obviously the conversion of input into output (the total throughput or IT in the enterprise) possesses complexity — often more complexity than the human operator and manager can comprehend and cope with at once. This complexity is reduced by breaking IT into unit operations, or meaningful "chunks," in order to put the technical system into human scale. This chunking takes the form of *changes in state* in the throughput that are *meaningful* to the members in terms of the mission and purpose of their enterprise. When the input changes in an important or significant way, we call that *state change* a "unit operation."

As applied to STS design, the concept of unit operations provides workers an appropriate common language; it enables employees to get out of focusing on machines, job, and tasks and start looking at the whole conversion process that really produces the product. Use of the concept also demands an unequivocal focus on the throughput and its course of completion. For designing appropriate and effective work systems, unit operations combines the best from information theory and from social organization theory. But the use of unit operations did not provide, at the time of its development, all of the conceptual tools needed — specifically, it lacked sensitivity to throughput variations re-

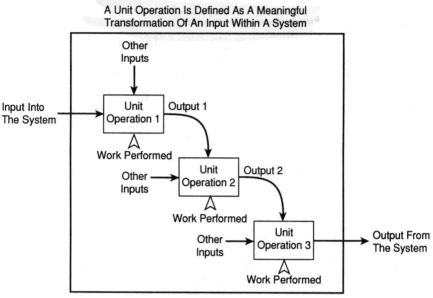

A Unit Operation Is Defined As A Meaningful
Transformation Of An Input Within A System

FIGURE 4.1
Unit Operations

sulting from the environment and from the process itself. As Emery (1966) concluded at the time, "analysis in terms of unit operations failed to encompass many of the critical variances for which production design

---

TECHNICAL VARIANCES ARE OF TWO TYPES:

1. **"Input variances" come in with the input—those emerging from the environment. Example: Presence of poisonous fungus in raw peanuts.**
2. **"Throughput variances" are generated during the normal conversion process—created by mechanical or human sources, or from interactions among technical operations. Example: Degree of "roastedness" peanuts attain.**

(or redesign) decisions have to be made. . . . [These] variances excluded by unit operations analysis were those emerging from the environment . . . and from the human input" to the process.

Technical Variance. Process or throughput variances were introduced into the technical system analysis in order to understand what effect environmental conditions and process runout (sometimes the result of human intervention) might have on subsequent (and eventually final) results. The term "variance" in this sense is used in the way that cost accountants use "budget variance." *It is a deviation from normal, expected, or average state of the throughput.* Once establishing that such variances could be listed for a product throughput, it is a direct step to examine the relationships among the variances. Understanding these relationships helps to examine the systemic nature of the full list, thus facilitating in the identification of key, or "critical," variances. Key variances are those having a significant impact on the product's quantity, quality, and cost. The identification of such key variances serves to further the understanding of process operators and aids in empowering them to respond effectively to unplanned events. In addition, the relationships among the variances can be seen as the major interconnections defining the systemic character of the "technical system." The important task for the investigator is to identify the myriad technical requirements or variances and from among those to select the most important, or *key*, variances. Those key variances are so called because they include not only the technical requirements that must be met in order to control their direct effects, but also they include the variances that, although having indirect effects themselves, are key to controlling those that do impact directly on the systems's primary task. Variances are defined, not as problems to be solved, but simply as deviations in "IT" around some central tendency or from some norm, or specified standard. The most important of these deviations (the key variances) represent technical system requirements to be controlled; the primary purpose of the variance analysis is to examine the manner in which those variances, or requirements for control, are met.

Key Variance Control. The next step in developing the technical system analysis is to link the key variances to the information system underlying the identified unit operations. This "key variance control" analysis is achieved by showing how the key variances are presently controlled by the social system. In so doing, it identifies where important organizational connections and other information loops exist or are required. It avoids placing blame where variances are not controlled. Successful sociotechnical systems are built on the premise that people are trying to do a good job and that the investigation should help to eliminate traps in the system that cause mistaken actions and omissions. This approach shifts the emphasis from trying to "fix" the people to trying to fix the system. Key variance control is the subject of Chapter 5, and the concept and its implications will be more completely developed there. One of the important points we will be considering in that chapter is controlling key variances as close to their "source" as possible.

STS, with its emphasis on product and purpose, permits the creation of work system designs that emphasize the centrality of employees' roles *to the delivery of the product*, along with the relevance of the system's mission to socially desirable ends. Thus, STS magnifies the value of skill training and competence for those central roles in a socially relevant system. These benefits are only possible if STS is seen as carrying with it a new view of technical systems and if that view is applied to enhancing organizational response to changing and turbulent environments.

Expanding the Technical System Application in North America: 1968-1980. The original assumptions and restrictions limiting the technical analysis methodology to continuous process industries (Emery & Trist, 1978) were largely ignored in North America as the techniques were applied after 1968. Of course, the STS methodology continued to be applied to continuous-process plants and to the linear process of manufacturing dimensional products like auto assembly. Further applications of the methodology, in information processing as well as service delivery operations, were undertaken by investigators outside the Tavistock Institute—many of whom were located in the United States and Canada.

Input in sociotechnical systems should be limited to what is actually converted into product or output. Common-sense thinking causes many practitioners to include much more as "input" to a system than should be included in STS. Consistent with the product/purpose focus of STS, the input to the technical system must be the raw material *to be converted* into the output or product. Clearly identifying the input requires one simple rule—include only what will be converted, and exclude what may be converted into a "by-product," or scrap and waste, or whatever is simply consumed in the conversion process. In food-processing technologies, raw fruits, vegetables, or nuts are input for cooked or processed products, just as milk, rennin, and "starter" are input for cheese. To carry the cooking illustration further, raw vegetables are washed in water and cooked in water, but water would not be defined as input on that basis alone because it is used up and/or discarded. If the cooking water is further processed (perhaps by mixing with seasonings or butter) as a sauce for the vegetables, then it would be considered "input" too. Like water, the intangible electrical power is required in many technical processes, but as it is normally employed it would be considered part of the technology and not input. In electronic data processing, for instance, electricity is required to create a data file on one personal computer (PC) and required to read the file from the data base on another PC. The electrical power is not the file itself, but simply the enabling technology. Often "people," "money," and "information" are incorrectly considered as "input" to a sociotechnical system when they are actually part of the technology. These important aspects of any business system are considered to be input if, and *only if,* they are converted directly into the product or output, such as in a modeling agency for people or a bank for money. Just as multiple outputs can be envisioned, so can multiple inputs—but they must be what is converted into the output that defines and is defined by the main business of the enterprise.

The Input-Throughput-Output Cycle. The technical system can be seen as the essential interplay between the components of input-throughput-output ("IT") and the human agent. These components can be described as the *tangible object* (the input as it becomes throughput), the *dynamic process* (the changes occurring in the tangible object as it becomes the output), and the *agent of change* (the purposeful human impact on the dynamic process).

So far, we have defined technical system understanding and the relationships of these components with one another. It is time to set these ideas into illustrations and examples of how to apply them as a methodology.

TOOLS AND TECHNIQUES OF TECHNICAL SYSTEM UNDERSTANDING

Overall the technical variance analysis is a way of "seeing" the conversion or transformation process—"seeing" all at once, but with much of the important complexity intact. It is a way for everyone involved in a purposeful system to "wrap their minds around" the purpose, product, and process for obtaining that product. This understanding becomes the common language for everyone in the system and others who have an interest in it as its suppliers or users.

❧ The Variance Matrix as the Central Tool in the Technical System Methodology

As described, the throughput and its unit operations (the "IT") can be further elaborated with the listing of variances, from which a smaller set of key variances is identified. These variances are arrayed in a graphic matrix that displays the unit operations, variances, and key variances on one sheet.

The typical variance matrix appears linear—the unit operations marching neatly down the page (or matrix) and the variances in the matrix relating downstream to further, later events. This is not surprising given its origins. Key variance analysis was developed for use in process industries, which are essentially linear and largely one-way processes.

Food processing has developed as either a batch process or a continuous process. As the latter, it, too, is largely linear and one way, although much can be done to correct for the effects of deviations introduced early in the process. Cheese making, in its basic form, provides a succinct example of food processing as a major type of continuous-process technology that produces soft, unripened cheeses such as American cheddar-type slices, or pizza-style grated mozzarella. Cheese making can also be used as an example of batch processing in the making of ripened or aged cheeses such as French Roquefort or other specialty cheeses like the hand-made Italian "bufalina" mozzarella. Over 2,000 varieties of cheese are known. They all have several common features: All are made from mammalian milk in a process containing five state changes (unit operations). In addition, they all rely on microorganisms for the transformation from milk to cheese. In fact, cheese contains the largest concentration of microorganisms found in any basic food. Much of the following discussion of cheese making was inspired by an article in *Scientific American* (Kosikowski, 1985).

A major source of throughput variances is the input itself. In the cheese example, real Roquefort cheese is made from sheep's milk, the bufalina mozzarella begins with the water buffalo's milk, and many other cheeses are made from special milk produced by herds of particular breeds of cows. In addition to these large differences in milk depending on the type of mammal from which it came, the milk can contain variances due to the condition of the herd, season of the year, and what has been used for feed and forage. The way the milk is handled before it reaches the cheese factory can introduce further variances into the milk input.

The second input for cheese is rennin, the coagulating agent. Rennin, an enzyme traditionally extracted from animal sources, can be more cheaply obtained from certain fungi—a product that has captured about half the market (Kosikowski, 1985). Obviously, the difference in source will introduce some variances into the rennin used, even if minor ones. In natural raw milk, the input to the process, there are billions of microorganisms (bacteria, viruses, and fungi) per gram. They are required for several phases of the process, such as conversion of milk into lactic acid (the presence of which results in the consistency of the cheese). Their numbers decline markedly during the process because of insufficient oxygen, high acidity, and the presence of inhibitory compounds produced as the cheese ripens. Microorganisms themselves are also input because some of them are transformed into enzymes required for creating the flavor and aroma of the cheese.

Several factors characterize the quality of the input. For example, the milk needs to be fresh (no more than 12 hours from milking), from herds of particular breeds of animals, containing no more than certain levels of microorganisms. The starter organisms (lactic acid bacteria) must be able to survive the temperatures reached in the curdling step in order to continue to convert milk into lactic acid. In this same way, the qualities of the output can be characterized as well—the cheese must have the appearance, texture, flavor, and aroma particular to that variety; it must be resistant to spoilage consistent with the type it is; and it must not precipitate a public health incident (food poisoning).

The five unit operations of cheese making are as follows:

1. The milk becomes pasteurized and combined with lactic acid bacteria to begin the fermenting process (and combined with coloring agents if necessary).
2. The prepared milk becomes curdled or coagulated through combination with rennin.
3. The resulting curds, separated from their whey, are changed by lactic acid and heat to a structure (form and consistency) resembling the final product.
4. The structured curd changes to a form and shape characteristic of the type of cheese it is (e.g., wheel, ball, or block).
5. Finally the formed cheese ripens or ferments over time to take on the flavor, scent, and texture of the final product.

A wide range of options taken during each unit operation or state change determine the variety produced and the quality of the results. The following illustration of a technical system analysis of cheese describes the nature of those options. Chapter 5 will more fully develop those options and the ensuing choices possible.

❧ *Importance of Throughput Variances*

Variances were defined earlier not as problems to be solved, but as deviations around a norm, or average. Incorrectly applied, the variance concept is often characterized as "problems." Correctly applied, variances are deviations from some established standard. Variances should be stated in neutral terms; for example, "temperature of throughput" rather than throughput that is too hot or too cold. A variance matrix lists all these deviations in checklist fashion, so that effects of variances upon other variances can be easily seen.

Table 4.1 presents a variance matrix for the cheese-making process outlined above. IT in this case is the milk, the rennin, and microbial agents (bacteria, viruses, and fungi), in conjunction with the heat and humidity, the pipes, vessels, and people of the cheese factory. The throughput is the cheese-in-becoming as it passes through the five state changes (unit operations) shown on the left margin of the matrix. The 34 variances listed along the diagonal of the figure represent many, but not all, of the ways the throughput varies in the manufacture of any of the 2,000 varieties of cheese. They represent a mixture of "input" and "throughput" variances. Most of these variances should be familiar from the preceding discussion, but others may be apparent in the context of the throughput flow. All cheeses must pass through this process and the variances shown are embodied in all of them. For instance, all cheese requires elevated temperatures for the various changes it goes through. The cooking process elevates the temperature of the throughput in unit operations I, II, and III, and its cessation reduces it in unit operations IV and V. This condition is shown or implied in Variances 3, 10, 17, 26, and 28. These are all examples of "throughput variances" created in the throughput during the normal process. "Input variances" are illustrated by the composition of the milk (Variance 2), the microorganisms (Variance 1), and the rennin (Variance 12).

Standards can be identified for each variance. For example, Variance 17 specifies the temperature of the cheese during cooking in unit operation III to be either up to 37°C or more than 37°C. This means that some varieties of cheese (e.g., Swiss cheese) contain lactic acid bacteria that survive the 54°C cooking temperatures that emmentaler and gruyere require; while many other varieties (e.g., cheddar) employ bacteria that make palatable cheese only when heated between 20°C and 37°C.

Table 4.1 displays relationships among the variances. The relationships among the variances are shown by "x's" in the matrix. They are not necessarily causal relationships (i.e., an earlier variance doesn't necessarily "cause" a later one to which it is related), but some of them are. For instance, the degree of pasteurization (Variance 3) is related to the number of microorganisms (Variance 1), since a large number of the latter will require a longer heating time for the pasteurization process to reduce the organisms to a suitable level for the intended cheese. However, Variance 1 does not cause a particular level of Variance 3. The degree of pasteurization does "cause" a certain proportion of microorganisms to die, thus influencing their numbers in Variances 5 and 6. Pasteurization is an intentional variable—a lower degree of pasteurization can make a positive difference in the taste and smell of the final product. However, whether through insufficient pasteurization or other cause, some microbial agents that may accelerate spoilage or cause disease in some consumers can remain after the cheese is made.

Note that the matrix shows many relationships between number of microorganisms (Variances 4, 5, 6, and 23) or more correctly their enzymes, and many important characteristics of the cheese such as softness and amount of amino acids. The ultimate consistency, flavor, and aroma of the finished cheese are direct results of the amounts and characteristics of the variety and amount of enzymes produced by the bacteria that act on the fats and proteins of the milk. Flavor, aroma, spoilage, and toxicity are not shown on the matrix because they are positive or negative characteristics of the output or product, not of the throughput. These output characteristics are the criteria for identifying and selecting some key variances to target for control. The other key variances are identified through their relationships with other variances in the matrix.

The Systemic Nature of Technical Systems.   Why check the effects of variances in other relationships and interdependencies? Because the methodology represents systems characteristics. Systems are interconnected sets of components that are more related to themselves (i.e., to one another) than they are to the environment—for the purpose of the system. The purpose in the cheese-making example is cheese, and the interconnection among the variances is in relation to cheese. Although

TABLE 4.1
Matrix of Variances: Cheese

O = Key Variance

Unit
Operations →

Variances

I — Prepared milk

```
 1 :1 Number of microorganisms in raw milk (bacteria, virus, fungi)
 2 : :2 Amount of fat, protein, carboyhydrates in milk
 3 :X: :3 Degree of Pasteurization
 4 :X: :X:4 Number of microorganisms for flavor
 5 :X: :X: (5) Number of microorganisms for disease (Salmonella, Listeria)
 6 :X: :X: :6 Number of microorganisms for spoilage (Fungi)
 7 :   :X:   :   :(7) Amount & Type of starter/microorganisms for consistency (lactic acid bacteria)
 8 :   :   :   :   :8 Amount of coloring
 9 :   :   :X:   :9 Amount of lactic acid
```

II — Formed (coagulated) Curd

```
10 : : : : : : :10 Temperature of curdled milk
11 : : : : : : :11 Time for coagulation
12 : : : : : : :12 Type of rennin (animal or fungal)
13 : : : : : : :13 Amount of rennin
14 : : : : : : :14 Surface area of curd
15 : : : :X: : :X:15 Moisture content of curd
```

66

:16 Amount of lactic acid
⑰ Temperature ($\geq 37°C \leq$)
:18 Time cooked (30 min $\geq$ 90 min)
: :19 Amount of whey released
X:X:X:X:X: :20 Hardness of curd
: : : : : :21 Amount of salt & water
: : : : : : :22 Amount of oxygen
X:X: : : :23 Number of microorganisms/enzymes
X: : :24 Compression of cheese
:X:25 Shape/size of cheese
X: : :26 Temperature & humidity of surface
X:X: :27 Amount of oxygen
X: : :28 Time & temperature in storage
X⑳ Number microbial enzymes
:30 Elasticity of cheese
X:X: :31 Amount amino acids
X: :32 Softness of cheese
X: :X: :33 Amount of CO_2
X: :X: :X:34 Amount of ammonia

III
Structured
curd

IV
Formed
Cheese

V
Ripened
(Fermented)
Cheese

67

milk is highly related to the cow while still in the dairy, it becomes more related to the lactic acid, rennin, and conditions in the cheese factory when it enters that system. In such a system, a seemingly small (or unimportant) variance early in the process can become very important later in the process, for the purpose of that system. For instance low amounts of starter bacteria (Variance 7) reduces the amount of lactic acid, which relates directly to consistency and hardness during ripening.

૨ Key Variances

A small subset of the variances identified while constructing a matrix (typically about 10%) will be considered "key" to the ultimate quality, quantity, or cost of the product. Furthermore, depending on the purpose and product of the enterprise, different technical systems will have different key variances. For every variety of cheese, there can be a different set of variances that will be most important to that variety (thus "key" variances to be added to those key variances identified for the generic process). For example, to produce French Roquefort, the presence of an enzyme from a special fungus during unit operation V is key. Concentration of that same microbial agent and its enzyme is not desired for most other cheeses—and in some unique cases it may be a key variance to reduce or eliminate rather than to nurture. Key variances are identified in either one of two ways—through their *direct* impact on the final product or through their *indirect* effects on many other variances, through a chain of events otherwise impossible without the originating variance.

Specific Examples of Key Variances in Table 4.1. *Variance 29*, number of microbial enzymes, is critical for the taste and aroma of the final cheese. Although it is related to many other variances in the matrix (e.g., composition of the milk [v 2], amount of microorganisms [v 1]), it is directly a function of conditions that reduce the bacterial population, since the enzymes are released on the death of millions of lactic acid bacteria. In successful cheese making it is necessary to keep the bacteria producing lactic acid as long as possible, yet to kill them via absence of oxygen and presence of salt and low temperature at the correct time to create the enzymes for flavor. These conditions for killing the bacteria are found primarily in unit operation V.

Variance 17, temperature of the cheese during cooking, is a key variance, since it is this, in combination with salt and water, that is most responsible for the elasticity of the finished product. Not much can be done during subsequent unit operations to suitably correct for variations in elasticity.

Variance 7, the amount and type of starter/microorganisms for consistency (lactic acid bacteria), is the most important for the final physical character of the cheese (crumbly, hard, dense, etc.) because of its influence on the creation of lactic acid and timely fermentation of the cheese during ripening.

Variance 5, the number of microorganisms for disease (*Salmonella, Listeria*), and for spoilage, which are initially present is affected by Variance 3, degree of pasteurization, but their number is normally not reduced to zero. Although contamination of the raw milk can be reduced by pasteurization, the total elimination of all bacteria (both harmful and helpful ones) through extreme levels of pasteurization would make the resulting food safe but would also reduce its palatability or taste. Of prime importance to a cheese maker are both to eliminate any possibility of food poisoning, as well as to win return business through superior taste and aroma. Distinctive and high-quality cheeses are normally enhanced through some "wild" microorganisms found in the raw milk. Historically, cheese has been among the safest foods to eat, in part because of insufficient oxygen, high acidity, and the fact that cheese produces its own inhibitory compounds. Although Variance 5 is shown early in the process, it can enter at nearly any time during cheese making, which reduces some of the effect of pasteurization anyway. As cheese making becomes a truly large operation, the danger of infecting a large number of consumers, even if they are a small proportion of the total, is increased. It is unfortunate that very small concentrations (e.g., 2,000 bacteria per ton of cheese) can be seriously toxic (if not fatal) to some proportion of the population (Hedberg et al., in press).

UNDERSTANDING THROUGHPUT IN SERVICE SYSTEMS

The technical system methodology (including the key variance analysis) is widely applied in transaction processing and customer service industries (such as insurance companies and banks), as well as in manufacturing and continuous process. The following section contains a brief example of key variance analysis in an insurance benefits authorization office — a service delivery system.

In a white-collar system the transformation of throughput takes place just as it does in a continuous chemical or food process or manufacturing system. "Transaction processing" is a term used to describe one common type of white-collar operation involving changes in information in banking (e.g., check processing), accounting (e.g., payroll tax calculation and withholding), many internal government operations, and other office settings where the information is remote or detached from its source. "Direct customer service," on the other hand, involves changes in information in direct response to client requests. Although retail sales, medical or dental care, and food service immediately come to mind as customer service agencies, many transaction processing systems can be seen (and define themselves) to be in direct service to a customer. In the white-collar system the input is information. Whether transaction processing or direct customer service, the input is still information. The difference between information processing and service, however, is that in the latter the input is defined as a customer's request for service rather than merely a piece of paper to process, a telephone to answer, a sample to test, or a computer screen to respond to.

SERVICE IS NOT SERVITUDE

There are two things to remember about customer service. First, service means that customer satisfaction is a major output *criterion*, but the value of the output must also take into account the dignity of the people providing the service. Second, customers are not throughput (except in the very narrowly defined group of "personal service" occupations like masseuse, hypnotist, or healer, for example). Customers provide information-as-input in the form of a request, and they expect the request to be transformed into information indicating some change to their satisfaction.

All requests for service are information, but not all information is a request for service. In other words, the service delivery system is a proper subset of information systems. The output of service systems is a fulfilled request and satisfied customer. The output of information systems is, naturally enough, transformed information, whether useful information from raw data, or persuasive knowledge from information. Both service delivery and information processing systems are largely routine, with most variances capable of being identified and controlled directly by the people doing the work. Like industrial or manufacturing systems, white-collar technical systems have been designed historically to optimize what people do. This use of the old paradigm in work system design puts white-collar systems in the same trap as other segments of North American enterprise—so long as they are looking at "what they do" they can't see what's happening to the service deliverable—or "IT." This life in the old paradigm makes white-collar systems good candidates for the sociotechnical system methodology to improve employee knowledge of the process, and to exert greater control over it in the pursuit of the purpose of the enterprise. Although professional work (or "knowledge work," as it is coming to be called) involves information processing as well, the specifics of a technical system methodology for understanding the process and product of that occupational segment are not the same as those used for more routine information processing applications. Knowledge work will be discussed in Chapter 11.

AN INSURANCE COMPANY CASE

One of the first illustrations of technical system methodology and key variance analysis applied to service systems featured a variance matrix developed for an insurance company pension claims department (Taylor, 1975). Table 4.2 shows an adaptation of that variance matrix, which illustrates application of the technical system methodology to insurance processing and customer service and the throughput-oriented focus of unit operations and variances.

This pioneering case involved the Pension Payment Department, a group of 18 people, in a large life and health insurance company as it existed in 1973. The work of the department was seen as follows. Payment examiners received requests for initiation of pension payments and determined if an award was warranted and its amount correct. Generally these requests came from the insurance company's agents or from the personnel clerks in the client companies that held the group policies. In both cases, the examiners' focus was on the benefits paid to the pensioner as a member (or survivor of member) of the corporate client "family."

The detailed group policy files were kept in a different division, the Records Maintenance Department. Individual claim information, however, was kept on a mainframe computer. Examiners often needed technical information from other departments (e.g., actuarial, accounting). Examiners had been given access to the mainframe through terminals where they could also calculate the payments, some of which were very complex. The Pension Payments Department also employed typists who acted as clerks and messengers, a supervisor, and a department manager.

The purpose of the payment system was to satisfy the client companies' responsibility to their employees and pensioners. The output was the correct and timely payment of pension benefits. In fact, examiners were dedicated to one-day turnaround of a claim (request for payment) from its receipt in their office. This work required that examiners cooperate and coordinate with client companies and others in their own company, as well as occasionally with the individual beneficiaries.

A sociotechnical design team of employees from this department was formed to address issues of productivity and employee turnover. Four examiners and their supervisor became the STS design team and undertook the sociotechnical systems analysis for their unit (see Table 4.2). The four unit operations they identified for the process were:

   I. A received and classified request or claim
  II. A claim collated with other information
 III. An approved or denied claim
 IV. Distributed payment and/or information

These unit operations hold a strong similarity to the phases of processed information used in computer systems analysis. It is no coincidence that systems analysts looking at information processing would focus their attentions on the same issues as would clerical employees who were encouraged to view their work in terms of its product and throughput (Taylor, 1979).

The key variances uncovered in the technical system analysis of the department were:

v1. *Volume of mail received.* Because their work all came in by U.S. or company mail, the examiners noted that their workload varied considerably from day to day—it depended on the number of pieces contained in the mailbag.

v4. *Volume of rush requests.* The speed of routing a claim through the office was sometimes too demanding—field sales agents would often request "rush" authorizations even when they weren't absolutely necessary.

v8. *Availability of Standard Policy File.* The paper policy files were not always

TABLE 4.2
Matrix of Variances: Pension Claims   O = Key Variance

Unit Operations →   *Variances*

I
Received, and classified
Request for payment

```
 1 (1) Volume of mail received
 2 :    :2 Type of claimant (primary beneficiary or survivor)
 3 :X:  :3 Correctness/completeness of policy # on mail
 4 :X:  :(4) Volume of rush requests
 5 :    :X:  :5 Number of requests per piece of mail
 6 :    :   :X:6 Complexity of request
```

II
Matched Policy
and Request

```
 7 :  :X:  :   :   :7 Timeliness of technical information from other depts.
 8 :X:X:X:  :X:(8) Availability of Standard Policy File
 9 :  :X:X:  :X:X:  :9 Availability of request
10 :  :X:  :X:X:  :   :10 Completeness of information in request
```

III
Approved or
Denied Request

```
11 :X:  :X:  :X:X:X:X:11 Timeliness of transaction
12 :X:  :   :X:X:  :X:(12) Number/type of terms in calculation (complexity)
13 :X:  :X:X:X:  :X:X:13 Accuracy of award amount
14 :  :X:  :X:X:X:X:X:X:  :X:  :14 Number and origin of required signatures
15 :  :   :X:  :   :   :X:  :15 Availability of materials to complete transaction
```

IV
Distributed
Payment and/
or Information

```
16 :  :   :   :   :   :X:  :X:X:16 Form of response (check, letter, form)
17 :X:  :   :   :   :X:X:X:  :X:  :17 Timely distribution of materials
18 :  :   :   :   :   :   :   :   :18
```

73

immediately available, or were difficult to trace, because they might be checked out to another examiner working on another request on the same policy.

v12. *Number/type of terms in calculation (complexity).* The calculations required for determining amount of benefit were, in some cases, very complex.

All four variances related to the department's ability to deliver timely and satisfactory decisions (either directly in the case of V1 and V12; or indirectly as with V4 and V8). The first key variance (V1), volume of mail, was an environmental effect that the department would simply have to continue to cope with in order to meet their criteria of timely payment. The variable (and sometimes complex) calculation

---

ASSURING THE PARADIGM SHIFT

The technical systems paradigm shift must be shared by the whole system. Even though employee members of the STS design team are clear about the product and throughput focus of the technical system methodology in a misguided effort to avoid misunderstanding or consternation of others in the company, they may choose to describe their process in more familiar activity- and problem-oriented terms.

When such a compromise is made, the resulting variance matrix usually contains unit operations presented as actions on the throughput, not intended changes in IT; and (some if not all) variances listed in the matrix are worded in such a way that they depict problems, or human errors, and not deviations in the normal process of transforming IT.

The consultant to the process must take a tough enough stand with the analysis team on this so that the methodology assures that the throughput- and product-oriented view is passed on from the team to the rest of their organization. Only in this way can the technical systems paradigm shift be shared by the whole system.

requirement (V12) was also something the examiners felt they could successfully contend with through innovation at their workplace. At the same time, several variances could not be controlled without cooperation and coordination with others in the company. Those variances included the assignment of (sometimes unnecessary) urgency (V4), together with the timely (sometimes difficult) procurement of the policy files (V8), which could slow down the entire process for all claims through interrelatedness of these and other variances such as V9, V13, and V14. The two key Variances 4 and 8 were largely under the control of people outside the Payment Department.

Design teams in this and other companies find key variances like these are simple to communicate. Relationships among the key variances themselves and with other variances in the system are explicitly portrayed in the matrix. Key variances are the raw material of "Performance By Design." In this insurance case, a system design based on better control of key variances resulted in a sustained 10% performance improvement (Taylor, 1977).

CONCLUSION

In sum, the technical system methodology can provide not only a deep and unique understanding of a system's function for members of the system (and outsiders), but a logical and measured basis for guiding change. When technical system data are compared with the expectations vocalized in the company's statement of mission and purpose, some of the requirements of change are highlighted in bold relief. In addition, technical systems results, as a list of key variances, can be used as the raw material for individual, unit, and system performance data. Such performance data, based on the common denominator of the system — reducing or eliminating deviation in the throughput and output — is novel, perhaps even revolutionary. By comparison, conventional performance indicators are activity oriented. They not only focus attention on the "wrong stuff," but conventional measures of production are typically unable to absorb the complexities of technical systems in order to be valid and fair to employees. New performance measures based on key variances become the common language of all people concerned with the product and purpose of the enterprise, and they include the tools (i.e., variance matrix) required for everyone involved to understand the complex of interrelations among the measures. Key variances are identified before the system is improved, and as such, they can become baselines against which to compare the performance results of the subsequent changes and improvements to the system. Technical system methodology, including key variance understanding, has started to become the basis of identifying the primary quality aspects and key performance indicators in total quality management (TQM) programs. If it is "owned" by the members of the organization, technical system understanding can be updated at any time. Once the unit operations and variance matrix have been created, they can be reviewed and revised, with little effort, to reflect the current state of the system and to compare it to variations and average results at any point before changes are made. The understanding of product focus is a continuous process.

REFERENCES

CHECKLAND, P. *Systems Thinking, Systems Practice.* Chichester, Eng.: Wiley, 1981.

DAVIS, L. E. & P. H. ENGELSTAD. "Unit Operations in Socio-Technical Systems: Analysis and Design." Tavistock Institute for Human Relations document no. T894, October 1966.

EMERY, F. E. "Unit Operations as a Unit of Analysis" (Originally published 1966) In F. E. Emery. *The Emergence of a News Paradigm of work.* Canberra: Center for Continuing Education, Australian National University, p. 99, 1978.

EMERY, F. E. & E. L. TRIST. "Analytical Model for Socio-Technical Systems." In W. A. Pasmore & J. J. Sherwood (eds.), *Sociotechnical systems: a sourcebook.* San Diego: University Associates, 1978.

ENGELSTAD, P. E. "Socio-Technical Approach to Problems of Process Control." In L. E. Davis & J. C. Taylor (eds.), *Design of Jobs.* London: Penguin Books, 1972.

ERIKSON, E. H. *Childhood and Society.* 2nd rev. ed. New York: Norton, 1963.

HEDBERG, C. W., J. A. KORLATH, J.-Y. A'AOUST, K. E. WHITE, W. L. SCHELL, M. R. MILLER, D. N. CAMERON, K. L. MacDONALD & M. T. OSTERHOLM. "A Multi-State Outbreak of *Salmonella javiana* and *Salmonella oranienburg* Infections Due to Consumption of Contaminated Cheese." *Journal of the American Medical Association, in press.*

KOSIKOWSKI, F. V. "Cheese." *Scientific American,* pp. 88–99, May 1985.

LITTLE, A. D., INC. "Analysis of Automation Potential by Means of Unit Operations." U.S. Department of Labor c-66411, 1965.

NEWSWEEK, "Blue Collar Blues in Lordstown," February 7, 1972.

TAYLOR, J. C. "The Human Side of Work: The Socio-Technical Approach to Work System Design." *Personnel Review,* 4(3), 18–22, 1975.

TAYLOR, J. C. "Job Design in an Insurance Company," *Journal of Contemporary Business,* 6(2), 1977, 37–48.

TAYLOR, J. C. "Job Design Criteria-Twenty Years Later." In L. E. Davis, & J. C. Taylor (eds.), *The Design of Jobs*, 2nd ed. Santa Monica, CA: Goodyear, 1979.

UNITED STATES SENATE. Hearings on Bill S. 3916, Worker Alienation, July 25 and 26, 1972.

WOMACK, J. P., D. T. JONES, & D. ROOS. *The Machine That Changed The World.* New York: Rawson Associates, 1990.

CHAPTER 5

𝖺 𝖺

Designing for Control: Understanding Success and How IT Is Unique

"'If you want to keep people working—and they do want to work, believe it or not—you have to cheat the system.' . . . [In cases like this] we are witnessing the creation of a new informal system, in which the role of the worker is to handle those frequent situations where the computer system, however technically sophisticated, is too crudely programmed to respond to the complexities of the real world."

(Schneider, Howard, & Emspak, 1985)

INTRODUCTION

Analysis of the management of key variances frequently reveals that they are often not controlled where they originate and that much of the control is undertaken long after the variance limits are exceeded. This is a design decision—whether by omission or by commission.

The designer must beware of a serious pitfall of traditional organizations: Managers cannot continue to intuitively design their organization's structure in a world that is increasingly chaotic—they thus fail to "identify and control variances at their source." With a sociotechnical system, work is designed to make the most of technology and of the people who control it, for conscious organization purpose. With STS designs, people in organizations can respond more flexibly and effectively to their turbulent and changing environments.

The key variance control analysis described in this chapter provides an important opportunity to see how conventional ways are often inappropriate because of the difficulty of communicating among groups.

UNDERSTANDING THE MARKET NICHE: WHY OUR SYSTEM IS UNIQUE

Each work system is unique in its output characteristics and in its mission and purpose. A more effective sociotechnical system has a closer correspondence between the characteristics of its product and its statement of purpose than does a less effective system. The links between product and purpose are the technical goals and objectives—those quantifiable and attainable measures introduced in Chapter 3. Goals, it will be recalled, are short-term statements of expected results. For example, in a sociotechnical system where quality of product forms its explicit mission, *daily, weekly, or monthly* measures of quality in terms of scrap, rework, or defects per 100 items are technical system *goals*. Objectives, on the other hand, are the longer-term performance expectations. To continue the same illustration, a baseline number of *quarterly or annual* rates of the same quality indicators used for goals, plus a defined rate of warranty returns, as well as measures of the longer-term, out-of-warranty reliability, could be some of the system's technical *objectives*. Employees and managers in the chemical plant introduced in Chapter 1 discovered that their originally stated objectives did not describe the bridge between product goals and plant mission. Their scan revealed that the plant's existing objectives were not intended to aid the pursuit of purpose, but rather to correct budget and performance problems from the preceding year. It was clear that they needed to create plantwide objectives to reflect the "business" they were in. New objectives were drafted and were reviewed by home-office executives as well as plant members.

> **Key variances are unique to each system, just as the outputs from each system are unique in the marketplace.**

Every purposeful system must have an output or product that is recognizably different from the output of other producers in the same marketplace. Such differences can be discerned in product quality, content, price, guarantee, speed of delivery, or some other characteristic. Different brands of automobiles, breakfast cereals, chemical fertilizers, or medical insurance can all be distinguished from one another by potential customers in the marketplace. Within the work system itself, it is important that employees and managers responsible for the product understand this distinctive difference in the marketplace and realize its direct connection to the business mission of the enterprise. If that connection is neither close nor clear, it is difficult for those system members to be able to make the decisions and then to take the necessary actions to control the overrun or deviation of key variances identified in Chapter 4.

Key variances must reflect those output features that define the technical goals and objectives and that pursue the system's purpose. Each system is in effect a "niche marketer" even though, in the case of a very large producer, that niche represents a majority market share. In order to remain successful in the marketplace and to keep up with changes introduced by competitors, the system must continually improve its technical system performance. In many organizations this continual improvement comes about through concealed or informal systems, or "cheating the system." With an open and visible sociotechnical design, it becomes "enhancing the system" because it's out in the open and everyone shares the solution.

The control of key variances is the way successful performance is achieved—the only way.

❦ Focus on Product and Purpose

Variance control employs the best that humans have to offer in guiding system performance toward mission fulfillment. The STS analysis methodology has the advantage of defining technology in terms of its input and product, rather than by its tools, processes, or techniques.

The chemical plant, previously discussed, benefited from the focus on product. For instance, one section of the plant had always been known as "the steam plant," although its principle part of the plant's product was refined sulfur. The STS design team challenged this terminology during the technical analysis and succeeded in convincing the employees in the sulfur section (the former so-called steam plant) of their role in producing "IT."

In identifying unit operations, managers and employees frequently find that they can establish fewer unit operations for their system than they at first thought. This is because many of the functions performed on their unique input are checking, verification, or inspection activities rather than fundamental *changes in the state of that input*. By carefully questioning and ultimately eliminating all of the steps and activities that were irrelevant to production of IT, the STS design team in the chemical plant eventually narrowed their unit operations down to five. This was despite their recognition of a large and complex technical system, in which they identified nearly 100 variances and 12 key variances.

Often the throughput variances that inspection catches at the end of the line may be better controlled by reexamining the relationships and boundaries that the system sets with its own suppliers. In the chemical plant a critical boundary condition was revealed with respect to the plant's major (and company-owned) supplier. The plant paid a flat price for its input material, even though the quality of the input varied greatly from day to day. This made it difficult for the plant to consistently produce good output. Prior to the plant's redesign, these results were not observed until delivery — customers sometimes had to return shipments to obtain the quality they wanted. A new, variable rate structure for the raw material was established, along with a new understanding of the input specifications wanted. Focus on product ensures that the technical system will be analyzed separately from the jobs and work of people on the one hand, and from the supervisory and control systems on the other.

❧ *Identifying Key Variances*

Following the listing of variances for all the unit operations, the key variances are identified as those that are most important in their impact on quantity, quality, or costs of their unique system output — *as defined by the purpose of the enterprise*. Table 5.1 illustrates a matrix that can be used to identify and evaluate key variances.

The most likely candidates for key variance are those variances thought to be the big ones — unique and special — and those consistent with the customers' expectations. In the chemical plant, one of these "big" key variances was identified as a previously little-regarded var-

TABLE 5.1
Identifying and Evaluating Key Variances

| Variances (Most Likely Candidates) | Impact | | | | Relationship With | | | Other Reasons | Total Impact (Sum all 7 Columns) |
	Quality	Quantity	Economic Cost	Social Cost	Same U/O	Other U/O			
List the									Identify
variances the									those
team feels are			Evaluate each candidate (1 = low, 3 = high) against the objectives and goals defined by the purpose of the enterprise						variances
most likely to									that are
significantly									key to the
impact the									systems
systems output									output
or product									

SOME GUIDELINES FOR SELECTING THE MOST LIKELY KEY VARIANCES

- Those variances that have impact "downstream" on variances in later unit operations
- Variances that have numerous relationships with other variances in the same unit operation
- Those single variances that, by themselves, if not controlled, will have significant impact on quality, quantity, or cost objectives
- Those variances one has a "hunch" about, that should be evaluated further

---

iance, the rate of crystal growth in a major ingredient, the control of which was worth an estimated half million dollars a year to the company. The plant's engineering manager immediately made that key variance a plant priority for engineering and production. Meanwhile, the STS design team published their technical systems report and held meetings around the plant to discuss that "big one" and to ask for any suggestions for improving its control, and that of their other key variances.

Other key variances are identified because they have a *systemic influence* on other variances. In the chemical plant's technical analysis, for instance, their variance analysis clearly showed that five of the key variances were important because they had major impacts within several unit operations and across existing unit operations and organizational boundaries.

If key variances can be automated out of existence through state-of-the-art technology, so much the better. Not all key variances can be eliminated that way. As the quote at the beginning of this chapter recalls, it is the rare automated or computerized system that is so self-regulating that it can run error free or without human adjustment and control.

CONTROLLING KEY VARIANCES

A well-designed system resolves the answers to the following questions. Technical system performance is a direct function of how well key variances are controlled within the system. Are key variances controlled as close to their source as they can be? Are key variances controlled in ways that enhance those characteristics of the product or output that truly pursue the uniqueness of its product? What role does the technology play in control of the key variances, and what roles remain for the human operator in the system?

Without informed and committed intervention by workers and supervisors, real-world complexity often defeats the effective application of modern computer-based office and manufacturing control systems. A study undertaken for the U.S. Office of Technology Assessment (Schneider, Howard, & Emspak, 1985) described a number of specific examples of management dependence on workers and foremen in a manufacturing resources planning system (MRPS II). These authors stated, "Despite the sophistication of MRPS II as an information system and as a production planning and control system, it is often too 'rigid' or too 'simplistic' to adequately reflect the complexities of production on the shop floor. As a result, the managers and workers in the [shop], as well as the supervisors and clerical personnel in the Production Support office, all have to devise 'end-runs' simply in order to get the work done," p. 51.

Variance control analyses frequently reveal that key variances are controlled close to their source by employees who are not recognized for their innovation or their efforts in developing these informal control systems. On the other hand, especially where there is ambiguity or conflict about the purpose of the enterprise and its connection to output, key variances are not controlled where they originate. In such cases, much of the control must be undertaken by management or support staff long after the variance limits are exceeded. The technical analysis conducted by the insurance office employees, as described in Chapter 4, revealed that two of their four key variances were under the control of people outside of their department.

> **Key variance control is focused on the control of IT rather than control of people.**

⚜ The Methodology of Variance Control Analysis

The key variances identified for a system must be examined one at a time to determine the manner in which they are currently controlled (or are usually controlled). This process of understanding the current condition helps system members deal with the paradigm shift. Key variance control analysis identifies which variances are controlled better than others, and whether some are not controlled at all. The analysis is accomplished through the use of a Table of Variance Control, which lists the unit operation in which each key variance originates, where it is observed and where it is controlled, who or what controls the key variance, what actions are used to control it, and the source of information used in that control. During this analysis, and particularly at the completion of analyzing each key variance, participants are encouraged to start brainstorming ways of improving performance through better control of the process. This is their first opportunity to suggest design ideas; they need to recognize that these early ideas are tentative and will be among many other alternatives developed after all the analyses are complete. As alternatives to process control are explored, it is important to challenge traditional methods and procedures, regardless of existing hierarchies and "turf." The focus is on breaking down the old blinding paradigms and discarding the bureaucratic model of machine-age thinking. This type of baggage must be discarded to liberate the thought process and really brainstorm possibilities. The common goal is to control variances in the process as quickly and efficiently as possible.

Some suggestions for improvement will come by examining and asking the following questions: Are key variances observed or presently controlled in a place different from where they occur? Can the control activities be given to the individuals or teams who first observe the variance? Is the control physically separated from the actual location where the variance occurs—and should it be? How many people and/or levels get involved in the control of a key variance—and are they necessary? What activities, tasks, forms, and procedures get in the way and consume time that could be better spent controlling the variance earlier? How often does the variance occur? Are current standards adequate? Can improved technology help reduce deviations? If the operators closest to the source of occurrence had the knowledge and skills, could they be empowered to control the variance?

Table 5.2 shows a form often used for assessing key variance control. The preceding questions often come to mind, and they should be asked as the variance control form is completed.

TABLE 5.2
Variance Control Table

| | Name of Unit Operation | | | |
Key Variance	Where Occurs	Where Observed	Where Controlled	Controlled By whom? (Role)

ẕ *A Process Manufacturing Example of Key Variance Control*

The key variance chosen for a first illustration is *Variance 5* in the cheese-making example from the preceding chapter. Variance 5 is the "number of microorganisms for disease (*Salmonella, Listeria*), and for spoilage," which are initially present. This key variance was recognized to be of critical importance to a cheese maker because it is essential to eliminate any possibility of food poisoning. As noted earlier, cheese is among the safest foods with respect to food poisoning, in part because cheese itself provides insufficient oxygen, high acidity, and its own

TABLE 5.2
Variance Control Table (*Continued*)

Activities Required to Control	Information & Sources of Information Related to Control Activities	Suggestions For Job or Organization Design	Suggestions for Changes in the Technology

compounds to inhibit the *growth* of dangerous microorganisms. Although Variance 5 is shown early in the process (c.f. variance matrix, Table 4.1), it can enter at nearly any time during cheese making. As cheese making becomes a mass-production operation, the danger increases of infecting a large number of consumers who are susceptible to a low level of contamination, even if they are a small proportion of the total. With such a widely distributed product as mass production permits, it is possible that very small concentrations of *Salmonella* or *Listeria* can be seriously toxic (if not fatal) to some proportion of the population (Blaser & Newman, 1982; New York State Department of Health, 1986).

Between February and May 1989, a cheese factory in a midwestern state produced 5 million pounds of shredded mozzarella cheese. The cheese produced during this period contained a low level of *Salmonella* bacteria contamination (as low as 2,000 bacteria *per ton* of cheese), but it was enough to sicken some 200 people in various locations around the country, producing symptoms that included vomiting, diarrhea, fever, and prolonged weakness (Hedberg et al., in press). At the end of May 1989, the company went bankrupt. Subsequent interviews with former production employees of the plant revealed that as bankruptcy grew closer, management emphasis on production increased while attention to sanitation decreased. It appeared that management's concern in the final days of the company was for as much income as possible while assuming (or hoping for) minimum spoilage. As the technical analysis of cheese making in the preceding chapter illustrated, spoilage is caused by one set of microorganisms, while food poisoning is caused by another set. In ignoring tests for *Salmonella* and relaxing efforts at sanitation during the final months, management loosened standards of housekeeping and product testing, as well as relaxing instructions to employees to observe health and hygiene codes. Health departments in several states cooperated to reveal the source of the contaminated food, and the adverse publicity caused the plant to close permanently. The game of "you bet the company" had been played and lost. The fate of the mozzarella factory is not unique — in fact a cheese factory in California had experienced a similar breakdown in control of toxic organisms in 1983, with very similar results (California State Department of Health, 1985; Fleming et al., 1985).

Table 5.3 presents an example of use of the control table for analyzing the organizational and technical control of that key variance (V5) in cheese making.

Variance 5, number of microorganisms for disease (*Salmonella*), originates in unit operations I through V. Although it can be a function of incomplete pasteurization of the raw milk, this contamination can be introduced at any point in the process through careless handling by workers who are sick or by the curds coming into contact with unclean tools or utensils.

In the present case, the contamination might have been observed in any unit operation and should have been seen and controlled during testing, which occurs frequently during the process. The microbiological tests must be oriented toward finding specific organisms in above-threshold quantities. The quantities present in this case could well have been overlooked or considered nonproblematic especially during the financial crisis the company was experiencing. The variance was, in effect, controlled by factory employees who performed some degree of unsanitary practices. It might have been observed by personnel in the test laboratory, but their methods were not sensitive enough to detect low concentrations of the organisms. Of course, if the information was not available to plant management, they could not use it as an added reason to practice better housekeeping. With or without specific laboratory results, however, something went wrong.

Suggestions for improving technical aspects include modern sanitary facilities, more sophisticated laboratory equipment, and better understanding of modern laboratory techniques and infectious disease for management. These technical improvements, although useful, are neither necessary nor sufficient to substitute for job improvements such as paid sick leave, which encourages employees to stay at home during sickness, and management encouragement and training in hygiene and sanitation for plant workers. The contamination was not controlled within the system, but it was finally controlled outside when tainted product was consumed.

In an actual sociotechnical analysis, all of the key variances identified in the technical analysis would be examined using the Table of Variance Control, as in the previous example, and thus would be listed in Table 5.3.

⸘ *A White-Collar Example of Key Variance Control*

A second example of key variance control analysis involves the pension claims process described in Chapter 4. All four key variances are illustrated in Table 5.4.

As Table 5.4 shows, Key Variance 4 was largely under the control of people outside the Claims Payment Department. Variance 4 ("volume of rush requests") originates outside the system either when the client company specifies that a claim is urgent, or when the insurer's own agent upgrades an otherwise routine request to urgent in an attempt to improve service. The speed requested for routing a claim through the office was sometimes too demanding—field sales agents would often request "rush" authorizations even when they weren't absolutely necessary. This assignment of (sometimes unnecessary) urgency (V4), together with the sometimes untimely and difficult procurement of the policy files (c.f. Variance 8 in the variance matrix, Table 4.3), could slow

TABLE 5.3

Variance Control Table: *Cheese Making*

	Name of Unit Operation*			
Key Variance	*Where Occurs*	*Where Observed*	*Where Controlled*	*Controlled By whom? (Role)*
# 5 Number of Microorganisms for disease	Unit Operation I: Prepared Milk	Unit Operations I–V	Unit Operations I, II, V	Production manager
				Production supervisors
				Cheese worker

*See Variance Matrix in Table 4.2

TABLE 5.3
Variance Control Table: *Cheese Making (Continued)*

Activities Required to Control	Information & Sources of Information Related to Control Activities	Suggestions For Job or Organization Design	Suggestions for Changes in the Technology
Stop production, or withhold delivery if *Salmonella* or *Listeria* are noted; set effective hygiene and sanitation policy.	Microbiology lab results; observation of hygiene and sanitation.	Increase sick leave benefits to encourage workers to stay home when ill.	Improve lab tests sensitivity; Develop higher temperature-resistant starter organisms to permit complete pasteurization and subsequent cooking of disease organisms.
Temporarily transfer or send home sick workers; encourage and enforce sanitary & hygienic practices.	Sick reports from company nurse; direct observation of employee illness.	Closer contact between supervisor and production worker.	
Wash hands and arms before returning to work; practice good hygiene & sanitation practices.	Multilingual hygiene practice notices in employee restrooms; training in hygiene and sanitation; awareness of hazardous disease symptoms.	Improved health screening for employee hiring and placement.	

TABLE 5.4
Variance Control Table: *Pension Claims*

	Name of Unit Operation*			
Key Variance	Where Occurs	Where Observed	Where Controlled	Controlled By whom? (Role)
# 1 Volume of mail received.	Unit Operation I, and before.	Unit Operations I–IV.	Unit Operations I–IV.	Examiner
# 4 Volume of rush requests.	Unit Operation I.	Unit Operations I–IV.	Unit Operations I–IV.	Supervisor or assistant supervisor, working with customer or sales agent.
				Examiners
# 8 Availability of standard policy file.	Unit Operation I.	Unit Operation II.	Unit Operations II–III.	Examiners
# 12 Number or Type of terms in calculation.	Unit Operation I.	Unit Operations I, III.	Unit Operation III.	Examiners

*See Variance Matrix in Table 4.3

TABLE 5.4
Variance Control Table: *Pension Claims (Continued)*

Activities Required to Control	Information & Sources of Information Related to Control Activities	Suggestions For Job or Organization Design	Suggestions for Changes in the Technology
Cooperate and coordinate with clerks and other examiners.	Clerks notify examiners of high loads; observation of multiple requests per envelope.	Daily meetings of all staff to equitably distribute all requests received.	Bar-coded requests and completion log for real-time feedback to examiners and supervisors.
Coordinate with client and agent and change priority if possible.	Client, agent, and examiners		
Cooperate and coordinate with clerks and other examiners to fit all the work in.	Identify source of request (always makes every job "rush?"); Roster of other work.	Sales agents and examiners set mutual expectations for urgent requests.	Computer automatically transmits summary of urgent requests to sales management.
Share with, or obtain file from, other examiner.	Records Dept. shows file "checked-out;" examiners broadcast files availability to others.	Combine Records Department with Claims Department.	Include all files in computer data base.
Apply special computer protocol; test results for accuracy.	Type of request.		Automate QC procedures.

down the entire process for all claims through interrelatedness of these and other variances such as V9, V13, and V14.

MANAGING IN THE VOID

A void is the absence of anything—in management terms a void is any unknown situation. Voids in this latter sense are becoming more common in organizational life. Increasingly, workers are relied upon to make decisions in situations that they have never encountered before. Often they don't have time to seek a management decision and must act on their own.

Key variances provide all members of a system with a common language of work: They provide measures of effectiveness that promote the delivery of appropriate output from the system, in preference to the performance of specified job behaviors, whether those behaviors be by departments, functions, machines, or people. Key variance control further provides members of the system with a public and visible process by which to address and cope with the key variances that they have previously identified as the most important aspects of the work their system does. Rather than expending time and energy hiding their informal behaviors to "end-run" ineffective organizational rules or technology, employees sharing a key variance control analysis are saving time coping with recurrent but unpredictable key variances. This allows them time and "peace of mind" to deal with novel events that no one has ever considered before. Rather than waiting for day shift or calling out managers from their beds, a night shift crew aware of their key variances and of the purpose and product of the enterprise can take action when it is needed and debrief later to learn more about what they did.

Systemwide knowledge of product variances in the chemical plant improved the effectiveness and increased the confidence of all employees. For instance, a night shift crew, aware of their key variances and of the purpose and product of the plant, took action on an infrequent but crucial variance when it was needed. They "debriefed" their action at the next shift change meeting when managers and engineers could confirm their work. The night shift did this in contrast to deferring the decision to the day shift, and in lieu of calling out managers or engineers from their beds. The peace of mind that planned and effective variance control gives provides an edge to an "average" player/member/system to compete in a world-class arena.

"Managing in the Void" is a concept coined by the late Richard B.

Byrne, professor and associate dean of the University of Southern California, Annenberg School of Communication (cf. Krier, 1982). To illustrate this powerful concept Byrne sometimes used a compelling and true sports story of a pole vaulter who was capable of championship performance but who was also fearful of height. With unusual training techniques (e.g., dropping onto a padded area from a 30-foot-high balcony) the coach helped this athlete overcome his fear of height. Thereafter, the pole vaulter achieved his first world's record, but not without an incident involving his "managing in the void." He reached a record height, but simultaneously nudged the cross-bar off with his shoulder. He then had the remarkable presence of mind (or peace of mind) to be able to somehow replace the cross-bar on its pins before he dropped to the mat. The athlete later explained the feat in terms of his ability to control his fear of height. Because of this "control" of his fear, he was able to "see" the bar come off, and to "see" the opportunity to replace it on its pins. He had thus "discovered" what had been a void — a region of consciousness between ascending and descending where additional control of the process was possible. This discovery itself was possible because the pole vaulter had peace of mind through effective control of his fear. The pole vaulter continued to exploit this "region" between his leaping upward and falling downward to behave in unusual ways that allowed him to continue to break records (Neff, 1983). The control over his fear (a known and anticipated element in his performance) permitted the athlete to be able to be aware of and to react to opportunities he couldn't see before — he had become a world-class competitor by managing in the void.

Average employees who are aware of key variances in their process and are trained to control them effectively also become central performers in world-class operations. They are able to make decisions about unanticipated events at the time decisions need to be made; they are not dependent on the coach or supervisor to tell them what to do at the moment. Once variances are under control, employees are freed to cope with events that were never predicted. They are prepared — ready for anything, as it were — for the unexpected in a chaotic world. In this way, they learn to welcome and embrace change as opposed to fighting it.

RESOLVING PARADOX: THE NEW MANAGEMENT SKILL

As the environments of purposeful organizations become more complex and turbulent, decision makers find themselves confronted with dilemmas to choose among, or paradoxes to resolve (Cameron, 1986; Quinn & Cameron, 1988). Changing environments force systems to reevaluate their missions much more often than they needed to or wanted to in the past. For example AT&T was able to function for nearly 70 years with the mission of universal service (i.e., telephone service in every home and business) before it was realized that universal service had been virtually achieved in the United States decades before (Toffler, 1985). AT&T needed to change its mission, but it found itself in a much more chaotic world than mere divestiture of its operating companies and a focus on research and development would satisfy. The years from 1985 to the present have seen AT&T swing from a focus on computer hardware and/or software, to semiconductor design and/or manufacture, to long-distance telephone carrier.

Management decisions have paradoxical consequences not visible at the time a decision is taken, *but the paradoxes become obvious by*

WILL THE REAL AT&T PLEASE STAND UP?

Since the government deregulation of many U.S. industries in the early 1980s, some large U.S. companies have considered new businesses to pursue. AT&T is by no means alone in its search for who it is, what products it delivers, and who its customers and competitors are. U.S. airlines have considered focusing on hotels and resorts. Savings banks considered, and entered, the equities investment and venture capital businesses. With the many mergers and acquisitions among the energy and other U.S. primary industries, steel companies have tried to become oil and alternative energy companies, tobacco companies have become makers and purveyors of fast food and packaged snacks, and automakers enter such businesses as electronic data processing, industrial robots, and computer-based manufacturing technology.

American workers, through all of this, have been wondering what their jobs really contributed and how they could possibly make a difference.

their consequences. One such consequence of interest in key variance control is the increasing use of informal groups and teams of people working together. As the environments of their enterprise become more chaotic, people cannot make variance control decisions by themselves. They must learn to work together in new ways. As once-clear missions of companies disappear, diffuse, or multiply, the adaptive processes (both formal and informal) of production employees are increasingly responsible for company success.

One example of dealing with paradox involves the finance department in a large U.S. manufacturing company. This organization recently used STS to address the dilemma of the multiple missions of: (a) Providing reliable and accurate reports, payment, and collections, and (b) providing financial consulting services to its in-house customer in a novel way. The department's director accepted the employees' view that conflicts caused by the two missions (both potential and actual) should be considered and resolved by members of combined product-focused teams in the financial department. Through these teams, all employees in the department would have the opportunity to participate in the consulting business as well as the production of routine reports. The teams considered the routine reports generated to be input to the non-routine consulting business. In order to provide the new consulting services, the specific issues resulting from the paradox between the two businesses would be resolved by the teams (often with the customer) before undertaking data or information processing. The joint resolution of such paradoxical issues was equally as important as, and contributed to, the joint control of key variances of the more routine functions for which each team was responsible.

Informal processes take place in companies where a system's consciousness is either unspoken or absent. A plant belonging to a large U.S. automaker exhibited the dual mission of manufacturing low volumes of a wide variety of drive axles while developing and testing new computer-based manufacturing technology. Management described this plant as operating on the teamwork of people in the various functional departments, who work together constantly throughout the day to manage the dual missions. This teamwork is an example of informal control of process variances. People working together this way are resolving the paradox of multiple missions by controlling key variances in "virtual groups," not fixed or formal groups. Management is resolving the paradox of multiple missions by keeping the missions themselves clear and before the operating people, as well as supporting and encouraging the creation and use of the flexible group process.

Variance Control and the STS Paradigm

Variance control actually forms a bridge between the technical and social systems analyses; it is central to the design process. The fulcrum or link-pin is the identification of the social roles that control key variances. The column in the Table of Variance Control where those roles are listed provides an appropriate target for examining the *most important communications* among people in the work system—*the information required and used in the control of key variances*. Table 5.4 shows the analysis for all four key variances in the pension claims service system introduced in Chapter 4. The roles identified in control of one or another of those key variances include file clerks and sales agents, but the control of all four variances also include the claims examiners in every case. The conclusion is that examiners are central to the system—they are the "focal" roles in those most important activities of controlling the most important variances. Control of those key variances is necessary to deliver the output that pursues the mission. Any appropriate examination of the claims department communication system must begin with the examiners.

The key variance control step is thus central in any sociotechnical methodology. It includes the treatment of key variances and focuses on people, as they can contribute to the success of the enterprise.

Summary and Conclusion

Technical Variances. Technical throughput variances are an integral part of the technical systems analysis. They are used to understand what effect environmental conditions and process run-out or deviation (sometimes the result of human intervention) might have on subsequent (and eventually final) results. The term "variance" in this sense is used in the way that cost accountants use "budget variance." It is a deviation from normal, expected, or average state of the throughput.

Key Variances. Once such variances are listed for a product throughput and relationships among the variances are understood, examining the systemic nature of this full set of technical variances aids in the identification of key, or "critical," variances. The identification of such key variances serves to further the understanding of system members and aids in empowering them to respond effectively to unplanned events.

Key Variance Control. The next step in developing the technical systems analysis is to link the key variances to the information system underlying the identified unit operations. This "key variance control" analysis is achieved by showing how the key variances are presently controlled by the social system. In so doing, it identifies where important organizational connections and other information loops exist or are required.

Key variance control analysis methodology was initially developed through the joint efforts of Australians, Britons, Americans, and Norwegians. It was first formally described by Emery, Foster, and Woollard (1967). STS, with its emphasis on purpose and product control, permits the creation of work system designs that emphasize the centrality of employees' roles *to the delivery of the product.* These benefits are only possible if STS is seen as carrying with it a new view of technical systems and if that view is applied for enhancing organizational response to changing and turbulent environments.

REFERENCES

BLASER, M. J., & L. S. NEWMAN. "A Review of Human Salmonellosis: I. Infective Dose." *Reviews of Infectious Diseases,* 4(6), November-December, 1982, 1096–1106.

CALIFORNIA STATE DEPARTMENT OF HEALTH. "Listeriosis Outbreak Associated with Mexican-Style Cheese." *Morbidity & Mortality Weekly Report,* 34, 1985, 357–359.

CAMERON, K. S. "Effectiveness as Paradox: Consensus and Conflict in Conceptions of Organizational Effectiveness." *Management Science,* 32, 1986, 539–553.

EMERY, F. E., M. FOSTER, & W. WOOLLARD, "Analytical Model for Socio-Technical Systems" (Originally presented 1967). In F. E. Emery, *The Emergence of a New Paradigm of Work.* Canberra: Center for Continuing Education, Australian National University, 1978.

FLEMING, D. W., S. L. COCHI, K. L. MACDONALD, et al., "Pasteurized Milk as a Vehicle of Infection in an Outbreak of Listeriosis." *New England Journal of Medicine,* 312, 1985, 203–206.

HEDBERG, C. W., J. A. KORLATH, J.-Y. A'AOUST, K. E. WHITE, W. L. SCHELL, M. R. MILLER, D. N. CAMERON, K. L. MACDONALD, & M. T. OSTERHOLM. "A Multi-State Outbreak of *Salmonella javiana* and *Salmonella oranienburg* Infections Due to Consumption of Contaminated Cheese." *Journal of the American Medical Association,* in press.

KRIER, B. A. "Breaking through computerphobia." *Los Angeles Times*, August 11, 1982.

NEFF, C. "One Flies High, One Just Flies: After Billy Olsen Vaulted to an Indoor Mark, Carl Lewis Set a 60-Yard Record." *Sports Illustrated*, February 14, 1983, 87.

NEW YORK STATE DEPARTMENT OF HEALTH. "Listeriosis." *Epidemiology Notes*, 1(1), September 1986, 1–2.

QUINN, R. E., & K. CAMERON, *Paradox and Transformation: Toward a Framework of Change in Organization and Management*. Cambridge, MA: Ballinger, 1988.

SCHNEIDER, L., R. HOWARD, & H. EMSPAK. "Office Automation in a Manufacturing Setting: A Case Study." Prepared for the U.S. Office of Technology Assessment, OTA Contract no. 4330055, Washington, DC, 1985, 50–51.

TOFFLER, A. *The Adaptive Corporation*. New York: Bantam Books, 1985.

CHAPTER 6

ҙ ҙ

Designing for Flexibility:
Understanding How It's Up to Us

"The young . . . want roles—that is, total involvement. They do not want fragmented, specialized goals or jobs."

(McLuhan & Fiore, 1967)

Understanding the throughput, or IT, in the big picture, is one basic requirement for any member of a high-performance system or organization. Understanding *one's role* in the creation and delivery of IT is another requirement of prime importance for system success. Understanding what is required for a system's survival, in both short term and long, must also be included for the effective organization. These understandings are built through the sharing of information. Effective understanding is guided, trained, sustained, and changed via information. Transmission and use of information require communication. Communication requires not merely an information system in a mechanical sense, but also a social system in which total involvement is possible.

COMMUNICATION AND THE
SOCIAL SYSTEM IN ORGANIZATIONS

In the social system we are interested in who talks to whom, and about what. It is a way of mapping patterns and content of communication among people who are central to transforming and delivering a product. It is also an examination of the degree of collective involvement people have in the essential work. Thus, the social systems analysis examines the work-related interactions among people in an enterprise. Further, it permits a description of the coordinating and integrating buffer between the technical transformation process and the demands and constraints of a chaotic environment.

But social systems understanding is more than a description. The social system provides the organization's flexibility. Technical flexibility is created by the flow of communication for cooperation and coordination among people who control the key variances identified in understanding how to make the product ("IT"). Social systems also provide flexibility to help improve the short- and long-term survival of the organization—beyond its product-related flexibility. Such survival includes reacting to changes in the general political, economic, and social environment, as well as maintaining and improving the internal infrastructure of the enterprise. Together, the technical coordination and cooperation and the adjustment and revision for survival combine to promote organizational flexibility.

Four Factors for Organizational Continuity. The social system can enable the organization to succeed and to survive. Any organization, if it is to succeed, must first set and attain performance goals. If it is to survive in turbulent environments, the organization must also perform three other basic functions (Cherns & Wacker, 1978). The three survival functions include adaptation in and accommodation to the external environment, integration of the activities and sentiments of people within the system, and attending to the long-term development and latent resources of the enterprise. The social system delivers the behaviors that are key to the pursuit of the purposes of the enterprise and its members that achieve these four functions. How well the behaviors are performed is in great measure a result of the design of the social system—decisions about who should talk to whom, and about what. Organizations are always our inventions. Whether we choose to actively and consciously design them or permit them to develop by accident or accretion is up to us.

This chapter discusses the impact of communication flow and information exchange within the social system for appropriate and flexible organizational performance. It also describes methods and techniques used for assessing communication networks and their relationships to performance.

❧ Importance of Communication

Communication of Information.   In Chapter 1, we noted that information is essential for understanding and empowerment. Obtaining information from others facilitates decision making. Sometimes staying with the "herd" is the best decision, sometimes it is not. Communication among members of an organization provides the same basic functions today that it did in ancient times when people began living in caves. The choice of fight, flight, or freeze in face of outside threat is determined by what is communicated and by whom. People also communicate to support one another and to provide information about the past and the future. Typically, people do not actively communicate when things are going smoothly and when information is not needed for understanding past events or anticipating future ones. Like our ancestors, we set boundaries around our "tribes," our "families," or our "work units" that determine who we communicate with, how often, and about what. Communication flow in such systems forms patterns that can aid or hinder the system's success and survival.

Complexity of Language for Communication.   Studies of primitive peoples reveal that they communicate most frequently about what is most central to their survival. Anthropologist Bronislaw Malinowski studied agrarian people on Pacific Islands who had hundreds of names for each of their varieties of yams. Malinowski pointed out that, "Some names [for yams] distinguish what might be properly regarded as real botanical varieties, others describe characteristics of size, shape, perfection and so on" (1935, p. 76). These islanders communicated frequently about this dietary staple, delicacy, and trading stock of their society; and they had complicated rituals and ceremonies in which yams had a central place. Eskimo peoples are known also to have an elaborate language about the various qualities of ice and snow; this makes sense given the proportion of nature it represents to Eskimos in their environment and how important information about snow would be to their survival.

Today, of course, information systems and languages are even more elaborate. As outside influences become more complex (some have said even "chaotic," Gleick, 1987) individuals' ability to deal with them requires that incoming information be correspondingly varied and elaborate. More complex information and language provide a conceptual and practical way with which to cope and adapt to external complication. This is an example of what Ross Ashby termed "requisite variety"

(Ashby, 1960), by which he meant that increases in environmental complexity require that an effective system increase its internal complexity to a similar degree.

Complexity of Communication Modes. Marshall McLuhan introduced the idea that "the medium is the message" (1964), that communication can take many forms and the particular mode (or medium) used itself adds or subtracts meaning. For instance, a simple declaration delivered verbally or in writing can take on a different meaning when combined with the visual cues of "body language or physical expression." Another example of McLuhan's insight is the influence of electronic communication to far-flung locations. The camel driver in a remote desert with his transistor radio or "Walkman" stereo joins with westerners as part of the "global village." He can hear the same news reporting (on CNN or BBC), or music (Brahms, Beatles, or Chicago blues), as do Americans—and they could in turn share in information and entertainment originating from his part of the "village."

What message is communicated depends on how it is received. The differential power of battle scenes described around the barracks stove, retold at the family hearth, or transmitted (live or taped) via television predicts how and whether the listeners are motivated, entertained, or merely informed. What was available to our ancestors is still available to us, but we are also offered (and sometimes burdened with) new media that send different emphases and that are themselves different messages. Throughout history, communication has been used to sway or influence human behavior, as well as to understand the world around us.

Specific and General Messages. Attempts to influence others can take place in either individual and unique conversation, or through general information channels. In the social system of an organization, these types of messages are examined to understand their influence among people.

Organizational communication is divided into two kinds — specific communication and general communication. The former refers only to communication from one person or group to another person or specific group. The latter refers to communication between one person or group and a general set of people.

The most easily identified medium in a social system is face to face, between two people or in small groups. These contacts fit the category of "specific" messages, but there are many other specific situations that are not face to face. For instance, business memos can be used for *specific* messages if their intended recipient is identified. Telephone conversations are also frequently encountered specific communications. A telephone conference call can involve several people, but they are usually a specific set of individuals.

Communication and Time. Communication is easiest thought of as immediate, but delayed or accumulated communication is very common. Even in ancient societies people communicated across time. Native American Indian lore describes the subtle signs of blazes cut in tree trunks, or bent leaves or twigs, that are intended to inform others of the direction of a little-used trail. The cuneiform inscriptions of ancient Assyrians (and others) were also intended as communication across time. Business memos are a traditional medium for cross-time communication. The rapid growth in use of telephone answering machines and voice mail in the business environment is but one example of modern technology increasing the ability of individuals to communicate across time. In the discussion to follow, the time dimension will be described as "synchronous" or "asynchronous." These terms refer to messages that occur in real time, or are deferred, respectively. Table 6.1 lists examples of both specific and general contacts, together with this time dimension of communication. Table 6.1 illustrates the point that the *choice of medium* narrows the *choice of message* sent.

The upper left cell in Table 6.1 illustrates the most immediate types of business messages—specific and synchronous. These messages are often the most important and/or personal. They also provide clarification and confirmation. Face-to-face meetings between individuals, small group meetings, and telephone conversations are examples of synchronous and specific media where people are talking to one another in the same (or "real") time. Interchanges between people on radios— for example, ship to shore, air to air, or walkie-talkies—are also illustrations of synchronous/specific media.

Today, specific messages often ask the receiver to interpret or contribute to problem solving on request. In other words, specific messages are often requests for help or information, to which the listener is expected to respond.

In traditional organizations, synchronous messages often do not require such a reply. This is particularly true with a directive or order

TABLE 6.1
"The Medium is the Message": Types of Communication Media
Used in Business

Types of Messages → ↓	*Synchronous*	*Asynchronous*
Specific Messages	Meetings Face-to-Face Conversation Telephone Conversation Person-to-Person Radio Contact	Business Memos Electronic Mail (EMail) Voice Mail Telephone Answering Machine
General Messages	Mass Meetings Public Address System Live Broadcast Television & Radio	Company Newsletter Job Descriptions Blueprints & Technical Drawings Videotapes Parts Manuals

from superior to subordinate. As organizations are becoming more participative, this situation is changing.

The upper right cell in Table 6.1 shows examples of asynchronous and specific media used in business settings. Specific and asynchronous communication is really quite common in organizations and is becoming more so. Examples include regular mail (and memo) correspondence, messages left on a telephone answering machine, on electronic mail (EMail), or on voice mail. In specific/asynchronous messages, the sender provides information and does not always expect a reply. More and more, however, a reply (often also asynchronous) is expected. This category of media is often used to bridge important messages over time zones or work shifts.

The lower right cell in Table 6.1 contains examples of asynchronous and general messages. These are very frequent ways in which the front office communicates to the work force in general. Very often the sender provides generally applicable information and does not require a reply —although some compliant action or behavior is often expected. For example, upper management or staff management groups (such as human resources or occupational safety) and, where relevant, the trade unions, inform the work force, or set policy or doctrine, through memos on the bulletin boards. Memos or letters to all managers, or even all employees, are additional ways of transmitting asynchronous and general messages. Memos and bulletins are seen as impersonal, and they are easily misinterpreted.

Job descriptions prepared by personnel departments and work manifests prepared by industrial engineering are also types of media for asynchronous/general messages. The influence on employees of television or radio broadcast advertising sponsored by the company is another form of asynchronous/general contact (albeit perhaps unanticipated) between employer and employee.

Memos broadcast from the top of the pyramid may not be the best way for chief executive officers to get a complaint recognized. Such blasts are useless unless there is some kind of support for how to approach the problem described in the memo; a plan, for example, of how to improve quality or decrease costs. A memo or other asynchronous and general communication in a low-trust culture is a one-way form of communication. People at the top of organizations must learn to expect and encourage a meaningful response from subordinates.

The class of general messages shown in Table 6.1 is associated with media that are used for direction and/or information only. Among the modern technologies for general/asynchronous messages are prerecorded television messages and computer programs. So-called expert computer systems are interactive (or at least input-responsive and context-sensitive) computer programs that will ultimately lead the human operator to directive instructions (or, more rarely, to advice) for specific task accomplishment.

The lower left cell in Table 6.1 contains the communication channels that are among the least used in U.S. businesses. Synchronous/general messages are best represented by live broadcast television and radio media. In business settings this is generally the use of closed-circuit television or freeze-frame video telecommunication or teleconferencing systems—and these are becoming more common. The use of public address systems on board ships or airplanes or in school rooms is also illustrative of synchronous/general media.

℥ *Importance of Information*

Information is essential for enhancing understanding and empowerment. Alvin Toffler's book *Power Shift* (1990) eloquently describes how information is replacing both brute force and sheer wealth as a powerful source of influence over others. The evolution of modern warfare illustrates the advantage provided by information available to technologically sophisticated armies against overwhelming conventional ground forces.

A documented case illustrating the power of information in business enterprise involves the Foremost McKesson Company, a distributor to pharmacies (Keen, 1988). During the 1980s the company obtained a significant share of the market by installing on-site computer terminals in 17,000 of its customers' pharmacies and in 32 of its main suppliers' offices. Success for McKesson resulted in part from customer-originated orders transmitted directly to primary suppliers for fast, accurate turnaround and effective sales advice. Saved from writing orders, the thus-freed McKesson sales force began to provide the pharmacies with merchandising advice and in doing so, they concurrently acquired prime display space for McKesson products. During this time the company's data base was filling with information from the 32 suppliers and also from over 2,000 manufacturers. This knowledge about manufacturers' and other suppliers' competitive status, coupled with its own ability to buy in volume, permitted the company to exert immense pressure on suppliers' price and delivery terms. McKesson's computer-based information permitted ever-increasing sales at ever-increasing profits.

Another demonstration of the importance (and difficulty) of communication is this example of a trucking firm examined a few years ago:

> In an organization concerned with the distribution of petroleum products, studied by Cherns and Taylor . . . the [dispatchers] who collected [and scheduled] customers' orders were organized in a department separate from that of the drivers for whom schedules were worked out. A driver would pick up a schedule allocating him to a vehicle and a route. Frequently, the receipt of the routing would stimulate a string of expletives from the driver: "If I do what this _____ has told me to, I [would] not be able to do half the job. I would arrive at Customer B just after 12 o'clock when the only man with the key to the pumps has gone off to his lunch break. And it's no use my turning up to Customer P until I have discharged enough of my load for his short pipe to reach my tank. And finally I would end up on the _____ road just in the middle of the rush hour. It would serve him right if I followed these instructions; I would run out of time [exceed the permitted number of consecutive driving hours] right in the middle of a [freeway]." There was no doubt pardonable exaggeration in all this; the point is that the drivers had acquired a great deal of knowledge about customers, routers, etc., but, being organized into a separate department, they shared very little of this knowledge with the [dispatchers] who, however, received the customers' complaints before the drivers. (Cherns, 1976)

Differences in logic and reason, illustrated between the drivers and dispatchers, is well known in traditional workplaces and they are becoming important aspects in newly computerized work systems as well. Shoshona Zuboff has recently described the emerging changes in the workplace attributable to information and communication. Workers in newly computerized but traditional industries (e.g., papermaking or food processing) find themselves replacing old tactile and intuitive skills, developed on the job, with informational skills that require different kinds of logic and reason for making on-the-job decisions and that require more communication among co-workers than did the well-developed traditional technology. The new information-based technology also provides employees with information about the product that simply was not available before. Zuboff calls the creation and application of this new information "informating" (Zuboff, 1988).

Informating offers new understanding and response flexibility but, according to Zuboff, it must be managed and organized to do so.

In summary. To reiterate, the social systems analysis examines the work-related communication among people in an enterprise. It permits description of the requested information and of coordinating and integrating buffers between the technical transformation process and the demands and constraints of a chaotic environment. The task for the social analysis is to describe the ways that the necessary social system actually functions in a specific organization and to evaluate how effective these methods are for satisfying the human and technical requirements of the enterprise. Finally, the methodology provides an opportunity to use this new understanding of the social system to build creative new designs for higher performance.

THE METHODOLOGY FOR APPLYING THE SOCIAL SYSTEMS CONCEPTS

Application: The Tanker Trucking Case. Throughout the descriptive section to follow, an oil delivery trucking system will be used for illustration. This trucking system contains 10 terminals spread throughout an area about the size of California. Each terminal employs about 100 drivers and accommodates 50 large tanker trucks. Drivers, working alone, deliver gasoline or fuel oil to commercial customers within a 75-mile radius of their assigned terminal. Figure 6.1 shows the organization chart for a typical terminal.

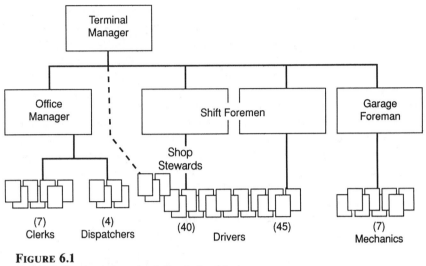

FIGURE 6.1
Typical Tanker Terminal Organization

Drivers work in two shifts, so the vehicles are driven up to 20 hours per day. Drivers report to their terminal each day and obtain their orders for the shift from the dispatcher. They may or may not see their shift foreman at start of shift. They then find the truck they will use, fill it with the appropriate products for the day's orders, and drive out to deliver the product. The drivers work rotating shifts, while the foremen work a fixed shift — either days or afternoons.

⅄ *Collecting and Using Social Systems Data*

Data collection for understanding the social system can take many forms. Direct observation by an outside expert is a very useful approach when research and knowledge about the system are the primary objectives and a reliable and consistent process is desired. The resulting data are small in quantity for the time expended, but the investigator's report of emitted behavior is beyond doubt.

Survey methods, including interviews and paper/pencil questionnaires, collect much more data for the time that they require. They can be designed to be quantitative (but not necessarily as reliable as observation). Survey methods can explore many topics (e.g., rarely occurring but significant events) that would otherwise be unexamined if data were collected only by observation. Survey methods can provide descriptions of events that have occurred in the past. They can also measure opinions and attitudes that reside inside the people in a system and may not be displayed during observation. Some recent efforts to apply Questionnaire Methods to Sociotechnical Analysis show promise (Geirland, 1990).

Interviews can be combined with observation by an outside expert to produce a very specific yet rational (i.e., explainable) view of social system behaviors. The resulting data are usually quantitative, but neither as comprehensive or as amenable to statistical analysis as questionnaire data. On the other hand, questionnaire data are more difficult to interpret, since the respondent may not understand the question, may not have an opportunity to query it, and may thus answer in error.

Whether interview, observation, or questionnaire methods (or some combination of them) are used, it is important to involve the members of a system in the survey design, data collection, and data interpretation if the main objective is the improvement of the enterprise as a sociotechnical system. Participative methods of data collection are further described in Chapter 7.

In the illustration which occupies much of the remainder of this chapter, a combination of interview and observation was employed by the investigator. The project was a combination of research and consulting—little was known about organization or management effects in that industry, yet both upper management and the industry's trade union council were interested to know if, and how much, sociotechnical systems concepts could be applied. A participant-observer approach was considered to be the best method with which to deal with the exploratory nature of the case. If done today, even with similar time constraints, the authors would opt for an approach that would more fully involve local management, unions, and the rank-and-file members in the design, collection, and interpretation of data.

The Concept and Application of Social Role.   The social system analysis focuses on the concept of social role as the basic link between organizational demands and employee competence and understanding. The social system is defined as a network of work-related actions and messages that are mediated by the reciprocal role expectations of individual employees. "Role" is a different idea from that of "jobs" or "work." The work role is defined as the behaviors of a person occupying an organizational position (or job) in relation to other people. These role behaviors result from the actions and expectations of a number of people in a "role set." A role set is comprised of people (occupying other roles) in the organization and outside of it who are sending expectations and reinforcement to the role occupant in question. People in the role set are known to the role occupant and their expectations are also usually known. Figure 6.2 shows a typical role set, together with examples of expectations set by each member.

Roles and Jobs and Work. Jobs, on the other hand, are not defined by behaviors, but by formal job descriptions. The job description usually does not specify or describe the social contacts experienced at work. Although the job forms a contract between persons and an organization, it is applied to persons individually—a job in an organization is rarely contracted with a team or group, and job holders are rarely expected to work as a team. Finally, work as occupation, employment, or business refers to the activities a typical member of that occupation is assumed to perform by a generalized audience. Unlike social role, work is a static concept. There is no common reason, mechanism, or urge to change that occupational behavior or to engage in social interchange when considering one's work. Role behavior, on the contrary, focuses on behavior as it is affected by the various (and sometimes conflicting) expectations of many people, including the role occupants themselves.

Social systems analysis addresses the work-related interactions among people in the work system that were detailed in the technical systems analysis described in Chapters 3 and 4. It is an evaluation of who talks to whom, about what, and how it's working. Social systems analysis is linked to the technical analysis because the most important messages are about the throughput and product, but the social system is also the wider mechanism for flexible response to a changing environment.

The social analysis focuses specifically on the primary relationships of a "focal role." In the trucking company illustration, the truck drivers are the focal roles around which the social analysis here is developed. They are focal because it is they who are finally responsible for the timely and accurate delivery of the product to customers' businesses. The drivers can and must accommodate to technical variances introduced earlier in the process. (Key variances here include such things as the availability of various products and their quality, the accuracy of the tanker's load for the final order, and overall demand for the product, as well as difficulty of delivery conditions.)

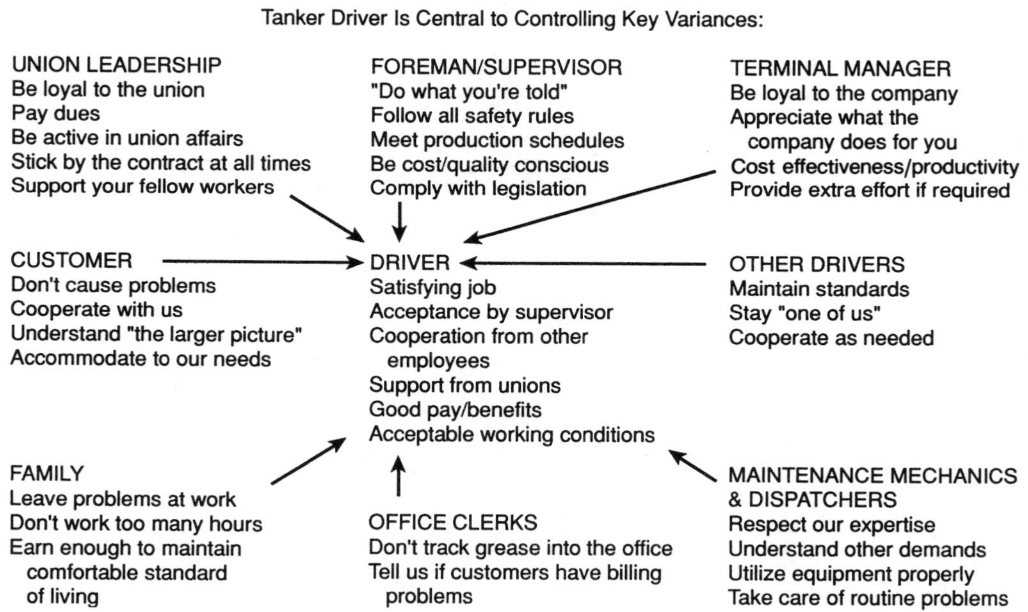

Tanker Driver Is Central to Controlling Key Variances:

UNION LEADERSHIP
Be loyal to the union
Pay dues
Be active in union affairs
Stick by the contract at all times
Support your fellow workers

FOREMAN/SUPERVISOR
"Do what you're told"
Follow all safety rules
Meet production schedules
Be cost/quality conscious
Comply with legislation

TERMINAL MANAGER
Be loyal to the company
Appreciate what the
company does for you
Cost effectiveness/productivity
Provide extra effort if required

OTHER DRIVERS
Maintain standards
Stay "one of us"
Cooperate as needed

DRIVER
Satisfying job
Acceptance by supervisor
Cooperation from other
employees
Support from unions
Good pay/benefits
Acceptable working conditions

MAINTENANCE MECHANICS & DISPATCHERS
Respect our expertise
Understand other demands
Utilize equipment properly
Take care of routine problems

CUSTOMER
Don't cause problems
Cooperate with us
Understand "the larger picture"
Accommodate to our needs

OFFICE CLERKS
Don't track grease into the office
Tell us if customers have billing
problems

FAMILY
Leave problems at work
Don't work too many hours
Earn enough to maintain
comfortable standard
of living

Figure 6.2
Focal Role Expectations

113

⚡ *Role Network*

The social analysis continues by developing a "focal role network" (i.e., a map of relationships indicating who communicates with the driver about what) that illustrates the activities taking place around the drivers and their supervisor. This network is constructed with the relative distances between the various roles reflecting the frequency and importance of their interactions. A role network for the tanker drivers is shown in Figure 6.3.

In this network figure, the shorter length of the lines between roles indicates a higher frequency of communication. The arrows represent one-way or two-way communication. Double arrows pointing in opposite directions (e.g., between drivers and dispatchers) denote equally frequent initiation of essentially one-way messages.

The most frequent contacts, which were usually several times a day (start of shift, on the road—if they met for breaks or lunch—and at end of shift), were with other drivers and the shop stewards. The next most frequent contacts were with dispatchers, whom the drivers would see through the dispatch window as they would pick up their orders for the shift. While at the window, drivers would often attempt to quickly review their routes, truck assignment, and customer orders in order to check errors or anomalies and, if found, have the dispatcher change the load. The dispatchers, in turn, would often attempt to ignore (or deflect) these comments and queries in order to serve the next driver in line.

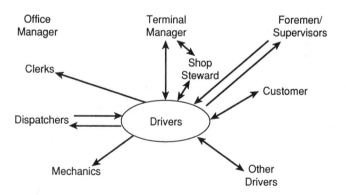

FIGURE 6.3
Role Network for Drivers I

Drivers may have gone on to complain to the shift foreman (or even the terminal manager), but they rarely had time to do this, and it was usually not successful. Informal complaints to the union steward would often be carried to the manager anyway. Drivers' contacts with individual customers (or customer representatives such as gate and scale guards or night watchmen) were obviously necessary for delivery, and sometimes information about changes in delivery conditions or in future orders was obtained. Sometimes this information was brought back to the terminal by the driver, who attempted to relay it to the office clerks for help in future orders and customer relations. The clerks (female) usually frowned on drivers (male) coming into the terminal office to do this because they "track in grease from their shoes, and stand around gaping at us."

Not all contacts between all roles in the terminal are shown on the role network. This is in the interest of clarity of focus. For instance, although the office clerks were in frequent contact with the office manager, this link is not shown, although one can infer it from the organization chart (Figure 6.1). On the other hand, drivers and the office manager were rarely (if ever) in contact with one another, and that link is deliberately omitted from the network.

Defined and displayed this way, the social system can be seen as not merely work or friendship behavior, but rather the source of adaptability and flexibility in coping with variances in the product and with changes in the system's complex environment. The demands of that environment go beyond simply satisfying a consumer market, coping with supplies of raw materials, or the other aspects directly affecting the technical system. The overall system's environment is actually many environments—legal, legislative, labor, cultural, competitive, climatic, and so forth.

The social analysis involves the examination of the roles and relationships within the whole work process. This activity actually includes mapping both the persons who have work-related interactions in the system and the reasons for those contacts. Because a comprehensive analysis of all positions would be too time-consuming, the social analysis focuses upon the role or roles most involved in the control of key variances, based on the assumption that every organization exists in order to meet the short-term goal of producing its product. This is the social system analysis, which maps the cooperation and coordination undertaken between the focal roles and others within and outside the work process.

❦ *Four Factors for Organizational Continuity (GAIL)*

Every organization exists in order to meet the short-term *goal* of controlling the variances that occur in the process of successfully delivering its product. However, in doing so it must not adversely impact its capacity to survive as an organization. To meet its goals, it must *adapt* to, and be protected from, short-term changes and pressures in its immediate environment. It must also combine or *integrate* (or avoid disintegration of) activities to manage internal conflicts and to promote smooth interactions among people and tasks. Finally, it must ensure the *long-term development* of knowledge, skills, and motivation in workers so that they can cope with goal-related, environmental and systems requirements in the future. In the social analysis the letters G, A, I, L stand for types of functions that are affected in contacts among people.

The four functions that any social system fulfills are as follows:

1. **Attaining the system's primary GOALS (G)**
2. **ADAPTING (A) to the external environment for immediate survival**
3. **INTEGRATING (I) internal environment for conflict management**
4. **Providing for the development and maintenance of the system's LONG-TERM (L) needs**

The role network for trucking terminals is further elaborated in Figure 6.4 to show the content of the various contacts and exchanges between the focal role of driver and the others, coded by G, A, I, and L.

Multiple classifications for a link can represent either multiple purposes served by each contact or numerous contacts, each with a different purpose. As an example of this, the symbols "G" and "I" shown between dispatcher and driver in Figure 6.4 can be explained as follows: a driver's attempt to convince the dispatcher to change the sequence of customers' orders for better fit of traffic patterns, product loading/unloading sequences in the truck assigned, as well as customer preferences, is an example of "G" (goal attainment function) as a method for controlling variances in the throughput. This same interchange can influ-

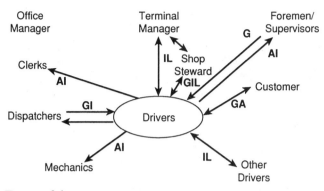

FIGURE 6.4
Role Network for Drivers II

ence the "I" (integration/disintegration function) if the driver perceives the dispatcher as uncaring or bureaucratic, and/or if the dispatcher perceives the driver as unruly or complaining. They will be less likely to want to interact with one another in the future, but because they must, the disintegration ("I") intensifies and their ability to solve problems dealing with key variances ("G") diminishes.

In an effective sociotechnical system, changes in a customer's demands need to be communicated from the customer and/or driver to the rest of the system. The contact between driver and customer can contain information about changes in delivery conditions, such as new construction blocking access to the tanks or filler caps, which will require adapting ("A") to the external environment by the tanker driver. Contacts coded "A" between driver and customer in Figure 6.4 can also signify information from the latter about future orders, or the reasons for likely changes in the future (e.g., forecasted decreases in the customer's business).

Information dealing with the adaptation function ("A"), as illustrated above, can have either short- or longer-term consequences. In either case, if the customer believes that telling the driver is enough, then it is obvious that the driver should carry the message to the rest of the terminal system, and the "A" between driver and clerk shown in Figure 6.4 illustrates that he does. The "I" (integration/disintegration) between driver and clerk further shows that the driver's attempt to communicate the customer-related information is met with misgiving, animosity, or denunciation—not necessarily based on the content of the information, but because of the driver's personal appearance or behavior.

The long-term development ("L") between drivers and other drivers signifies that the drivers try to exchange information about customers, locations, work practices, personalities, and other facts or processes that will help them to cope better in the future. This is training in the most elementary sense. Apart from a driving test and a new employee orientation session by the supervisor, no further formal training is provided a driver by the company. Since the contact between foremen and drivers is sparse, most driver training comes from shop stewards and other drivers. Drivers are informed of future developments in occasional meetings or written messages from the terminal manager — either directly or via the shop steward.

Many organizations have specialized departments to perform the GAIL functions. For example, industrial engineering (for G), sales and marketing and/or environmental safety departments (for A), personnel (for I), planning and/or training departments (for L), can have the formal responsibilities for one or more of the four basic functions. This specialization was true for the trucking terminal example illustrated above, although most of the specialized departments were located in the company's head office. Typically, this specialization acts to narrow and limit the ability of other employees to act appropriately when actions for the functions are required.

In spite of departmental specialists who exist in an enterprise, a good many of these functional behaviors are performed through informal activities at the level of the focal role — and this is obviously true for the drivers in the illustration. Not only are these behaviors informal, but they are often unrecognized, even though they may be more frequent and more influential in affecting performance (e.g., drivers' informal rerouting of customer orders to accomplish deliveries in a timely manner) than are the formal methods and policies of the organization.

The task of the social analysis is to facilitate a better understanding of the ways in which these necessary social system functions actually are carried out and to evaluate how effective these methods are for satisfying the human and technical requirements of the organization. This requires that the observer go beyond the descriptive focal role network and evaluate how well the social system meets organizational requirements.

The social system was described above as serving the four organizational functions of Goal attainment, Integration, Adaptation, and Long-term development. It can also be described in terms of the types of relationships between the focal roles and others.

⅋ Types of Relationships

For ease in analysis, four types of social relationships have been defined: *Vertical* (V) contact, or communication between people up and down the hierarchy; contact among *Equals* (E) (peers or co-workers) within a work group or unit; *Cross-boundary* (C) contact, or communication across unit boundaries with others (not necessarily at the same hierarchical level) in other work units or departments; and *Outside* (O) contacts outside the enterprise, with people such as final customers or vendors. These four relationships (V, E, C, O) permit inclusion of a wide range of possible real-world relationships yet limit the number of categories to allow for a manageable analysis. This helps to keep the social analysis in human scale.

In addition to these four social relationships, attention is also directed to the relationship between individual employees and their work or occupation. Although social relations account for most strong feelings about work, *Nonsocial* (N) and work-related perceptions cannot be ignored as potent determinants of performance and morale. Adding nonsocial relationships between individuals and work to the four social relationships (V, E, C, O) encompasses the minimal essential ways of viewing the variety of relationships at work. These five types of relationships (four that denote contact with other people and one that does not) form the acronym "VECON." The five relationships VECON describes will be used, together with the general/specific and synchronous/ asynchronous categories of contact, as the raw material of the social system analysis.

⅋ The Social System Grid

The four functions (GAIL) can be evaluated in terms of each of the five types of relationships (VECON) described above, and the results displayed in a 4 × 5 grid (a 20-cell matrix of four functions by five relationships) where each cell in the grid is used to specify a particular type of social contact or behavior. The grid also permits examination of the presence *or absence* of a set of functional relationships for particular functional requirements (GAIL). Conversely it allows testing for the presence or absence of particular relationships (VECON), describing the work process. Figure 6.5 shows a grid for the tanker drivers. Two cells, chosen at random, are shown in detail to illustrate the content typical of this part of the analysis. The two cells highlighted describe contacts

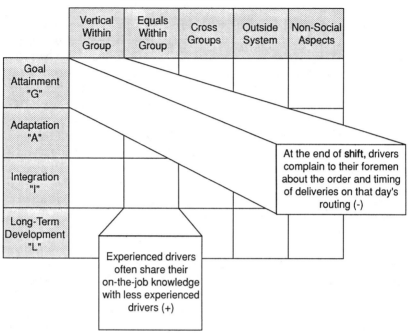

FIGURE 6.5
Social Grid

between drivers and foremen about key variances (cell "G-V"), and the informal "on-the-job" training among the drivers that helps them do the job (cell "L-E").

The observer performing the social system analysis evaluates the meaning of the data as classified. A positive sign indicates a favorable rating based on the responses surveyed, a zero indicates a neutral rating, and a minus sign indicates a negative rating. Figure 6.5 provides an illustration of the content and evaluative components of the social grid for the two cells described. A minus sign ("−") in cell "G-V" means that this communication is usually or typically ineffective, or possibly even disruptive to system performance. The plus sign ("+") in cell "L-E" signifies that this type of communication is effective in improving drivers' future performance at work. A further elaboration of the grid involves summarizing all evaluative signs derived from the data collected in the social analysis. Table 6.2 shows such an evaluative "GAIL Grid" for the tank truck terminal system. This table summarizes communication observed in the ten terminals in the system. It presents a picture of the average or typical terminal, but all individual terminals studied were quite similar to this normal case. Relative frequency of signs (whether plus, zero, or minus) in each cell represents the proportion of those observed contacts to those coded for the other cells. For instance cells "G-C" and "I-C" have more cell entries (of any sign) than do the other cells. This means that most contacts were observed between the drivers and dispatchers, mechanics, clerks, and others in the terminal (except their foreman)—and more of these contacts were evaluated as either neutral or negative than as positive in impact on the system. Table 6.2 shows that relatively few contacts were observed involving the drivers that dealt with either adaptation ("A") or long-term developments ("L"). Overall, Table 6.2 shows that there are a number of present social system activities (those coded "+") that deserve to be retained, reinforced, and acknowledged —located primarily in cells "A-O," "I-E," and "L-E." There are also a number of cells with a disproportionately high frequency of activities coded minus ("−") that warrant change, elimination, or improvement —primarily cells "G-C," "I-V," and "I-C."

Interpretation of Social System Results

In the case illustrated above, both the role network and the GAIL grid contribute to an understanding of cooperation and coordination among people in the system. The role network shows that the focal role occupants (the drivers, the people in the system who have the main responsibility for finally controlling key variances) work primarily alone throughout the day. Their contacts with others who stay in the terminal come in chunks at the beginning and end of shifts. Contacts with foremen are meager, and drivers' contacts with other drivers occur mainly while they are relaxing in locker rooms or cafes. Their contacts with customers are largely unplanned for by the system.

The GAIL grid adds further information to this picture. It demonstrates that there are few contacts beyond those in the service of delivering product each day. The grid also shows that many contacts lead to a

TABLE 6.2
Social Grid Summary "G.A.I.L." Functions Against Four Types of Social Contacts in Tanker Terminal Drivers/Fuel Delivery Service

	V. Vertical Contact: Between Supervisors and Subordinate	*E.* Equal Contact: Among Peers in the Same Work Groups	*C.* Cross Contact: Between Groups in the Same Terminal	*O.* Outside Contact: With the Terminal System
"G": Goal	+++ 0000000000	++ 0000	++++++ 00000000000 0000000	+++ 000
Attainment	- - - - -	-	- - - - - - - - - - - - - - - -	- - - - - - - -

"A": Adaptation To Environment	+ 0 –	000	++++++ 000 – – – – – – – – –	++++++++++++ ++ 00000000000 000000000 –
"T": System Integration	+++ 0000 – – – – – – – – –	+++++++++++ ++++++ 00000 – – – –	++++++ 0000000 – – – – – – – – – –	++++ – – –
"L": Long-Term Development	+ 0000 – – – – –	+++++++++++ + 0000 – – – –	+++++ 000 – – –	0 –

Legend:

"+" = Communication as observed is helpful or facilitative to the function or relationship.

"0" = Communication as observed is neutral to the function or relationship.

"–" = Communication as observed is detrimental to the function or relationship.

123

vicious cycle of distrust, anger, or hostility—the continuing disintegration of relationships between drivers and dispatchers, clerks and foremen.

CONCLUSION

In sum, the social systems analysis can provide not only a deep and unique understanding for members of the system (and outsiders too), but a logical and measured basis for guiding change. When social systems data are compared with the expectations vocalized in the company's statement of philosophy, the requirements of change are highlighted in bold relief. In addition, social systems results can be used as a benchmark, or baseline, against which to compare the performance results of the changes and improvements to the system. If it is "owned" by the members of the organization, a social systems analysis can be reapplied at any time (and in much abbreviated versions as required) to measure the current state of the system and to compare it to cooperation and coordination before changes were made.

These work-related interactions demonstrate the ability to design for flexibility. The results of the social systems analysis can provide an excellent opportunity to design a flexible social structure and network that enables those who are closest to the key variances to control them as quickly as they occur. This flexibility is based on members knowing who to talk to and what to talk about, so that they can talk directly—without the traditional layers, filters, and interferences.

REFERENCES

ASHBY, W. R. *Design for a Brain.* New York: Wiley, 1960.

CHERNS, A. B. "The Principles of Sociotechnical Design." *Human Relations,* 29, 783–792, 1976.

CHERNS, A. B., & G. J. WACKER "Analyzing Social Systems: An Application of Parson's Macrosystem Model to the Organizational Level and the Sociotechnical Perspective." *Human Relations,* 31, 823–841, 1978.

GEIRLAND, J. "Preparing for the Social Analysis: A New Tool for Manufacturers." Speech presented at the conference on Sociotechnical work redesign sponsored by the Manufacturing Institute, division of the Institute for International Research. Coronado, CA, December 1990.

GLEICK, J. *Chaos: Making a New Science.* New York: Viking, 1987.

KEEN, P. G. *Competing in Time: Using Telecommunications for Competitive Advantage.* Rev. ed. New York: Harper & Row, 1988.

MALINOWSKI, B. *Coral Gardens and Their Magic.* London: George Allen & Unwin, 1935.

MCLUHAN, M. *Understanding Media: The Extensions of Man.* New York: McGraw-Hill, 1964.

MCLUHAN, M., & Q. FIORE *The Medium Is the Massage.* New York: Bantam Books, 1967, p. 100.

TOFFLER, A. *Power Shift.* New York: Bantam Books, 1990.

ZUBOFF, S. *In the Age of the Smart Machine: The Future of Work and Power.* New York: Basic Books, 1988.

❧ ❧

## CHAPTER 7

Designing for Individual Satisfaction: Understanding Quality of Working Life

". . . As new technologies come into play, people are less and less convinced of the importance of self-expression. Teamwork succeeds private effort."

(McLuhan & Fiore, 1967)

INTRODUCTION

To say that individual quality of working life (QWL) is important is an understatement; but to say that positive feelings about one's work is an individual phenomenon, based on individual actions and experiences, is a misnomer. Morale is a group or team concept. Team morale, or experiencing one's work life with and by others, is fast becoming the norm in North America.

Complexity in technology, product, and environment all contribute to reliance on group action. Satisfaction with that group action, and with one's role in it, is becoming one (if not *the*) dominant "individual" experience of people at work. Few are the jobs and occupations that can be accomplished alone by the individual and those that come to mind — solo pianist, forest-fire smoke watcher, lighthouse tender, or skywriter — require technologies that originated in earlier times. Even computer programming (Kidder, 1981) and exotic electronic circuit design (Taylor, Gustavson, & Carter, 1986) have become so complex in modern application that these specialists must work with others, and are dependent on them, to successfully complete the work. In order to accomplish even the most straightforward work objectives, using modern technology, we need the help and cooperation of others. This chapter discusses the importance of morale (an individual's attitudes about jobs and work) as it affects and is affected by the sociotechnical understanding of work systems.

People find more meaning in work when that work is based on competence in, relevance to, some control over, and a belief in a meaningful and successful work system. Since complexity of technology and changes in work have put the individual contributor in a diminished role, the ability and value of working with others increases in importance.

Complexity of technology and the chaotic and changing world have dramatically increased the need for collaboration and teamwork.

Quality of working life is more than merely wages, hours, and working conditions; it is more than dignity and respect, social support, prospects for advancement, and challenging work. Employees (management and nonmanagement alike) have an opportunity to experience higher QWL through (a) a sense of the importance or relevance of their product to the larger community, (b) through the understanding of their place or direct role in creating the product, and (c) through the opportunity to become competent in dealing with those activities most central to the effective creation of the product. Finally, competence and centrality are greatly enhanced by designing work so that employees consciously control key technical variances as close to their source as possible. Viewed in this way, quality of working life is virtually synonymous with organizational effectiveness.

Sociotechnical systems methods provide organization and job design techniques that provide employees with greater control over their work, greater quality of working life through feelings of personal competence, a central place in the product stream, and a sense of the social relevance of that product. Further, STS designs result in higher performance.

Feeling a part of a winning team and sharing that success and its vision with others are overlooked dimensions of quality of working life. Historically this kind of work satisfaction came only to professionals — college professors, nurses, attorneys, and engineers, to name a few. Organizations designed to succeed, using sociotechnical systems methodology, can provide such satisfaction to all members.

DEFINING QWL

Interest in improvement of the quality of working life emerged over two decades ago as a dual area of concern. On the one hand, it represented a concern for the need to further increase system performance and operational effectiveness. On the other hand, QWL represented a move to prevent the waste of talent in the North American labor force. It was defined as a positive experience — to enhance employee options in a variety of dimensions. QWL was contrasted to employee alienation caused by the negative aspects of the job or workplace. It was thought that correcting negative aspects would merely return jobs and work to previous levels of industrial development. Now it is appreciated that by concentrating on improving what employees see as a positive experience at work, systems of work that are more suitable to turbulent environments and complex technologies will result.

The sources of positive feelings about work are important aspects of performance by design. All sociotechnical systems integrate the values of organizational members into the process of design. Data from a number of sources suggest that there will probably never be a "fixed" set of constructs for QWL (Boisvert, 1977; Davis & Cherns, 1975; Lawler, 1975; Levine, 1983; Levine, Taylor, & Davis, 1984). The organizational design process should deal with the values of its members about work as a special set of constructs that are unique to that system.

₹ *Job Satisfaction*

The job satisfaction survey is a remarkably robust idea, but one that has done very little to explain its tenacious grip in organizational development efforts. Job satisfaction measures were first applied during the depths of the 1930s economic depression (Hoppock, 1935). Initially hailed as an important bulwark of the new "human relations" management, job satisfaction research evolved in the following 20 years into a debate about the predictors of organizational productivity and the state of national morale (Brayfield & Crockett, 1955) — in effect, positive employee attitudes could not be established as a precursor of increased performance. Criticisms of job satisfaction measures have stated it does not and cannot measure how people feel *about* jobs and work and that it only provides a generalized reaction to a personal situation (Davis, 1971). Shortcomings include the tendency of individuals to answer idle questions dealing with selves or health in an offhand way. It is culturally acceptable to answer "How are you?" or "How's your job?" with the response, "Pretty good." "Pretty good" can mean many things, including ". . . about as good as a guy like me can expect" (Taylor, 1977). True feelings related to job satisfaction cannot be obtained at arm's length (Davis, 1971)—they include privileged information based on values, concerns, fears, and ambitions and, as such, require a collaborative and trusting relationship between subject and investigator. A worker cannot be expected to tell a remote investigator feelings about his or her complex and unique work situation by answering precoded questions framed by the investigator. In the early to mid-1970s, when employee absenteeism and turnover were at all-time highs, over 80% of North American workers surveyed by many sources reported being satisfied (or at least "not dissatisfied") with their jobs. This trend, that of an overwhelming majority of workers reporting satisfaction with jobs and work, was shown to be unchanged over the 20-year period 1954–73 (Taylor, 1977).

⚡ *Employee Participation in Measuring Morale Versus the Expert Models of Measurement*

To overcome the resistance and suspicion engendered by outside investigators applying precoded job satisfaction measures, questions about quality of working life must be communicable and believable to those involved. Employees and managers alike are cautious in their acceptance of survey results. In order to overcome this caution the product of research should be of interest to all of those involved in system design, and not only to other academics or to policymakers. Typically, job satisfaction research results are used to compare data obtained in order to evaluate the effectiveness of change programs with standards. As it is based on problematic measures, the job satisfaction survey is hardly appropriate to this end. Social survey data can and should be used for improving QWL and system effectiveness rather than for simply documenting their presence or absence. Such data can be obtained through measures created and administered by organizational members, to be used not only for creating improvements in the workplace, but also for rewarding and reinforcing those changes once they are in place.

Fixed-response job satisfaction measures coupled with job evaluation items are widely used because of their efficiency in application and because they require little additional development or customization. Considerable work has been done to establish the reliability and validity of such measures, but they may not provide as much statistical power, or account for as much of the true variance in the attitudes and perceptions measured, as user-centered measures do.

USER INVOLVEMENT IN THE DESIGN OF MEASUREMENT IMPROVES THE POWER OF MEASUREMENT AS WELL AS ITS RELEVANCE

The effective design of jobs and organizations requires that the construct of quality of working life be specific and concrete as defined by organizational members. Research into comprehensive employee-generated lists of quality of working life reveals that company-specific measures developed by these participative methods are as much as 50% more powerful as predictors of employee attitudes than are standardized, expert-created job diagnostic surveys. (Levine, Taylor, & Davis, 1984)

The power of participatory development of a definition and measure of QWL can be seen clearly in a study using the "Delphi" technique (Levine, 1983). The Delphi technique, named after the legendary oracle who "knew the unknowable," was developed at the Rand Corporation (Dalkey, 1969). The technique requires a "Delphi panel"—a group of experts, coordinated by a moderator—to answer a question of judgment. The criteria for Delphi panel-member selection are knowledgeability and expertise. In Levine's use of Delphi it was clear that all employees of an organization were experts in their own QWL and that a representative sample of employees on the panel would protect against bias while assuring opinions from a wide spectrum of the organization. In that study Levine engaged employees in a Delphi analysis of their

QWL and compared their responses to the highly regarded Job Diagnostic Survey (JDS), an expert-developed measure. The resulting composite, seven-item, QWL measure (developed by the organization's members) accounted for 56% of the variance in an overall QWL measure. In contrast, using the same sample of employees, the seven-item expert-developed short form of the JDS accounted for a lower amount of variance (34%) in the "global" job satisfaction measure in the JDS. This 34% is, incidently, identical to the normative reliability of the JDS measure reported by its authors (Hackman & Oldham, 1975). In addition, the employee-generated, seven-item, QWL measure predicted to the overall QWL measure better than did the seven-item JDS, and the seven-item QWL measure predicted the global job satisfaction measure at virtually the same level as did the JDS scale. This advantage in reliability of the Delphi-based measure over its expert-based counterpart as a predictor of QWL was thought to be because it was developed solely for the particular organization and by the employees who served as both developers and subjects (Levine, 1983). Additional predictive power of Delphi-based measures has been shown to be the result of analysis and application of the "latent structure" of the data obtained from the Delphi method (Levine, Taylor, & Davis, 1984).

❧ Using QWL Concepts and Applications

There has been considerable North American experience with computer-based manufacturing in the new high-tech areas of electronics and microcomputers. These industries often have rather specialized manufacturing technologies and use computers for fragmented portions of those processes. These North American high-tech industries, despite their use of computers at the workplace, are often no more advanced than their traditional manufacturing counterparts in their design of work or in the use of worker competence or potential. If they are to survive, these high-tech companies must use advanced technology—and use it wisely. The mobility of scientists, engineers, and manufacturing personnel makes maintenance of a high-tech firm's technical advantage difficult. If that mobility is caused by employees' distress and frustration with the quality of their current working lives, survival of the firm itself becomes an issue. Sociotechnical systems methods provide organization and job design techniques that provide workers in computer-based manufacturing settings with greater control over their work and greater quality of working life through feelings of personal competence, influence in the process, pride in the product, and a central place in the product stream. Further, STS designs result in higher performance as well (cf. Taylor, Gustavson, & Carter, 1986). Manufacturing managers (especially in the United States) must first accept that employees' values must play a role along with the values of the designers of the technology and with the values of the managers who adopt it.

QWL: THE FOUR "CS"

Taking a user-centered approach to measuring QWL (either the Delphi-based method or more direct and time-saving participatory techniques described below) in sociotechnical systems design projects has yielded a short list of four items that have not been included in most traditional expert-based scales (Taylor, 1986). The four qualities of working life appear together as important aspects for employees in nearly every successful STS change project. There are three interesting aspects about these four qualities. First, they nearly always appear together—if one is important to a system member, they all are important. Second, although one or another of the four have shown up on lists developed by behavioral science experts, they have not shown up together in any of them. Third, all four qualities require coordination and cooperation with others in modern and complex work systems.

The QUALITIES of Working Life for people in systems designed using sociotechnical methodologies go beyond the traditional lists of satisfiers. The four items below are interrelated concepts that together have been shown to be characteristic of a high quality of working life.

1. **Recognized COMPETENCE at the workplace**
2. **Acknowledged CENTRALITY, or real relevance in applying that competence**
3. **Shared COMMITMENT to the purposes of the enterprise**
4. **Joint CONTROL over the product and process**

❧ *Competence and Skill in Activities Performed*

Prior to the application of sociotechnical systems ideas to industrial and white-collar work, feelings of pride in one's abilities were found primarily among people employed in skilled trades and in professional roles (Centers & Bugental, 1966).

Since the earliest job satisfaction studies began, production-line maintenance workers, such as carpenters, electricians, millwrights, welders, and pipefitters, have expressed that their satisfaction with working life and job is based on their personal skills and competence acquired through lengthy training and apprenticeship. When the production process breaks down and their special skills are required, these workers feel very important to the enterprise, very needed by production workers. They are an elite group, often more highly paid than production workers, sometimes in different uniform, usually able to plan and execute their own work, and they adhere to a more flexible schedule. When machines are running smoothly these maintenance jobs can become boring, but workers often make the best of it by boasting about the time they can spend reading or playing cards.

Because of these "special" working conditions, skilled maintenance workers are often segregated and set themselves apart from production workers. This separation between the groups may lead to unintended frictions between them, and surely leads to misunderstandings about the work, consequences, and purposes of the other. Furthermore, maintenance workers in traditional organizations are often woefully ignorant about the basic production processes and throughput they work so closely around and about the key variances in the processes that lead to the success of the enterprise.

In turn, production employees typically don't feel competent—they don't understand their production and throughput processes either, nor do they understand the problems involved in scheduling or coordinating the various maintenance specialties required to repair complex machinery—often there is an absence of respect for one group by the other.

Professional workers include lawyers, physicians, engineers, nurses, clinical laboratory scientists, teachers, and others who earn a degree from an institute of higher learning and subscribe to a code of ethics. Their knowledge and the authority of that knowledge become their source of pride, and the respect they receive becomes their source of satisfaction. They are often well paid and usually have some discretion over work schedule and planning. Job satisfaction surveys comparing

various occupations often show university professors with the highest
satisfaction, with the other professions listed above close behind.
Maintenance craftspersons and professional workers account for a
small portion of the North American work force. Historically, competence has not been an important source of attitudes about the work
system for the large numbers of people employed by large and medium-
sized businesses. The Scientific Management model of dividing production work into small, easily trained tasks effectively eliminated competence as a source of pride for the American worker.

What has emerged, with the advent of sociotechnical work system
design, is the recognition, by employees and change agents alike, that
people who recognize and control key variances in the product stream
must have an understanding of the product, process, and purpose of the
enterprise, as well as the skills and abilities to control some of those
variances as close to their source as possible. Everyone in the system
must understand the throughput process, which key variances they
affect, and how they contribute to that impact. That combination of
skills and understanding is competence. People in control of key variances are good at what they do, and they know that they have this
capability because of training and learning on the job. In designing jobs
and work with this focus, competence as a source of self-satisfaction and
quality of working life becomes available to everyone in the system, and
not just to skilled craftspeople and people in professional occupations.

❦ Centrality to the Technical System of the Enterprise

It follows that if everyone in the system is involved in key variance
control (and recognizes it), then he will also recognize that they are at
the center of the "business" of the enterprise. This recognition is based
on the definition of key variances as the most important aspects of
producing the "product." This aspect of quality of working life has not
been well developed in prior job satisfaction surveys—and for good
reason. In 19th- and 20th-century organizations there was little opportunity for most employees to see themselves as central to the process or
important to the enterprise, or to understand how their work contributed to the whole process or "big picture." When worker values were
examined in a conventional white-collar organization, the importance
of being central to the enterprise was revealed, even though it was not
satisfied in the work force studied (Levine, 1983; Levine, Taylor, &
Davis, 1984).

When centrality in the process is tied to control of key variances, the connection between centrality and competence is self-evident. Learning to be competent in the skills and knowledge required to control key variances leads to high performance in tasks defined by everyone in the system to be central to its success.

ૐ Commitment to the Values and Goals of the Enterprise

This third quality of working life has been a part of the United States management copybook for a very long time. But for all the attraction that this concept has for managers, it has not been expected to be (or observed to be) necessarily associated with being competent and being central for the "average" North American worker. It is apocryphal to relate the story of a new factory design in which workers were central and were provided training in controlling the production process. But after becoming competent and understanding the business, these workers then "turned" on their employer by criticizing the product as "useless" and no better than similar products currently on the market. In an open sociotechnical system where employees are empowered by understanding, such "disloyal" behavior can only be prevented by making the purpose (both mission and philosophy) crystal clear to potential employees during the initial selection process. The purpose must be explained and discussed during initial training and continually reinforced during recurrent training and day-to-day work process. In dealing with the workers who challenged the value of their product, the employer was able to enable them to better understand the product in the marketplace and the technical mission of the plant within the enterprise. With the workers' help, the employer was able to adapt and revise the product formulation so that it was in line with their values as well as with their technical mission and with recent changes in the environment.

ૐ Control through Understanding of the Product and Process

The political process in any organization relies on the sharing of (and struggle for) power and influence. Power equalization through participation has been an idea of great interest to designers of organizations (Mulder, 1971), and the influence over work process has been defined as a tenet of sociotechnical system design (Cherns, 1987). In an independent evaluation of STS redesigns in four manufacturing plants, it was shown that the innovations introduced were associated with significantly higher levels of perceived control and influence for workers and supervisors in contrast to those perceptions among workers in traditional plants in the same organization (Denison, 1982).

The combination of control over process through understanding and influence over others through the authority of knowledge and competence has been found to be a potent source of individual quality of working life, and it is more likely to promote a consensual political process.

A CASE ILLUSTRATION OF QWL IN AN STS-DESIGNED PLANT

In 1979 a Silicon Valley electronics firm applied STS design to the start-up of an integrated circuit production plant in Idaho and revolutionized the way microprocessors are manufactured. This "greenfield" site reached full production in 13 months instead of the more typical time of 25 months, circuit yields were improved by 100%, and employee turnover was reduced to only a few percent per year (Gustavson & Taylor, 1984). The company subsequently applied STS management to improve white-collar productivity in the sales and engineering departments (Taylor & Asadorian, 1985; Taylor, Gustavson, & Carter, 1986). All of these applications followed the methods described in this volume — the product-oriented focus, the design for purpose (including technical mission and human philosophy), and the involvement of employees characterized all of the company's STS applications.

The cooperative work process designed at the company's Idaho plant was reflected in the high quality of working life measured during its third year of operation. In that measurement, developed by using the Delphi process described above, employees were asked to list the most important and significant aspects of their jobs. Some 70 individual items were generated and these were clustered into 26 composite measures (Levine, 1984). Those items and clusters are presented here as Table 7.1.

The four qualities of competence, centrality, commitment, and control were represented within the set of composites. The list of composites was converted into a questionnaire and each item was evaluated for its presence on the job and its contribution to employee QWL. Of the 26 items thus treated, 7 were found to be significantly related to QWL. The results revealed that QWL resulted from identification with the plant's product and purpose (centrality and commitment), good wages, security, and good working conditions. Similarly, good growth

TABLE 7.1

QWL Items and Clustering Using the Delphi Method: Smallest Space Analysis: Empirically Derived Conceptual Framework of the QWL Definition

Conceptual Framework of the QWL Definition

1. Identification with product quality
   - (47) Quality of production
   - (60) Product identification
2. Identification with product quantity
   - (46) Quantity of production
   - (60) Product identification
3. Relationship of home life and working life
   - (6) Social environment
   - (36) Relationship of work to home life
   - (48) Personal stress
4. Individual control at work
   - (1) Work ethic
   - (17) Control over working life
   - (33) Individual responsibility and accountability
   - (53) Working with a variety of people
5. Building social relations at work
   - (40) Support, trust, respect, and helpfulness of co-workers
   - (42) Cooperative social relations
   - (43) Disruptive behavior of co-workers
   - (63) Dealing with social problems
6. Effectiveness of face-to-face communication
   - (32) Frequency and effectiveness of meetings
   - (44) Effectiveness of communication
   - (61) Giving feedback
   - (62) Receiving feedback
7. Growth potential of work related activities
   - (9) Job mobility
   - (10) Using acquired skills
   - (14) Job variety
   - (21) Training and learning opportunities
   - (57) Challenges of work
8. Meaningful future at company
   - (12) Advancement and promotions
   - (16) Knowing where my career is going and how I can get there
   - (26) Sense of purpose

- (54) Opportunity for increased responsibility
9. Working in a team-oriented system
   - (35) Working in a team-oriented/open system organization
   - (51) Team boundaries
   - (56) Problem-solving process
   - (64) Working with competent people
   - (65) Team development
10. Participative management decision-making system
    - (5) Management/employee relations
    - (11) Distance from corporate headquarters
    - (37) Participative management
    - (39) Organizational decision making
    - (41) Presence of supportive leadership
11. Discretionary work schedule
    - (20) Flexible work schedule
    - (24) Work load and scheduling
    - (38) Autonomous decision making

Continued

137

Table 7.1
QWL Items and Clustering Using the Delphi Method: Smallest Space Analysis: Empirically Derived Conceptual Framework of the QWL Definition (*Continued*)

Conceptual Framework of the QWL Definition

12. Basic individual needs
- (3) Safety
- (7) Job security
- (15) Direct pay
- (18) Fringe benefits
- (50) Physical environment, working conditions

13. Individual contribution at work
- (19) Recognition
- (58) Personal contribution to organization
- (59) Self-accomplishment

14. Role and job clarity
- (8) Role clarification
- (34) Job goal clarity

15. Dealing with equipment and documentation
- (45) Working with equipment
- (67) Preparing and using documentation

16. Company goals, policies, and procedures
- (2) Company policies and procedures
- (4) Company goals

17. Staffing process
- (30) Selection and deselection process
- (66) Adequacy of staffing

18. Equal rights; fair and just treatment
- (23) Status differentials
- (28) Personal appearance and dress code
- (29) Equal rights
- (52) Company cares about employees' human needs

19. Open architectural area
- (25) Open architectural area

20. Use of buzz word language
- (27) Use of buzz word language

21. Committee representation
- (31) Committee representation

22. Performance evaluations
- (55) Performance evaluations

23. Enforcement of norms
- (68) Enforcement of norms

24. Company's image to outside community
- (13) How outside people look at company

25. Availability of recreation activities
- (22) Recreation

26. Transportation to and from work
- (49) Transportation

SOURCE: Mark F. Levine, "A Self-Developed Measure of Quality of Working Life: Case Study in a Microchip Manufacturing Facility" (Unpublished, California State University, Chico, 1984).

138

potential from work activities, pride in one's skill (competence), and good relations between work and home were significant aspects of jobs at the plant and highly related to employees' QWL. Control (although found as one of the list of QWL item clusters) did not emerge as a significant predictor of the omnibus QWL measure, and commitment to purpose (although manifested in four composite item clusters) was found significantly related to QWL in the rather oblique cluster of identification with productivity. This case illustrates that successful STS designs do not always evoke all four qualities of working life as significant predictors of current QWL, but that these aspects are realized in unique ways for each system.

METHODS FOR COLLECTING DATA ON QWL

The Delphi method of involving employees in their own measurement of quality of working life has been shown to be effective in developing a statistically powerful measurement to be used for quantifying the individual experience of work and working. The resulting QWL questionnaire can be used repeatedly to test the relationships between QWL and other attitude and performance variables using sophisticated causal modeling techniques. A company must invest time in developing the measure. More direct and, in many ways, equally effective measures are available and are widely used in sociotechnical design projects.

❦ *Using the Social System Interview*

These direct methods rely on ongoing data collection such as the semistructured employee-managed interviews described in Chapter 5. Adding just two open-ended questions toward the end of the interview protocol that the STS analysis team devises for collecting the data to fill the GAIL communications grid can provide relevant and valid data on QWL. As used in many STS design projects, these two questions are: "What are the things (name as many as you want) that you really like about working here?" and "What are the things (list all you need to) that you'd really like to see changed or improved?" These questions elicit a unique set of positives and negatives for each person interviewed, but the combined lists (especially when combined by occupation or hierarchical level) show substantial similarities across people. These similarities, if consolidated for the whole system, become the short list of QWL items for the enterprise. The short list is used to guide the (re)design efforts of the analysis team. It can also be used as a bench-mark when the system is remeasured, particularly if the remeasure is applied to continue to improve the system over time. Compared with the Delphi process for obtaining QWL items for a system, the more participative face-to-face interview is considerably more direct and less time-consuming.

⚶ *Participative Data Collection and Analysis*

The use of interviews for such data collection is not new, but to have co-workers who are members of the STS analysis team conduct the interviews and analyze the data is new. When an outside expert conducts the interview or leads the Delphi process, the level of trust of employees for one another is less important to the reliability of the results than when the process is conducted by insiders. In the case of the internally conducted interviews for quality of working life, such trust must be high. In general, the level of trust is high.

What is it about the interview process as promoted here that would assure such trust? Basically, trust results from the open process of the interview itself and by the nature of the questions the social system analysis employs. As described in Chapter 5, each co-worker being interviewed is informed that the session is voluntary and confidential, that there are no "trick" questions, and that most questions ask about descriptions of contacts with others during the normal work day. During the course of the session, the interviewee is invited to review the answers for correctness as they are written down. It is obvious that the two QWL questions are not used by themselves. Furthermore, they are not asked near the beginning of the interview. The interview process to collect data for the social analysis takes about 30 minutes. By the time the QWL questions are asked, respondents are typically comfortable about the form and content of the interview, trustful of its consequences, and usually eager to continue talking about themselves and their work.

Table 7.2 shows the QWL list obtained from the analysis for redesign in a chemical manufacturing plant (Taylor & Christensen, 1990). The data presented contain the overall short list for the whole plant system. Note that the four qualities (competence, centrality, commitment and control) are contained in the short list. Also important is the number of items that link quality of working life with the social system and working with others. It is clear that the purely individual experience of work is a limited part of quality of working life.

TABLE 7.2
Measuring Quality of Working Life
with Employee-Managed Interviews

Summary of Most-frequent Responses to Open-ended Question "What helps and hinders you on the job?" Chemical Plant Redesign (N = 240)

What Helps?

Recognition — "a pat on the back" (50% of all respondents volunteered this; coded as centrality)

"Teamwork" (35% of all respondents volunteered this; coded as commitment)

"A sense of pride in their work — a feeling of accomplishment" (12% of all respondents volunteered this; coded as competence)

What Hinders?

"Poor communication and cooperation between workers" (60% of all respondents volunteered this; coded as control)

"Lack of understanding of how and why management decisions are made" (30% of all respondents volunteered this; coded as control)

"Lack of recognition" (10% of all respondents volunteered this; coded as centrality)

CONCLUSION

This chapter opened with the assertions that teamwork succeeds private effort and that working with others is an increasingly dominant part of each individual's feelings about work. The kinds of positive experiences engendered by sociotechnical systems designs have been reviewed. The results of several different methods of measuring and assessing quality of working life confirm that wages, hours and working conditions, individual control, and career are augmented by the systems-related constructs of competence, centrality, commitment, and control in a shared work setting.

REFERENCES

BOISVERT, M. "The Quality of Working Life: An Analysis." *Human Relations,* 30, 1977, 155–160.

BRAYFIELD, A. H., & W. H. CROCKETT "Employee Attitudes and Employee Performance." *Psychological Bulletin,* 52, 1955, 415–422.

CENTERS, R., & D. BUGENTAL "Intrinsic and Extrinsic Job Motivators among Different Segments of the Working Population." *Journal of Applied Psychology,* 50, 1966, 193–197.

CHERNS, A. B. "Principles of Sociotechnical Design Revisited." *Human Relations* 40, 1987, 153–162.

DALKEY, N.C. "The Delphi Method: An Experimental Study of Group Opinion." *Futures*, 1(5), September 1969, 408–426.

DAVIS, L. E. "Job Satisfaction Research: The Post-Industrial View." *Industrial Relations* 10, 1971, 176–193.

DAVIS, L. E., & A. B. CHERNS (eds.) *The Quality of Working Life: Vol. I. Problems, Prospects, and the State of the Art.* New York: Free Press, 1975.

DENISON, D. R. "Sociotechnical Design and Self-Managing Work Groups: The Impact on Control." *Journal of Occupational Behaviour*, 3, 1982, 297–314.

GUSTAVSON, P., & J. C. TAYLOR "Socio-Technical Design and New Forms of Work Organization: Integrated Circuit Fabrication." In F. Butera & J. Thurman (eds.), *Automation and Work Design.* Amsterdam: North Holland, 1984, 697–713.

HACKMAN, J. R., & G. R. OLDHAM "The Development of the Job Diagnostic Survey." *Journal of Applied Psychology*, 60, 1975, 159–170.

HOPPOCK, R. *Job Satisfaction.* New York: Harper, 1935.

KIDDER, J. T. *The Soul of a New Machine.* Boston: Little, Brown, 1981.

LAWLER, E. E., III "Measuring the Psychological Quality of Working Life: The Why and How of It." In L. E. Davis & A. B. Cherns (eds.), *The Quality of Working Life: Vol. I. Problems, Prospects, and the State of the Art.* New York: Free Press, 1975.

LEVINE, M. F. "Self-Developed QWL measures." *Journal of Occupational Behaviour*, 4, 1983, 35–46.

LEVINE, M. F. "A Self-Developed Measure of Quality of Working Life: Case Study in a Microchip Manufacturing Facility." (Unpublished, California State University, Chico, 1984).

LEVINE, M. F., J. C. TAYLOR, & L. E. DAVIS "Defining Quality of Working Life." *Human Relations*, 37, 1984, 81–104.

McLUHAN, M., & Q. FIORE *The Medium is the Massage.* New York: Bantam Books, 1967, 123.

MULDER, M. "Power Equalization through Participation." *Administrative Science Quarterly*, 16, 1971, 31–38.

TAYLOR, J. C. "Job Satisfaction and Quality of Working Life: A Reassessment." *Journal of Occupational Psychology*, 50, 1977, 243–252.

TAYLOR, J. C. "Job Design and Quality of Working Life." In R. Kraut (ed.), *Technology and the Transformation of White Collar Work.* Hillsdale, NJ: Erlbaum, 1986.

TAYLOR, J. C., & R. A. ASADORIAN "The Implementation of Excellence: Socio-technical Management." *Industrial Management*, 27(4) 1985, 5–15.

TAYLOR, J. C., & T. D. CHRISTENSEN "Employee Guided Design and Implementation in a Chemical Plant." In H. L. Meadow & M. J. Sirgy (eds.), *Proceedings of the Quality of Life/Marketing Conference.* Blacksburg: Virginia Polytechnic Institute & State University, 1990, 540–547.

TAYLOR, J. C., P. W. GUSTAVSON, & W. S. CARTER "Integrating the Social and Technical Systems of Organizations." In D. D. Davis (ed.), *Managing Technological Innovation.* San Francisco: Jossey-Bass, 1986.

CHAPTER 8

ใ ใ

Designing for Whole Systems Capability: Understanding How It All Fits Together

"Most existing organizations were not born but 'just growed.'"

(Cherns, 1976)

The analysis is done and suggestions abound. It's time to put it all together and design a new organizational system. How do all the pieces fit together? How does the design team integrate and make sense of all the individual ideas generated during the analysis? The analysis process to date can seem exhausting and painstaking. The analysis was specific and detailed. It's time to stop and put systems theory to work and begin designing.

The beginning quote from Albert Cherns helps us understand just what sociotechnical systems design is all about. The "birthing" of a new sociotechnical organization is the *consciously conceived* purpose, structure, and processes to permit an organization to excel in what it intends. Without using sociotechnical design this consciousness is not a part of most organizations, because it has to be done by people who know, and who want, to change and improve. This is designing for performance.

STRUCTURING FOR DESIGN

Now that the analysis has been completed, the team of people responsible for that phase must consider the requirements of design.

Often, because the analysis process is so highly structured, it seems

143

to the analysis team that design must also result from one more table or matrix or grid—but it does not. The design process is manifestly unstructured when compared with the process of understanding the system. The design "structure" then involves creative thinking. Such creativity should directly involve as many stakeholders as possible. This means at least employees and managers together.

❧ Creating the Design Team

It is often helpful to mark the passage from the phase of "understanding" to the phase of "design" by creating a new team of people including people from the analysis team (for continuity and for in-depth knowledge of the analysis), and the system's "gatekeepers" (who may include management and supervisors, trade union officials, and/or Human Resources Department representatives). Sometimes members of the analysis team have "had enough," either because workmates have taken up the day-to-day load long enough, because they feel others should have a chance to participate, or because of other, purely personal reasons. In any event, the departure of some members of the former analysis team can make room for different kinds of stakeholders to join in the effort. If the analysis team was composed mainly of workers, then some managers on the re-formed team will bring the ability to advocate direct action or to confirm the importance of structural, technical, or plant changes that nonmanagement personnel may be reluctant or fearful to seriously propose.

This newly formed design team can be larger than the analysis team (sometimes very large) because much of its work can be accomplished in subgroups. It is important, however, that its members feel empowered to create an innovative and practical work system design.

❧ Thinking Big, Not Piecemeal

Thinking whole systems and not piecemeal is essential. It's not a decision of what piece should be designed first, but rather a process of looking at the larger whole. Designing for whole systems capability requires returning to the primary purpose of the organization and asking, based on the technical and social data gathered, what needs to be changed and how.

This requires a balanced and joint view of the technical and social systems. It has been asserted that, apart from STS design, the design of work continues to rest "firmly in the hands of technical experts who report to management" (Alic, 1990)—and our experience bears this out. Turning to engineers and technicians for ways to optimize the technical system will only force a process of having to adapt the social system to fit. Only by jointly exploring each subsystem can joint optimization occur. Joint optimization needs design team members who are involved in both the technical and social systems analysis. This knowledge base is essential in exploring alternative designs that jointly accommodate an understanding of the technology requirements of machines and equipment as well as the individual and group behaviors and dynamics. Through the sharing of both systems' uniqueness and alternatives, a new creative system can be designed that jointly optimizes both while fulfilling the primary purposes of the organization.

Joint optimization focuses on both the technical and social subsystems by looking at purpose.

Figure 8.1 portrays the joint optimization as three overlapping distributions—the far left curve represents the typical social investment and its payback, and the second curve is the typical technical investment (further to the right of the graph because it is always greater in dollar terms than its social counterpart) and its payback. The third and larger distribution represents the greater effectiveness, or higher payback, from an investment in *jointly optimizing* both the technical and social investments simultaneously. The third distribution shows that results are best when the technical system and social system are jointly optimized. But Figure 8.1 only tells of costs and benefits and that is just half the story. The fact that investments in technology can usually be reduced, but the investment in people is increased, is shown in Figure 8.1. This shift away from "typical" levels of investment is because extensive automation is usually not a centerpiece in successful sociotechnical system designs; and employees must be trained to effectively use new and existing technology in intelligent ways and to work with one another as effectively as conditions will allow. The other "half" of joint optimization is not so rational and orderly; in fact it is sort of "messy," in that the design really starts as a creative act.

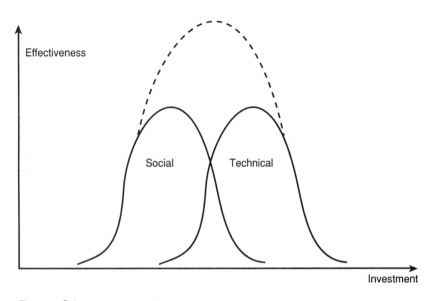

FIGURE 8.1
Joint Optimization
Adapted from James C. Taylor & Robert A. Asadorian. The implementation of excellence: STS management. *Industrial Management*, 27 (4), 1985, pp. 5–15.

THE PROCESS OF DESIGN

"The art of organization design is simultaneously esoteric and poorly developed" (Cherns, 1976). There is no one best way to design. Recent developments toward an automated approach to sociotechnical design, in which artificial intelligence (AI) is used to facilitate organizations in performing their own systems integration (cf. Majchrzak & Gasser, in press), suggest that automation may be useful even here. As with any application of automation, the replacement of humans (designers) with technology (AI), the role of people in the larger system is a primary STS concern. Even when tools and technologies are used to enhance their design process, organizations are human inventions that are organic and iterative in nature. The initial design will continue to change and evolve over time, regardless of its excellence or appropriateness at the time of its creation. The design process itself must reflect the values found in the new paradigms and held by the members of the system.

ᴚ *Taking the Leap*

Before any rational decision making takes place, the members of the design team are invited to make a leap—to consider the organization as it might be in an ideal state, without consideration of any real-world or practical guidelines. The STS map we presented in Chapter 1 showed all four phases of the process as part of conscious sociotechnical system design. The design phase was shown beginning "nowhere," or more accurately in a "cloud." Figure 8.2 presents that map again. We can see from Figure 8.2 that the creation of the "ideal" organization is in a cloud, but it soon turns into a practical exercise when it is tested against the results of the analysis or "understanding" of the system. In a section to follow, we will study how to design in a "constraint-free" mode while living in a world full of constraints.

ᴚ *Participation in Design*

Participation of members within the organization is essential, not only for acceptance and commitment to the new design, but, more importantly, to develop and build the new design, taking into account all of its unique elements identified in Chapters 3 through 7.

Two major hurdles are confronted in participation with STS programs, once the risks of empowering employees have been faced. The *first* is the problem of total participation during day-to-day operations. That is, how can all employees participate at the same time and still get the work out? The *second* is the large organization problem. That is, how can everybody participate if the organization has 150 or 1,500 people?

Solving the first problem of total participation requires that additional resources be obtained. If all 25 people in a work system are to be involved in an STS redesign, they must be given time off the job to do so. Ready solutions (that also cost money) include overtime, contract employees, deferred or delayed production. Less financially costly solutions include choosing a usually slow period so that reduction in productivity has a minimum impact, or the short-term exercise of improved efficiency by employees to do their regular work, together with the extra study and design. Such efficiency and extra effort can sometimes be obtained for the short period of time required for redesign. It is expedient, and often effective, to use a smaller subgroup of people to do

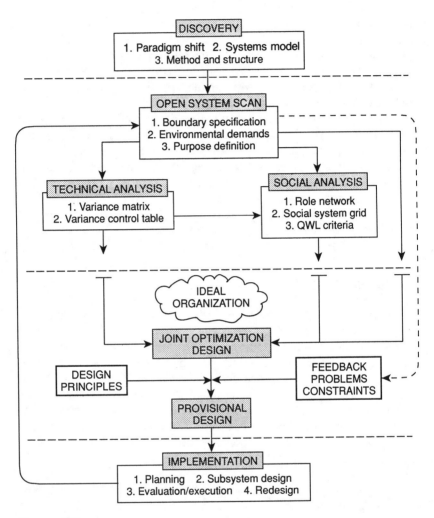

FIGURE 8.2
The Process of STS

much of the study and to meet and encourage the participation of their co-workers. But in the long run, the communication and involvement become the most crucial aspect in successfully implementing the resulting design.

The role of the first-line supervisor is a crucial one in STS redesign. The supervisor's job is often the most changed following a redesign, and it is far better to involve those people as early, as directly, and as sensitively as possible. This involvement can take the form of an STS facilitator or member of the study subgroup, but it must be direct.

Solving the second problem, that of participation in large organizations, requires the above, plus some additional considerations. These include finding a meeting place large enough, managing initial participation by everyone, and selecting an appropriate product or deliverable and its associated core process. Often, plants and administrative locations can be as large as 3,000 employees or more, and the general manager in charge and the trade union leaders are convinced that empowerment is required. What can be done?

If STS is to be used for the creation of a participative design, all members are to participate. This compatibility between means and ends has long been a principle of STS design (Cherns, 1976, 1987). The problems of shutting down production are the same, but quite large when organization size increases. Special methods of carrying out large-scale changes have been developed, and in these it is important that the initial meetings and communications truly engage employees and managers.

One example of this involved the design of a new fabrication plant (2,700 employees) to replace an existing adjacent facility. Two hundred fifty employees were selected from all pay codes to provide design ideas. Some 70 of those people later formed focus groups to explore and evaluate the ideas from the 250. To establish communication back to the 2,700, a communication team was formed to plan and coordinate the effort. The focus teams held meetings for roughly 250 employees each over all shifts to describe the proposed design. Following these reviews a survey of all employees was conducted to determine the degree of support for each proposed design idea. The communication process was judged a "great success" (Hoffman, 1990).

CONSTRAINT-FREE DESIGN AND THE REAL WORLD

The three steps of the design phase, ideal design, joint optimization, and provisional design (see Figure 8.2), each contribute to the creation of the most innovative, effective, and practical design possible for any given organization. The design phase is the culmination of what has gone before, not merely in the sociotechnical process, but also in the history of the organization and its predecessors.

❦ *The Ideal Design Step*

The design team is brought together for the first time by a facilitator and, after a period of introduction, acquaintance, or team building, is given an assignment. Each member, individually, is asked to think about (and list, write, or draw on no more than one page) his or her "ideal system" for the organization. Individuals are encouraged not to put their names on "their" design because once shared, they belong to the group. At this stage, justification of these individuals is also discouraged. What is important is that all members reveal what they would do with the organization if they were a "king" or a "queen" with a magic wand. Typically this assignment is given for completion overnight, for presentation to the whole team the next day.

Once having reassembled the next day, the facilitator explains the agenda as follows: (a) Individually and silently review all the other "ideal systems," (b) discuss, as a group, elements of an ideal design they all like (this is usually based on points drawn from many of the individual ideals), (c) reach consensus as a team on one (and sometimes more than one) ideal design for the organization.

In practice, the first agenda item is accomplished as follows. Each member is instructed to post his or her one sheet "multimedia" presentation on a wall of the meeting room. All members then circulate around the room reading each sheet and making notes to themselves. The second item is always achieved with a positive discussion, listing clever, novel, and appropriate ideas noted in the individual work. Even if there are cynics on the team, they are subdued in their behavior as the overwhelmingly positive energy of the other members is revealed. The usual admonitions against criticism of others' ideas are not needed here because design team members are highly motivated to create, to build, and to move forward *without constraints*. The third agenda item follows a predictable pattern of behavior in which a brief, but comprehensive statement of an ideal design (or occasionally more than one) is created that all members state that they can "buy into." The whole process usually requires no more than three hours—and usually without mention of the sociotechnical analysis. Often design team members will create an ideal for the organization that is totally new and original. Sometimes the ideas will be "old favorites" for organizational improvements that a team member has promoted for years. Others may bring ideas that represent new versions or modifications of their "old favorites," changed to fit the member's new (but unstated) sociotechnical systems understanding. Both of these latter cases are appropriate, first because those individuals have a good sense of what would/could improve things (even if they have been discussed previously), but can't express why; and second, because raising "old chestnuts" may permit "clearing the air," and allowing new ideas from others or from the team to have fresh impact.

ॐ *Joint Optimization as a Design Step*

At this point in the process, the facilitator would guide the team to briefly review the major learnings from the STS analysis—the purpose, objectives, boundaries, environments, key variances, focal roles, performance in GAIL functions, and the quality of working life "turn-ons" and "turn-offs." After the team has done this, the facilitator prompts the team members to test their ideal design (or designs) in its ability to control key variances better than existing designs and its capability in improving important social relationships and quality of working life. If the design is found wanting in any of these aspects (and it usually is), then it must be changed in order to do so. This step truly produces a joint optimum that involves the people and the production process simultaneously. Some have noted that because many practitioners lack knowledge of one side or the other, the central principle of a joint optimum remains a conceptual dream rather than an operational reality (Alic, 1990). Carefully exercised, however, joint optimization does become a powerful design step, even though it employs only the most direct operations described above.

It is important to note that these direct actions of testing an ideal against the technical and social system requirements from the analysis may be repeated several times. First, the resulting changes are tested against the new system's pursuit of its purpose (both mission and philosophy) as well as addressing the specific key variances and GAIL functions. Sometimes this process requires several iterations before the team and facilitator are satisfied with the design (it still feels good to them), and with its promise of performance (it still provides good variance control, cooperation, and coordination). Like the ideal design step, the joint optimization step also takes little time and is often completed in a day or two. With this step, the first, but *most important*, of many constraints has been applied to the new design. The design is, above all, the organization for the routine, the day-to-day, and not the solution to problems, or other peoples' solutions that solve no present problems. There are other constraints to be faced on the way to provisional design, but the conviction that the joint optimization has honed the design into something to succeed in the pursuit of purpose will make the practicalities of the real world simply obstacles to overcome or incorporate as important aspects to cope with a complex world.

⚵ *Provisional Design*

By provisional design, we mean it is the design to use "providing" it works. This means that a sociotechnical system design is not an "experiment," merely undertaken to see if it works. Of course, the design will work if and when the members of the system are convinced that they have addressed the critical aspects of organizational success and quality of working life. Too often, in the past, managers were only able to consider all the things they could do when an organizational experiment "failed." It seems ironic, but with sociotechnical designs these same managers were often caught unprepared for doing all the things they could do when the design "succeeded." Sadly, not being prepared can often cause a successful design to founder due to a lack of institutional or corporate support.

Organizational improvements, whether sociotechnical or not, are never complete successes. There are always critics who are happy to point out the real and imagined flaws in concept and/or in operation of a new system design. With provisional design, success is measured against the vision. The design is continuously improved in order to better live up to that vision. Such changes are expected to be slow, and although the specifics will evolve, major changes in direction are unlikely.

In the preceding discussion, we have noted that several alternative ideal designs can be created by the design team. Alternative designs can provide advantage to single proposal through comparison and choice, but they can also introduce "noise" instead of variety to the process. Alternatives can also result in added expense and delays in the design process, and they can even cause designers to measure their effectiveness more by the quantity of ideas than by their quality (Cherns, 1987). Sometimes when alternatives are generated, it is clear that only one is really attractive to the design team, and that should cause the process to concentrate on their most appropriate or attractive one. It is important that the decision to further develop and pursue bona fide design alternatives be delayed until an initial design (if attractive enough to the whole design team) has been suitably challenged, and the obstacles to it have been logged. It is vital that the assumptions behind a design proposal be clearly stated and that attractive alternative assumptions be given voice in the design team's discussions, if not in actual alternative designs.

Before the joint optimum of design (phase 2, step 2) can become the provisional design to be implemented, it must be tested against the further constraints and obstacles of the real world: such things as "it will cost too much," ". . . and take too long," and "we've tried it before and it didn't work," as well as the more subtle resistances that can result from power shifts, and the clash of strong egos. But the obstacles don't merely represent a blind resistance to change. They can be the legitimate and valid concerns of co-workers, staff specialists, and managers. All of this means that the process of sharing the design with the rest of the organization is the main way of determining constraints and adjusting or justifying the design as appropriate. Changes made in the design at this stage will improve its effectiveness, and the reasons used to justify the design help to strengthen members' commitment to it.

Another aspect of testing the potential of the joint optimum is to review the "presenting problems" listed during the scan phase to see which of them remain "unsolved" by the design. It is usually found that most, if not all, of the problems listed are solved by addressing the cause, not the symptoms. Table 8.1 presents a checklist to help log the evaluation of a joint optimum design against the "presenting problems" generated during the system scan.

Not all tests of the design need to be negative. As shown earlier, in Figure 8.2, problems, constraints, and feedback on the joint optimum design are counterbalanced by the application of STS design principles. These principles can be thought of as the positive aspects of sociotechnical systems designs in other organizations, which should be affirmed in the new design, built into the design, or confirmed as not appropriate for the design. These design principles form an invitation to the design team to consider "copying" other organizations' solutions, but only after they have developed their own design quite fully themselves.

PRINCIPLES OF STS DESIGN

The design is directly linked to the scan, social, and technical system requirements and will not succeed if the design content does not address certain principles. These principles have been summarized and are intended to help guide the design, as opposed to saddling one with restrictions. They are offered as a "checklist, not a blueprint" (Cherns,

TABLE 8.1
Evaluating the Design — "Presenting Problems"

Presenting Problems	Design Alternatives		
	1	2	3
1.			
2.			
3.	Bring out the presenting problem identified in Chapter 3 and select the key problems the design team wants to ensure the new design will address.		
4.			
5.			
6.			
7.			
8.			
9.			
10.			
11.			

1987). These principles give the design team the opportunity to think about others' solutions, even generic ones. The 11 principles that follow are drawn from the work of Cherns (1976, 1987), and Davis (1982). This list reflects the best features of sociotechnical designs in North America and Europe over the past 25 years. For more comprehensive detail and background, the interested reader should refer to these original sources. The point of any of these lists is merely to remind a design team that others have introduced good ideas into organization design, but an original design should only be augmented by the principles and not founded on them. Table 8.2 presents a checklist to help log the evaluation of a joint optimum design against the 11 principles.

❧ *Principle 1: Compatibility*

How the whole design process is carried out should be compatible with the design's objective — in other words, the means should fit the

TABLE 8.2
Evaluating the Design — 11 Principles

	Key Design Alternatives		
Design Principles	1	2	3
1. Compatibility			
2. Minimum Critical Specification			
3. Variance Control			
4. Boundary Location			
5. Information Flow			
6. Power and Authority			
7. Multifunctional/Multiskills			
8. Support Congruence			
9. Design and Human Values			
10. Bridging the Transition			
11. Incompletion — Build in Continuous Improvement			
Summary/Total			

ends. The earlier discussion of participation in the design process illustrates one very important manifestation of "compatibility." If the desired outcome is real and meaningful participation where all members of the organization work together toward common goals and objectives, then no one should be omitted from the process. Other examples can be readily drawn from the application of the remaining principles. For example, all phases of the STS approach should follow the principle of minimum critical specification in order to allow flexibility and adaptive use throughout the organization. The degree to which this first principle of compatibility is respected and adhered to will greatly influence long-term success and commitment.

ǰ *Principle 2: Minimum Critical Specification*

Specify as little as possible, and identify only *what* is essential and critical to the organization's success. It is important that the design team be precise and get everyone together on *what* has to get done. *How* to do it should be left up to the individual teams. In the assignment of tasks, application of rules, policies, procedures, and so on, only the key minimum requirements should be specified so options are not closed off and new improvements or changes can be developed by those who are involved in doing the work. It's so easy for the design team to define and specify everything each team should do in its new design. A good team design should not specify more than primary purpose and key responsibility, and all should fit on one page. This will allow team members the opportunity to create their own processes on *how* they plan to fulfill *what* the design demands of them.

ǰ *Principle 3: Variance Control*

Controlling the variances identified in Chapters 4 and 5 at points *other* than their source has the effect of trying to correct their consequences rather than preventing them from accruing. This third principle simply states that variances not removed or eliminated through technology should be controlled by the organization closest to their point of origin. Key variances should not be allowed to cross unit operations. The less variances are exported beyond their point of occurrence, the more control and empowerment is provided to the individual on the line. A good example is product quality. Quality cannot be inspected into the product. It clearly needs to be built in by the person(s) responsible for building the product or performing the service.

ǰ *Principle 4: Boundary Location*

Setting internal organizational boundaries—that is, the division between units, functions, and so on—is important in the design of any system. Boundaries should not be drawn that inhibit the sharing or flow of information, knowledge, and skills. Boundaries should be set so that:

- The team and its members have access to and control of variances that occur in their work area.
- Team members have or can generate the information they need to solve the

team's problems and evaluate its performance; that is, if they receive continuous feedback, they can generate and track their own data.

• The team should be responsible for a complete process and produce a whole and identifiable output; that is, boundaries should not be set in the middle of a process.

• The team possesses all the knowledge, skills, and abilities needed to perform its work and fulfill the team's responsibilities to the larger whole.

By locating boundaries that allow the team the means to regulate itself, the need for external control becomes minimal.

❧ *Principle 5: Information Flow*

Information should go first to the point of action. This empowers the workers. But when managers get the information, they are sorely tempted to give in to the urge to micromanage. This external control will rob teams of their ownership and performance ability and will make it difficult to hold them responsible. Management cannot tell a team it's responsible and then withhold data that's critical to the team's ability to self-manage. The key to effective information flow is to design systems with the involvement and participation of the team using the data. After all, they are the ones who need accurate and timely data to control variance and take action to resolve deviations.

Information used to control individual behavior is an element of external control or traditional design and, when used in the new design, should be given to the team as part of its data base for self-management.

❧ *Principle 6: Power and Authority*

Cherns (1987) added this principle in his later version of the principles, and for good reason. Every successful sociotechnical system design has acted to increase the degree of power people have over their work and the control they have over their part of the product. Earlier, in Chapters 1, 4, and 7, we have discussed the importance of employee empowerment, the crucial contribution employees make in the control of key variances, and the role that power and influence play in employee quality of working life. Any of these aspects of power and authority, individually, would cause the idea to be included here as a principle of sociotechnical design, but together they form an indisputable element in the well-constructed sociotechnical design.

⅋ *Principle 7: Multifunctional/Multiskills*

The traditional form of organization relies very heavily on division of labor. It requires people to perform highly specialized, fractionated tasks. There is often a rapid turnover of such people, but they are thought to be comparatively easily and inexpensively replaced. Each is treated as an expendable or replaceable part.

But people are not seen as quite so expendable today. Higher technology has led to greater investments in training. Fast-changing markets have demanded a flexible and well-skilled work force. And employee expectations have risen, too. Boring throw-away jobs are not much sought after anymore. It then becomes more adaptive and less wasteful for each team and person employed to possess more than one function. The same function can be performed in different ways by using different combinations of elements. There are several routes to the same goal — the principle sometimes described as equifinality. Complex organisms have all gone this route of development. Complex organizations are also living systems (Katz & Kahn, 1966) and will improve in effectiveness by applying this principle.

⅋ *Principle 8: Support Congruence*

This principle states that the systems of social support should be designed to reinforce the behaviors which the organization structure is designed to elicit. If, for example, the organization is designed on the basis of group or team operation with team responsibility, a payment system based on individual members' loyalty would be incongruent with these objectives. Not only payment systems, but systems of selection, training, conflict resolution, work measurement, performance assessment, timekeeping, leave allocation, promotion, and separation can all reinforce or contradict the behaviors that are desired. The attention and support of others, managers and employees alike, can also provide powerful reinforcement of appropriate behavior. This is to say that the management philosophy should be consistent and that management's actions should be consistent with its expressed philosophy. Virtually all STS designs employ "pay for what you know" and/or "pay for results obtained," instead of the traditional pay for what you "do." The craft model of high pay for maintenance workers reminds us that the value isn't ever what skilled professionals "do," and it isn't always what they "accomplish," but always what is "in their heads." This value is appropriate for operations workers in sociotechnical systems in any industry and the eighth principle—support congruence—keeps that value appropriately focused.

❧ Principle 9: Design and Human Values

This principle states that an objective of organizational design should be to provide a high quality of work discussed in Chapter 7. We recognize that quality is a subjective phenomenon, and that not everyone wants to have responsibility, variety, involvement, growth, and so on. The objective is to provide these for those who do want them without subjecting those who don't to the tyranny of peer control. In this regard, we are obliged to recognize that all desirable objectives may not be achievable simultaneously. The company's philosophy statement provides guidance in creating a design for human values. That philosophy must accommodate the varied interests of system members by employing what all of them share, including human choice and flexibility of rewards.

❧ Principle 10: Bridging the Transition

As discussed in Chapter 9, implementing a new design involves a lot of stress. Keeping the balance of pushing forward without invoking adverse stress needs to be consciously and continuously reviewed. Rolling out a new design should be handled in a way that is congruent with the design, its objectives, and its philosophy. If not thought through and planned, it could send a negative message into the system and undermine the success of the implementation, as well as violate the future design that's envisioned.

❧ Principle 11: Incompletion—Building Continuous Improvement

Design is a reiterative process. The closure of options opens new ones. At the end, we are back at the beginning. The new paradigm is that of an organization flexibly adapting to its environment. Although a certain degree of stability is necessary to operate, the organization must be prepared to review and revise its design. Being prepared means having mechanisms built into the structure of the organization at all levels to deal with changes it must make on a continuing basis. The members of a sociotechnical system must be unafraid to change their design once it is in place. Everyone in the organization must appreciate that the design is never finished—it is always incomplete.

A Case Illustration: Sociotechnical Redesign in a Chemical Plant

The following description of STS design process is drawn from (and continues) the case of the participative redesign of a chemical plant (Taylor & Christensen, 1990) which we introduced in Chapter 1. Before design can take place, the processes of discovery and system understanding are required. These steps for the chemical plant have been described, but for further reference see Figure 8.2.

To briefly review, the chemical plant was considered a candidate for redesign after only one year of operation. The plant's original design had been assembled from the best elements and ideas of other plant designs, but without a systematic regard for the whole. The "no-expenses-spared" technical system and physical plant had been designed by a contractor specializing in that type of plant. The plant's social system had been copied from elements of several "innovative" organizations the original start-up team had seen during visits to other companies in North America.

After a six-month period of searching and "discovery," followed by a six-month period of learning and "understanding" (already described in Chapter 1), the original STS analysis and design team found itself ready for the next phase in the process.

ৠ *Phase 3 of the STS Process, "Designing the System" (September–November)*

While the phase 2 analysis activities were still under way in the analysis/design team, two other groups were brought together by the plant manager in anticipation of creating a new sociotechnical design for the plant. The first of these was the group of production and maintenance foremen, who were concerned about their jobs as the analyses progressed and had voiced their concern to the plant manager. The other group that met as the analysis was completed included middle managers and professionals. Although some of this latter group had served on the steering committee, few of them had much to do with the STS process since the initial system scan. The plant manager wanted to see all of his supervisors, managers, and engineers more deeply involved in the STS design process, as the analysis hadn't touched most of them in any direct way for several months. The foremen-group was guided by an external consultant who helped them draw up a list of things they'd like to continue to do and things they would like to see the production workers do for themselves. The other managers and professionals met together to confirm their values and to list specific response capabilities that the plant system should exhibit in responding to its complex environment. Although they did create a list of requirements and values, these managers additionally (and significantly) came back with a process which successfully involved the employees in the plant in inventing their own set of "requisite response capabilities." The managers' lists, together with one created by the foremen, would later be used as (positive) constraints and feedback to the design process. These two group activities were further useful as they energized the foremen, managers, and professionals to volunteer for further design activities.

Phase 3, Step 1: Creating the Ideal System (September). Upon completion of its analysis, the analysis/design team produced its "ideal design" using the process described above. Immediately following that, the design team was expanded to include several managers and additional foremen, while some of the original members of the analysis/ design team either retired from the new team or were replaced by others from their individual work units. The final composition of the "new" design team included five original members and seven new members. The original members of the design team reviewed and summarized their entire analysis results for themselves, and particularly for their seven new members. The original members also reviewed their "ideal" design for the team as a whole, and obtained the consensus of all members to that constraint-free, "pie-in-the-sky" design.

Phase 3, Step 2: Creating the "Joint-Optimum" (October). Having summarized the analysis results, the design team then tested the ideal for its control of key variances, its ability to provide for optimal performance of all four social functions (GAIL), and its provision of important qualities of working life. Certain features of the design were changed to accommodate for their understanding of the plant as a sociotechnical system. In doing this, the design team members also assured themselves that they had designed for its purpose and for the performance they desired.

Phase 3, Step 3: Creating the "Provisional" Design (October–November). It was now time for testing the joint optimum against the constraints, problems, and design principles. The new members of the design team reviewed the two lists of opportunities the foremen and managers had created during the preceding month. These lists acted to further shape and modify the evolving, but always incomplete design. By this time, the design was taking shape in an exciting way. The design team's meeting room had become the focus of attention throughout the plant, and many visitors from the front office, as well as from the operating units, sat in to listen to the team's discussions. Although visitors were always welcome, the team was eager to get the evolving design out for further feedback from the plant, lab, and offices, and they held a series of meetings to assure complete participation in testing their design ideas. Soon the ideas began to seem like a viable blueprint for change. Top management from home office, including human resources managers and wage specialists, were invited to the plant for a formal presentation and informal discussions about the emerging design.

In an effort to provide better control of the process and improve quality of working life, the design team proposed a structure of five plantwide production teams. These would be teams with multiskilled members, doing away with existing boundaries between the production units. They wanted no permanent supervisors. The design team further proposed additional skill training, skill-based pay, a gainsharing system, direct involvement in setting goals and objectives, budgeting discipline, career planning and development, and personal evaluations. In a move to accomplish this, the team recommended changing the work schedules from four shift cycles to five cycles. This new schedule would allow each team one week in every five for skill training and development, including both social and technical skills. Included in each new team would be one person with maintenance knowledge and skills and one with lab/QC skills. Use of external contract employees would be reduced and some of these former contractors would be selected to join the teams as regular full-time employees. Daily shift-overlap meetings between production teams were also recommended. A single "management" team that cut across disciplines and hierarchical levels was developed along with an "organizational support" team made up of the clerks who formerly served in separate departments, and a "production support" team made up of engineers and former line supervisors. Finally, a "plantwide coordinating team" (PWCT) was developed to provide overall guidance and coordination of day-to-day operational issues like plant production scheduling. Representatives (REPS) to the PWCT came from each team in the whole plant. This design was pictured as a wheel with the product (IT) as the center and the teams circled around IT and focused on the center. (See Figure 8.3.)

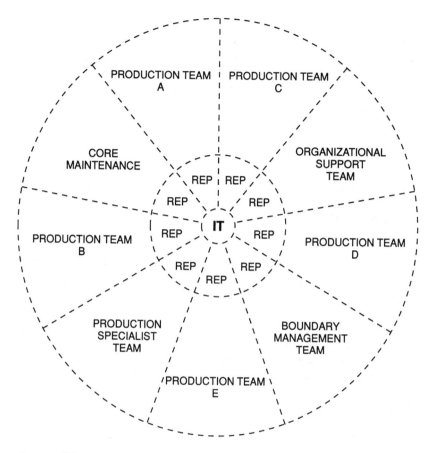

FIGURE 8.3
Chemical Plant Organization

At start-up, some of the chemical plant operating teams requested and got former supervisors as coaches (limited to several months) to help them better manage some of their new functions. The new design provided the challenge everyone wanted and the results they intended.[1] Consistent with design principle 11, "Incompletion," the plant remains

---

[1]This chemical plant design was implemented during the 12 months following design. Some 30 months later, overall plant effectiveness had improved 48% in productivity, 21% in operating expenses, and 15% in labor costs reduction (cf. Taylor & Christensen, 1991).

in continuous improvement. Managers and workers overcame their natural reluctance to change what they had created and in doing so they discovered the power of continuous improvement of their design. Some four years after their STS redesign, all teams participated in a thorough redesign, with emphasis on role redefinition and mechanisms for further training.

CONCLUSION

Designing a new organizational system is both an exciting and scary time—with so much involvement and change one may wonder how anything could get done, let alone produce a product or service. However, high-involvement designs can produce dramatic results.

The design process must be driven by the design team in concert with all members of the organization. This provides the members opportunities to live, in action, the new values and processes so essential to understanding the new organization paradigms. Technical experts cannot design organizations in a vacuum, nor deal with the stresses of start-up nearly as effectively as those living in the system responsible for the system's success.

Designing requires a balance, a "fit" of many variables. STS is not a program, not an add-on to the usual way of doing business (e.g., quality circles, total quality management, manufacturing resources planning, and management by objective). It is a fundamental change in the way the organization is structured and managed to create a high-commitment, high-performance work system. Whole-system design requires a lot of work and activity. Everyone in the work system must be informed and knowledgeable if high performance is desired, and it takes many months of design and redesign to create an environment of high performance.

REFERENCES

ALIC, J. A. "Who Designs Work?" *Technology in Society,* 12, 1990, 301–317.
CHERNS, A. B. "The Principles of Sociotechnical Design." *Human Relations,* 29, 1976, 783–792.
CHERNS, A. B. "Principles of Sociotechnical Design Revisited." *Human Relations,* 40, 1987, 153–162.
DAVIS, L. E. "Organizational Design." In G. Salvendy (ed.), *Handbook of Industrial Engineering.* New York: Wiley Interscience, 1982, 2.1.1–2.1.29.

HOFFMAN, K. M. "Evolution of a sheet metal plant from a control oriented environment to a high involvement organization." Unpublished M.B.A. Thesis, Seattle University, January 1990.

KATZ, D. R., & R. L. KAHN *The Social Psychology of Organizations.* New York: Wiley, 1966.

MAJCHRZAK, A., & L. GASSER "On Using AI to Integrate the Design of Organizational and Process Change in U.S. Manufacturing. *AI & Society,* in press.

TAYLOR, J. C., & T.D. CHRISTENSEN "Employee Guided Design and Implementation in a Chemical Plant." *Proceedings of the Third Quality of Life/ Marketing Conference.* Blacksburg: Virginia Polytechnic Institute & State University, 1990, pp. 540–547.

TAYLOR, J. C., & T. D. CHRISTENSEN *A High Involvement Redesign.* South Bend, IN: STS Publishing, 1991.

CHAPTER 9

₹ ₹

Designing for Design Success: Understanding How to Make It Succeed

"Begin with the end in mind, as all things are created twice."

(Covey, 1989)

Implementation begins at the beginning. Performance by design follows this simple rule. There is the mental (design) phase, then the physical (implementation) phase. For a new design to be successful, there needs to be understanding, ownership, and commitment to its success by a large majority of the people impacted by the design. This includes groups outside the immediate location; that is, functional ties such as corporate purchasing and engineering. They need to understand the process as well as the product and its implications for them. This understanding needs to begin early in the process and continuously developed and nurtured. In essence, all those impacted by the design need to know the end result. It's not acquired through company publications, all-employee meetings, or bulletin boards. Involve as many as possible, as deeply and as early as possible. It is their active and visible involvement that builds the common shared understanding and the ownership required to implement and adapt. The more one is able to do this, the easier is the transition from the old and familiar to the new and unfamiliar.

Success doesn't come without some challenge and cost. Some may even view it as confusing and chaotic. Transitioning organizations are often characterized by the following:

- Lack of predictability and stability
- Emotional stress
- Misdirected and misguided energy
- Perceived, as well as actual, loss of control
- Defensive tightness
- Fear of structural changes
- Longing for past systems
- Increased conflict

Although the benefits ultimately outweigh the costs of transition, these characteristics often drive increased fear and anxiety, as opposed to optimism and anticipation. Implementation is a time when reality sets in. It hits individuals right in their own backyards or heartlands. Forms of resistance and avoidance occur. Individuals rationalize the irrational. Selfish desires and concerns surface and slow down the process. Separating the smoke screens from the real issues can easily cloud what's right. Be extremely open to adapting the design, but be aware of and avoid compromise that violates the basic design principles and analysis that have produced the new design. The organization may need to take transitional steps that increase the understanding needed, but this can be done without building obstacles to progress.

EVOLUTION OR REVOLUTIONARY IMPLEMENTATION

The pace an organization chooses for implementation of its design is often driven by its key stakeholders. For example, if the economic return on investment is low, the stockholders or investment community may push for a quick turnaround.

Deciding how fast and how much change an organization can handle can be evaluated by the amount or degree of competitive pain the organization is currently experiencing.

Swift, Radical Change. If, in fact, the performance indicators are extremely negative and a company is losing significant amounts of money, the decision for radical, swift change may already be made. Survival is a strong driver for revolutionary change. If one wants major improvement and communicates the need for it with a sense of urgency, it needs to be backed up by significant actions. This type of approach will bring about higher degrees of verbal resistance and stress, but in most cases, the actual performance indicators improve at a more rapid pace than a slower evolutionary process would produce.

Planned Change. Deteriorating performance, which will eventually lead to lost profitability, can be an effective catalyst to move organizations toward planned change. General Motors, which once owned over 30% of the car market, resisted changing until its market share plunged by 10%, primarily to foreign imports (Grayson, 1988). The Saturn Company is, in essence, a pain-driven enterprise. Bridging the transition can be at a slower pace, allowing the organization to digest each phase and adapt prior to moving forward. The fear here is that one will see improvements as one goes along and may settle for less than is possible, just to avoid the perceived or actual pain encountered in moving forward.

Avoided Change. Organizations not experiencing pressure from their outside stakeholders can be the most resistant to changing the status quo. These organizations may be tempted to take small steps over time and lose the momentum so critical to success. "It's a long-term effort" becomes an excuse or avoidance technique for not moving ahead and not making the tough decisions or confronting the sticky issues. These types of situations require extremely strong leadership, motivational faith, and a visible vision for what can be. The question "Why change?" really needs to be addressed and defined in visionary terms, painting a picture of a more profitable future. Remember: One doesn't have to be sick to get better.

⅋ *Change*

Change brings about decisions, and decisions bring consequences. These consequences often cause a sense of loss. Organizations and individuals often focus more on protecting than achieving. Thus, the fear of loss is greater than the desire for gain.

The trust level within the organization also impacts an individual's willingness and ability to accept and work through the change process. "I know they wouldn't do anything that would be harmful to the organization and its members. I've worked with them for years and have learned to respect and trust their leadership." This level of trust, earned over time, through honest, intimate, and open dealings, is difficult to establish. Especially when one recognizes how the old paradigms of maximum profitability through technology at the expense of human growth impacted employees. Organizations have used people and allowed technology to drive their decisions, undervaluing the employees' learning capabilities and intelligence.

One's reactions to change are dependent on one's acceptance of the change. This can be significantly impacted by the degree of involvement in creating it. If individuals don't genuinely feel part of the change process, denial and even anger can appear. Kubler-Ross' (1969) change cycle applies, not only to individuals, but to groups and organizations (Bridges, 1988; Grayson & O'Dell, 1988). These stages are characterized by the following feelings and emotions:

Denial. Denial is a means of protecting oneself from issues that violate an individual's view of reality. Characteristic responses illustrating denial include:

- It can't be.
- Change isn't really required.
- It won't really happen.
- Here comes another program, fad, or gimmick.
- Just wait and see; it'll blow over.

Resistant managers like this phase because they don't have to deal with the actual pain of loss. They often will form cliques with others to fight the change, in an effort to keep from facing the new design. Again, keeping people involved in the basic rationale and facts helps individuals understand the real need for change.

Anger. Anger is a secondary emotion that develops from frustration, fear, or anxiety and is often misdirected. Anger is often a good sign that the individual's defensiveness is beginning and the basic need for change is recognized. It is expressed by "I can fight it and maybe stop it." Once people realize it's inevitable, they can begin hearing.

Bargaining. Bargaining is a time of yearning and searching; a time of hope, along with discouragement; a need to hold on, but a willingness to face the change. It is an in-between stage, the attempt to cut a deal so the loss is minimized. Illustrations of bargaining include:

- Excessive cooperation or placating behavior
- A willingness to take on some or a few new assignments
- Actions and behaviors that have an unreal quality, lack authenticity

This is a critical period during the change cycle. Managers find this discouragement and sadness hard to deal with and try to make it go away, as opposed to viewing it as healthy and normal. Trying to make the need for change go away doesn't do much good, and blaming may drive the behavior underground. Encourage open dialogue; it's the best solution for working through the difficulties.

Depression.   Depression is the neutral zone, a time of confusion and emptiness. One feels disoriented, alone, powerless, unable to control. It's that strange valley in the gap between the old and the new. No more excuses, each must look inside himself as an individual and organizations, owning the incompetencies. It's an opportunity for creating the new design about which each has dreamed. The more one is able to leave behind, the more room one has for the new.

Acceptance.   During acceptance one can come to beginnings only at the end. There's a new energy released by letting go of the old. There is a real readiness to move forward. People will say, "It's really going to happen, and I can have a significant role in making it happen. Let's get on with it."

The real evidence that people have let go of the old way is characterized by:

- Lack of bargaining and negotiating
- Less chasing after simple solutions
- Genuine interest in exploring new alternatives
- A real understanding that they must create the new

These new beginnings call for a clarification of the roles and responsibilities that go beyond our traditional understanding of manager, supervisor, employee, and so on.

Defining Roles

If the workers are going to organize and manage themselves, what do the managers do? Understanding what's expected and how to fulfill these expectations is critical to success. Management's roles shift from controlling the work force to supporting the new desired culture. Some mental shifts required for management are:

From	To
Placid	Chaos
Directive	Enabler
Push	Pull
Control of people	Control of product
Suspicion	Trust
How and when	What and why
Efficiencies	Effectiveness
Status quo	Challenger
Doing things right	Doing right things
Obedience	Autonomy
Maintain	Develop
Bottom line	Big picture
Short term	Long term
Administrators	Initiator
Authoritarian	Empowerment
Reward and punishment	Encouragement and support

Some of the responsibilities that go along with these shifting roles are:

- Keeping the vision
- Maintaining clear focus (especially through the tough times)
- Managing the external environment
- Anticipating the future
- Building a coalition of understanding and support among:
  - Customers
  - Suppliers
  - Union officials
  - Corporate staff groups
- Overcoming the resistances to the redistribution and sharing of power
- Letting go of:
  - Methods and details
  - Authoritarian symbols
  - Day-to-day operations
- Providing support and service functions

When managers do step inside the work system, they need to serve as teachers and facilitators by:

- Highlighting concerns
- Tracking outcomes
- Providing knowledge and fostering learning
- Encouraging cooperation and teamwork
- Suggesting new ways, alternatives
- Making decisions the team cannot (will not) make
- Stimulating creativity

⚱ *Learning New Roles and Behaviors*

Learning these skills can be difficult when one considers they were not reinforced in the past. The first task is unlearning, not necessarily learning anew. Being taught by experience means to live in the past. We must initiate and do new things in new ways. Practice is required before becoming good at it, and practice means one probably won't do it so well the first several times. People may even retreat to the old, familiar, comfortable ways of behaving, without even being aware. It's what they have always done or the way they have always done it—it's second nature. And people don't feel too good about making mistakes while they practice. They're expected to be good at what they do.

The model outlined in Table 9.1 may be helpful in understanding this learning process. This adult learning process (origin unknown) has been a useful tool used in the human resource development field for over 15 years.

Quadrant 1, Unconscious Incompetence, is when individuals are unable to perform differently because they are unaware of the alternatives. A person's experience base does not include the knowledge or skill level required. They haven't discovered a different way, a new way, of performing. Once new alternatives are recognized, one moves to *Quadrant 2*, Conscious Incompetence. Getting there isn't always easy. A person's background and previous experiences make it difficult to see or recognize new alternatives. In fact, the past may even blind one's ability to let in new knowledge or approaches. Barker (1985) in his book and video *Discovering the Future* has done an excellent job of illustrating this phenomenon. Once areas of incompetence are discovered, the journey to *Quadrant 3*, Conscious Competence, gets clearer but ever more difficult.

Moving to Quadrant 3, Conscious Competence, requires new awareness, then actions. To understand there's a new way is tough enough, but to understand how to do it requires another shift, needing both mental and behavior action, not just mental challenge. How one is

TABLE 9.1

The Four Stages of Adult Learning

		Unconscious		*Conscious*
I N C O M P E T E N T	I.	Unconscious Incompetence ------ "Unaware" of alternative management styles and design processes. (Don't know shoelaces exist)	II.	Conscious Incompetence ----- "Discovers" new ways of managing and how effective they can be. (Aware they exist, but can't tie them)
C O M P E T E N T	IV.	Unconscious Competence ------ "Performing" new roles and management patterns. (Doing it well and not thinking about it much)	III.	Conscious Competence ----- "Learning" how to implement new patterns of management. (Have to concentrate and practice to do it)

Example: The Process of Learning "Performance by Design" and the Process of
Learning to Tie Shoelaces

to do it doesn't come easy. Through trial and error, one must extend the
effort to explore new ways, adapt what others have done, and do it
consciously. Consciously means thinking about it when individuals least
expect they need to. One doesn't always remember and therefore easily
retreats to the familiar activities of the past. The paradox of "They don't
walk their talk" is better said, "They haven't *learned* how to do what
they know needs to get done." Cut them some slack and get in there and
support and help explore new ways together.

Moving into Quadrant 3 requires consciousness, repetition, risk
taking, reinforcement, and willingness to make mistakes, learn from
them, and move forward. Once people have done it a number of times,
the comfort level increases along with the skill level, and they move into
Quadrant 4, Unconscious Competence, the phase of mastery where

effort is hidden and tasks look easy. However, complacency can set in and before long, in this chaotic environment, one can easily move back to Quadrant 1 and the cycle repeats itself. The more one recycles through the four quadrants, the easier renewal and continuous improvement become part of the culture.

A typical example of moving through the quadrants would be a manager of manufacturing who has learned from experience that one of the ways to increase profits is by controlling average hourly pay rates. The paradigm is "the lower the cost of payroll, the higher the profitability" (Quadrant 1 mentality, Unconscious Incompetence). This mental set extends itself into other areas of one's role and how one thinks about work; that is, to control labor costs, one needs to have as many individuals as possible at the lower levels of pay. Keep hourly rates as low as possible. To do this, managers have learned to break jobs down to the lowest level of skill, and the scenario goes on violating the whole principle of empowerment. Until the manager becomes aware of other methods—that is, labor cost as a percentage of units produced and skill-based pay and gainsharing—and acquires the skills to implement them, he or she remains locked into the only way available—what he or she knows. This requires a number of reassessments challenging what had seemed tried and true.

TEAMS

So often, designs include teams. This is not difficult to understand, since complexity of technology and changes in work have decreased the individual contributor's role and increased the ability and value of teamwork. This increased interdependency has also demonstrated how synergistic team efforts can significantly improve the quality and creativity of decisions. However, understanding and developing productive and mature teams is not an easy task. Outside of collegiate sports, few universities provide an in-depth curriculum in team development.

First, one needs to be clear on what a team is. In general, a group is thought of as any set of people who happen to work together. But from a systems perspective, we need to be more precise about what really constitutes a team. To be able to move from a group to a team, the following conditions need to exist:

- Several individuals who are jointly responsible for their performance.
- Their tasks and activities are interdependent.

- The interdependence centers on a whole work process, flow, or product.
- Members bring differing skills.
- High need for integration of skills.
- Members share a common and conscious purpose.

⚛ *Team Development and Performance*

A team is only as strong as its members are mature. Individual team members with qualities of strong self-esteem and collaborative problem-solving skills will significantly impact the group's ability to grow. Build teams around those individuals who are self-confident, personally secure, and broadly capable, with low status and power needs. Those inspired by the vision and design are far more desirable than brilliant soloists. Don't allow technically related expertise to become blinding to the value of these human qualities.

In allowing teams to self-organize around their purpose, it is important to provide them with support. This vehicle of support can come in a number of ways but is usually done through facilitators or mentors, individuals who have lived the experience several times and understand the growth stages important to team maturity.

Facilitators.   These are agents of positive change, results-oriented generalists, flexible and adaptable as opposed to narrow specialists. One of the facilitator's most valuable contributions to a team's growth and development is helping the team members become aware of the team's own process, enabling them to discuss their own communication, problem-solving, decision-making, and conflict-resolution practices. Helping the team learn how to work more effectively to fulfill their charter, roles, and responsibilities—not doing it for them, but not allowing them to run from it.

Not just anyone can become an effective mentor or facilitator. It's an art developed and mastered through practice, not by formal education. What counts the most is willingness, real experience, desire, and motivation to help themselves and others learn. The best criteria for selection is those who have been doing it naturally all their lives. And many have. Most people have been helping others grow since the beginning. Some better than others, but one can continue developing these interpersonal competencies by practicing:

- Empathy
- Acceptance

- Authenticity
- Active listening
- Artful intervention

Forming Teams. This is like giving birth. The fact that six or seven people have gathered together does not guarantee effectiveness. Teams, like individuals, need to grow up, move through developmental stages, from formation to maturity. There are a number of practitioners and researchers who have proposed any number of clearly definable stages or phases of group life. Teams don't experience these stages exactly as they are identified, but the general descriptions are helpful. The stages are normal, to be grown through just as individuals go from adolescence to adulthood. As teams struggle through these growth pains and become more effective as a team, they'll even find their personal lives richer, fuller, and more satisfying.

During the early formative and dependent stages, it is not surprising that individuals are concerned about membership, belonging to the group, being included. There is a strong need to be liked and accepted. Conflict is usually avoided at all costs. Personal needs and wants are characterized by the following:

- There is conformance to the established company line.
- Feelings are hidden and suppressed.
- There is little listening and caring for others.
- Personal inadequacies or weaknesses are kept hidden.
- Objectives and action plans are poorly done and communicated.
- Hidden agendas remain hidden.
- Cliques and alliances begin forming.
- Feedback and disclosure are at a minimum.
- There is a strong need for approval.
- Mistakes are often used as evidence.
- Real feelings are shared outside the meeting.

Control. Once the team members get the lay of the land and begin to feel comfortable, they usually want to figure out who's in control and how much influence they will have on the team. Look for the following characteristics:

- People do not work in a unified way.
- The cliques grow and wield influence.
- Conflict intensifies and is generally resolved through voting.

- There are a lot of win/lose interactions.
- Infighting exists.
- Personal strengths and weaknesses become better known.
- Commitment is debated.
- Self-centeredness becomes evident.
- Team identity is low.
- Self-disclosure is still cautious.
- Close-mindedness is evident.
- People are defensive.
- Ground rules are ignored.

This is a critical time for teams and some may even self-destruct. If there is order without freedom, team members will rebel against the rigidity or formality. If there is freedom without order, the chaos will produce confusion and frustration. Member freedom within an orderly process to which the team has agreed is the best result desired.

Effectiveness. To arrive at this point is the real struggle. It provides the team with the vehicle for becoming an effective team. It allows them to dig in and be truly productive with their time. This stage is characterized by the following:

- There is an attitude change.
- Real constructive cooperation begins.
- People are more open-minded.
- Better listening is evident.
- Cliques dissolve.
- Leadership becomes more shared.
- Previously dormant people contribute.
- There is willingness to experiment.
- Conflict is viewed as needed to explore all sides of an issue.
- Methodological processes begin developing.
- Operating methods are reviewed.
- Problem-solving skills are developed and utilized.

Maturity. As the team continues to constructively explore and struggle developing orderly processes and methods, task accomplishment becomes much quicker and easier. The work team begins functioning as mature, interdependent members. Leadership becomes less of an issue; anyone can take the lead role when appropriate. The team will appear to have less structure because the discipline is internally understood and monitored by the members themselves. This level of maturity can be recognized by the following:

* Close relationships
* Resourceful and economical
* High spirits and morale
* Informality and respect
* Happy and rewarding
* Encouragement of outside help
* Mistakes still made, but eagerly examined
* Cohesiveness
* Common spirit
* High goal attainment
* Intense loyalty
* Open relationships with other teams
* Flexibility, adaptability
* Individual needs recognized and met
* Continual review and feedback
* New members welcomed and included

The mature team, like a mature individual, is able to learn from its mistakes, reflect on itself, and organize its own continuous growth and development.

These stages are not tied to time. Some groups never achieve maturity. Some get so bogged down at stages that it is difficult to move on. Even mature groups may have to recycle to work out some new issue or problem, or simply lose their willingness to work together.

❧ *Training and Development*

The old Chinese proverb "I hear and I forget, I see and I remember, I do and I understand" seems to apply here.

The training requirements for supporting a team's ability to grow and mature are continuous, not event centered. Sending someone off to a five-day workshop on facilitation or conflict resolution does not make him or her an expert. Awareness and understanding of what is required is the best one can expect. It is not wasted, but it's clearly not enough. It's simply the beginning. The adult learning process, discussed earlier in this chapter, illustrates the difficulty in acquiring new knowledge and skills. The traditional training program needs to be taken to the team, where real application on real live issues can be addressed. This can be done by those who are already unconsciously competent (facilitators) at the skills required. It's not that training programs aren't helpful; it's that our overreliance on them for producing all the new skills required without follow-up and reinforcement is not well founded. A Canadian chemical company designed an extensive 32-hour course in group dynamics, problem solving, decision making, communication, and developmental discipline, and gave it to all employees prior to start-up, only to find significant deficiencies in individuals' abilities to effectively transfer learning to the workplace (Halpern, 1982). Employees learned the concepts, but they did not learn how to apply them. As a result, skilled facilitators were identified who could work with the teams on a continuous basis, to assist them in acquiring and upgrading essential skills while dealing with real issues.

Although many training programs offered by outsiders promote success formulas, the results are rarely achieved. The major cause of failure to "put the words in action" is a lack of opportunity for many to be able to experience timely and practical application of the concepts and tools to real team issues. The program focus also shifts away from the key STS elements identified in Chapter 1.

Since the team's structure is designed around an open STS systems model that holds that, over the long haul, the organization and its teams can develop the ability to adapt better to changing internal and external demands. These adaptations and processes need to be developed by every team by exploring each of the interdependent processes discussed in the previous chapters (see Figure 9.1).

- *The Search for Purpose*—provides the team members with a sense of identity and direction, outlining critical minimum standards and values.
- *Technical Production Processes*—by which the meaningful work required by the team's purpose and objectives gets done. The processes developed by the teams make sure the available resources—that is, equipment, facilities, money, and so on—are well used in pursuit of its primary output.
- *Individual Processes*—employed by the team members to satisfy their personal needs, interests, and expectations.
- *Social Processes*—where team members explore and develop the processes essential for interaction and teamwork among themselves and relating to other teams in the pursuit of their individual needs, team purpose, and responsibilities.
- *Environmental Processes*—by which the team goes about influencing and being influenced by its external environment.

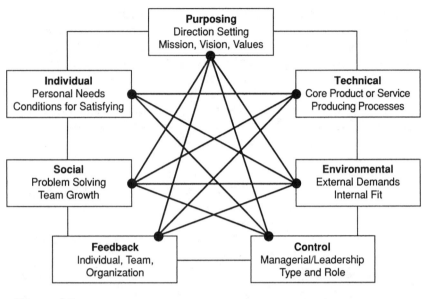

FIGURE 9.1
STS Core Team Processes

- *Control Processes*—that provide the team members with the leadership, organization, and control that ensure the team's purpose and objectives are fulfilled and variances controlled.
- *Feedback Processes*—where the team and its members learn to collect data in order to make assessments and corrective adjustments and adaptations.

All of these "how to" processes are highly interdependent and dynamic. They need to be first developed and then maintained in a balanced and steady state. Each team needs the autonomy to work through the processes and develop the methods and procedures that are right for them. The development of these processes is based on individual team member's strengths, needs, and shortcomings. Therefore, the skills required to support the team's development of these processes are going to vary significantly based on overall composition and competencies. The level of skill development needed for any basic skill area must be sensitive to the team's real needs, not some predetermined module or program content. For example, a team needs to have the skills essential to resolve conflict. Some team members may already possess these skills and be able to help other teams when the need arises, or they may have the knowledge of how to do it but have never really done it, or they may know very little about what it takes to resolve conflict.

The other issue for the trainer or facilitator is understanding how and where conflict resolution skills apply to the basic core processes. There's little payoff in developing skills that are unrelated to the core team processes.

The facilitator who truly understands the concepts and theory and who possesses the skills required in developing teams won't need the packaged step-by-step training module. He or she will already understand that there are many such packaged approaches.

The facilitator helps the team explore and understand the principles, concepts, and pitfalls applied to their real needs, while the team members develop the methods and procedures that are right for them. The focus changes from predetermined and developed methods to team-developed processes that fit the team's needs and fulfill the basic elements of STS.

CONCLUSION

STS design implementations are trying times. They require the faith and commitment discussed in Chapter 1. There are many paradigm shifts to make, shifts away from traditional learning models and training programs that provide recipes and step-by-step formulas. The real skill acquisitioning comes from the struggle of developing one's own recipes or step-by-step processes. These struggling experiences provide the understanding and commitment essential to building real adaptability and ownership. Organizations need to understand that struggling can produce mistakes and errors. If they are embraced, real learning and growth can occur. "Adults learn best when they take charge of their own learning" (Bennis, 1989). To take charge of their own learning, employees need continuous learning opportunities that provide broad exploration, reflection, and challenging applications.

REFERENCES

BARKER, J. A. *Discovering the Future*. St. Paul, MN: ILI Press, 1985.
BENNIS, W. *On Becoming a Leader*. Reading, MA: Addison-Wesley, 1989.
BRIDGES, W. *Surviving Corporate Transition*. New York: Doubleday, 1988.

Covey, S. *The 7 Habits of Highly Effective People.* New York: Simon & Schuster, 1989. p. 99.

Grayson, C. J., & C. O'Dell *American Business: A Two-Minute Warning.* New York: Free Press, 1988.

Halpern, N. "Sustaining Change in the Shell Sarnia Chemical Plant," *QWL Focus*, 2(1), May 1982, Ontario Ministry of Labor, Quality of Working Life Center.

Kubler-Ross, E. *On Death and Dying.* New York: Macmillan, 1969.

CHAPTER 10

ॐ ॐ

Redesigning for Renewal: Understanding Adaptability

"There's no law that says anybody has to improve. It's all voluntary. It's only a matter of survival."

(Deming, 1982)

The design principle of incompletion recognizes that the design process for organizations is an activity that is never complete. Organizations should constantly monitor and evaluate developments internally and in the external environment. The assessment of stakeholders' needs should be continually designed into the organization and institutionalized so that it occurs automatically.

This chapter deals with this continuous process of renewal, highlighting major areas of concern, as well as providing some alternative tools and processes for assessment.

THE PROBLEM

ॐ Vulnerability

Ironically, organizations that have gone through an STS design and implementation process can be discouraged by the thought of renewal. The energy and commitment in giving birth to the original design make its organizational members extremely resistant to the need for renewal until the principle of continuous improvement truly becomes part of the organizational culture. Members also recall the pain and disruption they went through in implementing the new system and building the level of commitment needed for success. Unfreezing and refreezing are painful exercises because each disrupts the current state. Until this feeling of discomfort can be viewed as healthy growth, renewal is difficult.

> **Another way of assuring "incompletion" in design is to implement before every "i" is dotted and "t" is crossed.**

One way to help offset this vulnerability is to view change as growth and an essential survival element. This will be frustrating to those who like to plan everything out and make sure it's right before implementation. This concern with making sure that everything is thought out and that detailed plans are developed is an element in closed system thinking. It is the very cause that locks people into not wanting to change or adapt when the need arises.

One of the strongest needs humans possess is that of belonging. Individuals in organizations develop intense feelings of belonging to the organization's structure and norms. To attack the organization is, in essence, to attack them. In addition, there is a need for recognizing that personality traits can either inhibit or encourage renewal. The Myers-Briggs Style Inventory points out that certain "types" of people resist change (Meyers, 1980). Assessing team types can be extremely valuable in developing this need for unfreezing.

❧ *Adaptability*

Learning to be flexible within a specific organizational design is really no different from learning to adapt an organizational design to fit changing demands from the external environments. In both cases, adaptation becomes easier once there is a recognition that organizations are an open system of relationships that involve many interdependent elements. Circumstances no longer encompass just machines (technology) or profitability. A cause-and-effect relationship must be considered in every change or adaptation that is made to the system design. The end result of adaptation is the continued pursuit of purpose.

The results an organization is getting are based on its current design, so why not periodically examine in depth the current organizational results? Reviewing daily, weekly, or monthly results can lead to complacency. But to stop and ask the tough questions and explore major trends over time takes time, commitment, and discipline. Most managers tend to wait until they are in trouble and the indicators are significantly down before they stop and take a seriously hard look at what they are doing. It's hard to generate a felt need when everything is running smoothly, but that is precisely the discipline that's required.

PROCESS FOR RENEWAL

Renewal requires systematic and continual feedback processes from both internal and external sources. The capacity to maintain leadership and success will occur when an organization can adapt more quickly than can its competitors. This requires building in the continuous feedback loop that forces organizations to learn from experience. This feedback loop is more than a procedure or process. Individuals must continuously look back and ask what was learned from previous events.

> **"Continuous feedback is the heart of renewal."**

Chapter 8 identified the first generation issues and hurdles that need to be dealt with early on in the design and implementation process. Renewal brings another set of growth issues and paradigms that few are equipped to handle without some struggle and hardship. Learning is change, and this learning and relearning process helps to build a culture of incompletion and continuous improvement. The second- and third-generation issues can be handled more easily when it is recognized that the process is a journey, not a single event, and that the journey itself is the destination.

❧ *Data Collection/Methodology*

Chapters 3 through 6 demonstrated the importance and power of data and feedback created and gathered by members of the organization (user centered). The approach presented assures that the methods used for data collection and diagnosis are congruent with the overall values and practices of the organization. The collection methods add believability, balance, and ownership of the data gathered.

To assure that organizations continually gather relevant data from their external and internal environments, it is important to set up a vehicle that encourages feedback. The leadership team of a medium-sized manufacturing plant (250 employees) chartered a Standing Committee for Assessment (SCA). The initial committee included 10 volunteers selected by management from the 20 teams in the plant. The SCA met monthly to gather and analyze the division's performance. Working with an external consultant for facilitation, objectivity, and experience, the SCA produced analyses covering topics such as the following:

- Long-term-trend analysis for quality, cost, market share, and profitability
- Revisitation of the mission, vision, and values to make appropriate changes
- Update of the technical systems analysis, both the matrix and the table of control
- A visit to other STS-designed organizations
- Recommendations for basic design changes
- A review of social systems problems and concerns

The SCA presented its information for review at the plant's quarterly State of the Business meetings for all employees. These meetings went beyond just information sharing. The SCA would present its findings and recommendations and then break the total group up into small discussion groups of seven or eight. The SCA members facilitated discussion within these small groups to assure understanding and then to gather everyone's opinions. This feedback was then reviewed by the SCA and modification to its recommendations were made prior to implementation. Membership in the SCA could last up to two years. Generally, one to two members were rotated out every six months and a new volunteer added. The new members were selected by the SCA and reviewed with management.

In the 1970s, a new chemical plant, designed as a sociotechnical Greenfield site, set up a Team Norm Review Board (TNRB) to provide a formal mechanism for self-management (Halpern, 1982). The plant employed about 200 people. Membership of the TNRB consisted of representatives from each team and a member from management and union leadership positions, for a total of 11. Their charter was to edit, interpret, and share plant norms by providing consistency, suggestions, modification, as well as support in helping teams live up to their norms. The TNRB also monitored the teams' roles—that is, work schedules, chairperson, secretary/recorder, and so on—to assure that internal team tasks were handled. In summary, the TNRB dealt with all issues that could not be handled at the team level or by the union/management committee. It provided a valuable service contributing to the plant's sustained success of over 15 years.

STARTING THE RENEWAL PROCESS: RENEWAL LEVERS AND APPLICATIONS

The opportunities for renewal begin by assessing three different but interrelated levels of growth and maturity: the individual, the team, and the organization.

ᖜ *Individual Maturity*

The field of human resource development provides many insights that are useful for understanding and structuring employee development. The STS work design and team experiences are generally new to most employees. When people join an organization, they are still in the process of growing, maturing, and developing. This is the human process of continuous learning, unlearning, and relearning.

A framework for exploring the maturity process that occurs during the development of these new relationships is taken from Erikson's "Eight Ages of Man" (Elkind, 1970; Erikson, 1963). Individual developmental stages continue throughout the entire life cycle and reappear whenever an individual is thrown into new situations that are both challenging and threatening; that is, being promoted, getting transferred, or joining a new team. These stages of development are stated in terms that are relevant to the work situation when one considers that the team as well as the organization has an influence over how a working adult comes to terms with self and others (Walton, 1975). Assessing maturity should begin with team members themselves understanding their own personal growth and development needs within the team. How well they have made the following shifts will greatly impact their performance as a team member.

> **Trust:** *From Mistrust to Trust.* Building mutual trust is essential. The degree to which team members trust one another depends largely on the care and support they receive from their fellow team members. However, when care and support are nonexistent or sporadic, an attitude of fear and

suspicion prevails and leads to basic mistrust. This can occur within a team or between teams and the organization and can arise at any stage of development.

Autonomy: *From Suspicion to Autonomy and Self-Control.* Team members want to have a sense of autonomy—to do things for themselves when they have the capability and skills to do them. The degree to which fellow team members and their leaders allow them to act independently develops the sense of self-control and autonomy. However, if fellow team members and superiors continue to act for them, members will retain a sense of doubt. It should be noted, however, that too much autonomy can be just as harmful as too little. Giving individuals or teams a task for which they are not equipped to handle (due to lack of knowledge or skills) can be just as detrimental as doing it for them. Doing it with them, on the other hand, will develop their skills to allow independent action in the future.

Initiative: *From Doubt to Initiative.* The manner in which team members' initiatives are viewed by others either encourages them to freely contribute or makes them feel hesitant and uncommitted. This lack of mutual support can develop a sense of doubt and guilt concerning self-initiated activities or suggestions. Differences will not be shared and resolved; team product acceptance and support will be hindered. The extent to which team members take on new tasks and activities can be greatly influenced and enhanced by how others respond to their inquiring questions. If ignored, cut short, or ridiculed, new initiatives will become fewer and fewer.

Accomplishment: *From Inferiority to Accomplishment.* If team members are encouraged to take on and complete projects and are rewarded for results, then the sense of accomplishment and industry will grow and develop. But if the efforts are overly criticized, the result can be an increased sense of inferiority. The core of self-esteem is accomplishment through difficult sustained effort. Each defeat or the taking of the easy path deteriorates the individual's self-concept.

Identity: *From Role Confusion to Identity.* New team members need to bring together their past experiences and learning and integrate them with the needs of the team and fellow members. The extent of the integration of individuals with fellow team members' strengths and weaknesses builds a sense of identity, a sense of who they are, where they have been, and where they are going. The varied background and experiences create a diversity of opinion. These differences can create conflict between members if not resolved openly as a team and viewed as helpful and essential to synergism. The degree to which the previous four stages have developed greatly influences the team and its individual members' sense of identity.

Intimacy: *From Isolation to Intimacy.* The ability of individual team members to care about one another without the fear of losing their own identities develops intimacy. If individuals fail to establish sharing and caring relationships, the result is a sense of distance and isolation from fellow team members. Intimacy is essential to real support and encouragement. Team members that have worked with one another under difficult and stressful circumstances develop a strong commitment to each other that embodies this sense of intimacy.

Wholeness: *From Self-Centeredness to Wholeness.* When team members are preoccupied by their own needs and comforts as opposed to being concerned about the larger system and its members, survival and growth are threatened. Team members who fail to establish a sense of wholeness fall into a state of stagnation where personal needs and wants are more important than the needs of the team. The team must be viewed as an integrated system whose very survival and success are dependent on the integration of its parts. Team synergy can be realized only through involvement of each team member. Team members need to grow together through the team's goal attainment processes, doing whatever needs to get done for the team and the larger whole.

Integrity: *From Despair to Integrity.* A sense of integrity develops over time when individual team members can look back with satisfaction and know that he or she has cared for others while doing the things needed for the team and the organization. Growth comes in learning to adapt to the tough trials and victories of the team. The other extreme is looking back upon the time with the team and organization as a number of missed opportunities; feeling that it's too late. Such feelings lead to disgust and "disgust hides despair" (Erikson, 1963, p. 232). To reach a satisfactory level of maturity and wisdom, an individual needs to develop through the previous seven growth stages, gaining the ability to respect and recognize the quality and uniqueness of others. Members of a successful team truly integrate their strengths and weaknesses and are willing to actively participate in doing whatever needs to get done for the whole, as well as accepting leadership responsibility when it's required.

The level of integrity versus despair within a team and an organization can really manifest itself in how individuals are treated and treat each other during highly emotionally charged situations (i.e., discipline, reductions, demotions, promotions, deselection, etc.). During these times, an individual's sense of worth and previous work contributions can either build integrity or result in a feeling of injustice and despair.

Regardless of how an organization or team approaches these issues of *individual* growth and maturity, one must recognize that they are *individual.* Each team member is unique and brings his or her own history of preferences, strengths, and weaknesses. These differences in experience help to define and build the team culture. They provide the diversity essential to creativity. In building a team, each member needs to be provided the opportunity to be his or her own person, contributing to the larger whole. This can take on as many different forms as the team has different individuals with different backgrounds. Some team members may prefer to be specifically directed and guided in their activities (McWhinney, 1992), while others may wish to receive only general direction. Some members enjoy subgroup or team problem-solving activities, while other members may enjoy working alone on certain types of tasks. Team members can learn to accommodate these differences within their group by providing work assignments that match individual preferences. The organizational design needs to handle this diversity by allowing the teams to organize how they wish to accomplish what gets done. This approach will lead to consistency in purpose and product (what gets done), while allowing the teams and their members to select the norms and patterns of work life they prefer.

Individuals who have learned to grow and mature by integrating these differences will be better team members and people. Their lives will be more effectively disciplined through principles and values, not situations. Members come to realize that while the team provided support and strength, it only enabled them to use what each already had. Individuals now can continue to empower themselves and others. The Individual Maturity Index (Table 10.1) can assist individuals in evaluating themselves. Sharing their results with fellow team members can help them validate and confirm their results. Discussing personal needs and

TABLE 10.1
Individual Maturity Index

Instructions: Circle the number on each of the eight scales that best reflects your own level of development within your team environment. Then list any actual examples of instances that aided or inhibited your growth.

1. Trust	0	1	2	3	4	5
2. Autonomy	0	1	2	3	4	5
3. Initiative	0	1	2	3	4	5
4. Accomplishment	0	1	2	3	4	5
5. Identity	0	1	2	3	4	5
6. Intimacy	0	1	2	3	4	5
7. Wholeness	0	1	2	3	4	5
8. Integrity	0	1	2	3	4	5

wants in this way provides team members with a vehicle for integrating differences, while building new norms, understandings, and expectations of each other.

A team from a small group office of a large casualty insurance organization found that Varney's (1977) Characteristics of Effective Teams helped to integrate and bridge individual maturity with team growth. The team modified the characteristics, gave them definitions, and called it "The Individual/Team Growth Questionnaire." Their questionnaire is presented as Table 10.2.

TABLE 10.2
Individual/Team Growth Questionnaire

Instructions: Decide first the degree or extent to which each characteristic applies to you. Then, based on your first answer, decide what result or impact your behavior has for the team.

Team Characteristics	*Degree/Extent* *Lo_____Hi*	*Result/Impact* *Neg_____Pos*
Mutual Trust. I can state my views and differences without fear of ridicule or retaliation. I encourage others to do the same.	1–2–3–4–5	1–2–3–4–5
Mutual Support. I can obtain help from others on the team and give help to them.	1–2–3–4–5	1–2–3–4–5
Openness. I can say what I feel and how I am reacting, knowing the team is listening. I listen and try to understand other team members.	1–2–3–4–5	1–2–3–4–5
Team Objectives. No objective will be assumed by the team until it is clearly understood by all members.	1–2–3–4–5	1–2–3–4–5
Conflict Resolution. I accept conflicts as necessary and desirable. I don't suppress them or pretend they don't exist.	1–2–3–4–5	1–2–3–4–5
Utilization of Member Resources. My individual abilities, knowledge, and experience are fully utilized by the team, and I use those of other members.	1–2–3–4–5	1–2–3–4–5

Continued

TABLE 10.2
Individual/Team Growth Questionnaire *Continued*

Team Characteristics	Degree/Extent Lo———————Hi	Result/Impact Neg———————Pos
Control Methods. I accept the responsibility for keeping discussions relevant and for the integrity of the team operation.	1-2-3-4-5	1-2-3-4-5
Individual Diversity. I respect individual differences. I don't push others to conform to central ideas or ways of thinking.	1-2-3-4-5	1-2-3-4-5
Feedback. I accept and give advice, counsel, and support to others while recognizing individual accountability and specialization.	1-2-3-4-5	1-2-3-4-5

Each individual team member anonymously completed the questionnaire by first circling the number that reflected the degree to which the statements applied to them. Then, based on that assessment, each member decided what impact or result this behavior had on the team. These scores were plotted on grids (Table 10.3) by characteristic, each dot representing one team member's opinion. Each grid was then reviewed and discussed. Each team member then developed a list of actions that he or she felt were needed, together with specific support required from the team. Members then shared their agreements and needs from the team, reached a consensus, and set follow-up dates for review. This follow-up process replaced the organization's traditional performance appraisal process but did not replace the team performance review.

⚕ *Team Maturity*

The process of maturity begins with the team members assessing their own growth and the degree to which they have assumed functions formerly handled by supervisors. As the individual team members grow and mature, one can observe the team's growth from dependency on others to true interdependence between team members and other teams. A first step to renewal can come from assessing how the team is cur-

TABLE 10.3
Individual/Team Growth—Posting Grid

1. Mutual Trust—I can state my views and differences without fear of ridicule or retaliation.

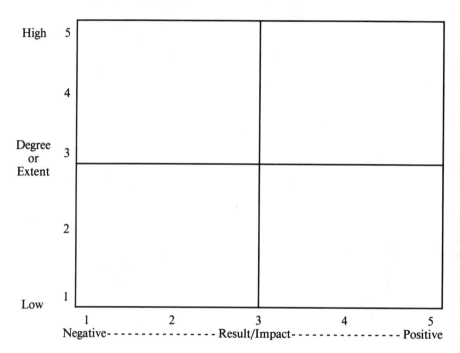

rently functioning. Table 10.4 is a list of the characteristics identified in Chapter 9, but condensed into three basic categories:

- Dependency
- Counterdependency
- Interdependency

Dependency. The beginning stages of dependency on others is initially characterized by adventure, apprehension, excitement, and enthusiasm. Team members attempt to clarify their hopes and fears and identify the norms and ground rules by which they intend to operate. At this stage, members usually feel that they have little or no control. They are polite and submissive and look to the "established line" for direction and leadership.

TABLE 10.4

Questionnaire on Team Maturity

Instructions: Check as many of the following characteristics as you feel your team is currently experiencing.

1 Polite Conversations	—	33. Burnout —
2. Selective Listening	—	34. Pride and Satisfaction —
3. Strong Need for Approval	—	35. Trust and Openness —
4. New Members Welcomed	—	36. Little Thinking —
5. Flexibility	—	37. Real Feelings Shared Outside —
6. Bids for Power	—	38. Evaluations Made Outside
7. Outside Help Expected	—	Meetings —
8. Not Working in Unified Way	—	39. Mistakes Used as Evidence —
9. Failure and Mistake		40. Social Aspects Considered —
Expected	—	41. Conformance to Established
10. Adaptation Is Easy	—	Line —
11. Hidden Agendas	—	42. Conflict Resolved by Voting —
12. Confusion and Stress	—	43. Misdirected Energy —
13. Lack of Trust	—	44. Suspicion —
14. Members Protect the Team	—	45. Shared Leadership —
15. High Goal Attainment	—	46. Views Change —
16. Active Listening	—	47. Personal Weakness Covered
17. Feelings Kept Hidden	—	Up —
18. Little Care for Others	—	48. Authority Is Central —
19. Happy and Rewarding	—	49. Leadership Discussed —
20. Dormant People Begin to		50. Interest in Climate —
Contribute	—	51. Cohesiveness —
21. Success Emulated by Others	—	52. Mistakes Made but Eagerly
22. Social Aspects Important	—	Examined —
23. Unresolved Conflict	—	53. Informality and Respect —
24. Lack of Stability	—	54. Second Guessing —
25. Infighting	—	55. Alliances and Cliques
26. Common Objectives	—	Formed —
27. Strong Need for Structure	—	56. Strong Opinions —
28. Little Listening	—	57. Continual Review —
29. Fuzzy Goals	—	58. Outside Help Welcomed —
30. Nit-Picking	—	59. Personal Weaknesses
31. Self-Serving Team Members	—	Covered Up —
32. Objectives Poorly Set	—	60. Commitment Debated —

Counterdependency. As team members gain a better appreciation of their new roles and become more comfortable with their own work requirements, they begin to challenge the existing authority structure. Some decide that they no longer need superiors and bosses. This counterdependence toward others outside their team is displayed rebellion, blaming others and management for their problems, as well as challenging the new design. So much energy, both physical and emotional, is expended in resolving these issues that a "burnout" or "peaking out" syndrome often follows. **Interdependency.** As team members begin to resolve internal conflicts and discover that they must take responsibility for their own behavior, a new sense of dependency on others outside their team is realized. External relationships are revisited and revised and the larger purpose is viewed in light of the interdependent parts. The team itself stabilizes and views the new design and the organization more realistically. The excitement, "easy fix" mentality, and the fighting are gone. New, redefined attitudes and approaches toward other teams, departments and management begin to emerge. Teams begin to accept responsibility for solving their own problems.

The Questionnaire on Team Maturity, Table 10.4, is an instrument that allows a team to assess its current state of maturity in all three categories.

To begin this process of assessment, team members must complete the questionnaire by checking as many of the characteristics as they feel currently apply to their team. All the responses are summarized and categorized per the scoring key in Table 10.5.

A summary sheet is prepared showing total number of responses by category as well as high and low response items. This summary is shared with the entire team for feedback and discussion. Action can then be taken by having team members identify what they and the team need to do more of, and less of, to make the team more effective (Table 10.6). The team should also make a list of those activities that they are doing well and do not want to change. The team can use this opportunity to review its ground rules, team norms, and team processes to see if revisions, additions, or deletions need to be made.

The process that accompanies these types of activities is extremely helpful and meaningful. The content of what is learned is helpful, but it is the process and discussions that really build common understanding and team maturity.

TABLE 10.5
Scoring Key

Dependency Items: 1, 3, 7, 12, 13, 17, 18, 24, 28, 29, 32, 36, 37, 41, 44, 48, 49, 54, 55, 59.
Counterdependency Items: 2, 6, 8, 11, 14, 20, 23, 25, 27, 30, 31, 33, 38, 39, 42, 43, 47, 50, 56, 60.
Interdependency Items: 4, 5, 9, 10, 15, 16, 19, 21, 22, 26, 34, 35, 40, 45, 46, 51, 52, 53, 57, 58.

TABLE 10.6
Team Development Grid

Instructions: Each team member completes his or her own sheet using specific descriptions of actions which each is willing to do more of, less of, and keep doing, to help the team mature. Sheets are passed around to other team members for their feedback. *Specific description examples: "**Keep** asking questions and clarifying when some things are not clear." "**Less** joking all the time when the team is working on serious business; **More** willingness to help out in subgroup problem-solving tasks." "I will agree to help the subgroup problem-solving team that just started working on reducing rejects."*

More Of	*Less Of*	*Keep*

Agreements: I will _____

_____

_____

ĩ *Organizational Maturity*

The organization as an entity, providing more collectively than its individual members could ever do alone, has a need to renew the processes of working toward its purpose. As an open system of interrelated, interdependent parts, the organization depends primarily on its external environment for survival and growth. The renewal process must start outside the organization itself and assess its stakeholders' expectations and demands, then check congruency with internal systems to assure alignment and fit. This can be done by building into the system the scheduling and funding of quarterly or semiannual mission reviews and renewal conferences. This compels the organization and its leadership to hold formal renewal sessions and allows problems to be faced promptly. It gives the organization an opportunity to be proactive versus reactive. It enables the organization to review progress against design objectives as well as holding individual members and teams responsible for the commitments made since the last review.

⚑ External Sources for Renewal

Feedback sources and strategies for renewal initially come from the external environment. They can be the most objective.

Three of the most important and valuable external sources are the customer, competitors, and external consultants.

The Customer. Some difficult questions may appear simple in solution, but to search out real, in-depth answers requires customer involvement, not just input. Determine:

- The customer's acceptance of the products and/or services—obtain input from the end user, not just from distributors, representatives, agents, and so on. What do they think about the product after one year, after three years? What was the customer led to expect versus actual reality?
- How well have market share and profitability grown compared to total market or industry?
- The degree of product improvement, innovation, and creativity that has occurred.
- The trends that have developed in customer indicators (like number of complaints, warranty costs, returns, etc.) over an 18- to 24-month period.

Competitors. Determine the trends around:

- Quality, quantity, and cost of product
- Dollars spent on research and development as a percentage of sales
- Product to market time frames
- Service warranties and reputation

External Consultants. Third-party support and neutrality are essential in providing an independent objectivity that is difficult to find internally. A third-party consultant can:

- Tell it the way it really is without reservations
- Raise those difficult issues often ignored or hidden
- Observe conditions that aren't so obvious to those involved in day-to-day operations
- Provide an experience base not available inside an organization

Other Stakeholders. Just like the customer, other stakeholders can provide feedback relative to how well an organization is fulfilling their needs and expectations. Some examples of other stakeholders and the types of issues that should be explored are the following:

The Vendor. Is a long-term relationship valued? Can the vendor develop a relationship that encourages innovation and economy in his or her production process, or does the vendor only see short-term business to the lowest bidder? Has a partnership been created? Have the vendors achieved better quality and productivity?

Governmental Agencies. Do the various agencies (such as Department of Transportation, the Environmental Protection Agency, and Occupational Safety and Health Administration) see the organization as helpful and cooperative? Do they view the organization as a company doing as little as possible to comply, as opposed to a progressive and responsible organization, concerned about health and safety of employees and the environment? Do the organization's actions set new trends in going beyond compliance? Is there a partnership with these agencies?

Corporation and Sister Plants. Are they hostile toward the innovative organization and see it as different and threatening? Does the organization communicate an air of superiority and indifference? What has the organization done to help them understand the organization's design? How do functional counterparts (i.e., Purchasing, Engineering, Marketing, etc.) view one another's performance?

Community. How do the community and its leaders view the company's contribution to the local area? What has the company done to support the local charities and educational institutions? Are key members of management and employees actively involved in the community?

⅂ *Internal Areas for Renewal*

After the external sources for renewal have been evaluated, the organization can have a consultant join with a cross section of organizational members to review and formally provide feedback on the congruency and fit of the following elements:

Individual Development Processes. Processes need to be examined to ensure that organizational members are provided the tools for continuous growth and development. Do the people have the knowledge and skills to do what needs to get done? Are they provided training so that they can continue to learn and to contribute more and more to the team? Are new technical knowledge and skills being developed to enable employees to maintain a competitive advantage?

Key Variance Control. Are key variances being tracked and trend lines developed? Have they been continuously reviewed to ensure that they are controlled? Do the outputs continue to add value to the product and for the customer? Have other key variances been described or have new ones emerged? Have some factors originally thought to be key variances proven to be less important?

Reward Systems. Are individuals supported intrinsically (internally) and extrinsically (by the system) for spending their energies doing the "right" things? Is the reward system encouraging and rewarding the types of behaviors desired?

Information Systems. Are the appropriate categories of qualitative, quantitative, financial, and relational information being gathered and shared by the appropriate people in the organization?

Decision Making. Are the appropriate types of decisions being made by the assigned people closest to the source? Do decisions reflect competence through knowledge and experience? Are they made in a timely fashion with a bias for action or bias for precision?

Philosophy/Values. Is the organization adhering to its principles, or is it falling into the trap of protecting methods/procedures?

In chartering this joint renewal group, the team must be given autonomy. Group members need the ability to use their own knowledge and intuition and to rely on their own perceptions.

CONCLUSION

STS-designed organizations are human inventions that need to be continuously reinvented, reassessed, and renewed. All of an organization's interdependent parts must be examined, redefined, and integrated for both internal and external congruence with the environment's many and changing needs and demands. Organizations that develop their own processes of renewal will survive and grow; renewal is a process built on principles, and not a method, tool, or technique. The renewal process will continue to improve and become easier and easier for those organizations committed to continuously developing cultures that provide individual self-worth.

REFERENCES

DEMING, W. E. *Quality, Productivity, and Competitive Position.* Cambridge, MA: MIT Press, 1982.

ELKIND, D. "Erik Erikson's Eight Ages of Man." *New York Times Magazine,* April 5, 1970, p. 25.

ERIKSON, E. H. *Childhood and Society.* 2nd rev. ed. New York: Norton, 1963.

HALPERN, N. "Sustaining Change in the Shell Sarnia Chemical Plant." *QWL Focus,* 2(1), May 1982, Ontario Ministry of Labor, Quality of Working Life Center.

McWHINNEY, W. *Paths of Change.* Beverly Hills: Sage, 1992.

MEYERS, I. B. *Gifts Differing.* Palo Alto, CA: Consulting Psychologists Press, 1980.

VARNEY, G. H. *Organization Development for Managers.* Addison-Wesley (May 1977), 156–157.

WALTON, R. E. "Criteria for Working Life." Davis, L. E., and A. B. Cherns (eds.) *The Quality of Working Life.* Vol. 1. New York: Free Press, 1975.

Knowledge Work and the Future of Sociotechnical Systems: Living with Paradox

". . . the one certainty about the times ahead, the times in which managers will have to work and to perform, is that they will be turbulent times."

(Drucker, 1980)

INTRODUCTION

This final chapter addresses future trends in organizational design, but the roots of these trends can already be found in our world today. As a society we face many uncertainties, but we also have many "signposts" for the future around us. It benefits us to recognize them and to prepare for them.

North America as an Information Society. Even though physical products will continue to be manufactured in North America, increasing computerization of the process will eliminate the monotony and drudgery of much manual labor. Computerization will also substitute human mental and cognitive processes for the sensory, tactile, and physical ones of the past (cf. Zuboff, 1988). For many years the information age has been hailed as the "postindustrial society" (Bell, 1967). Seven major and simultaneous patterns that characterize our future as an information society are examined in this chapter. These seven patterns are described first, then addressed more fully by using case examples to illustrate new work models and opportunities.

MAJOR EMERGING PATTERNS AND TRENDS OF WORK IN NORTH AMERICA

THE FUTURE OF WORK IN NORTH AMERICA

1. Managing organizational paradox
2. Nonlinear technical process
3. Information and knowledge processing
4. The product-focused system
5. "Professionalization" of the work force
6. Nonroutine and ordinary work
7. Organizational change in form and function

❦ *Paradox*

A high commitment to paradox is required for organizational effectiveness. Cameron (1986) argued convincingly that a foremost attribute characterizing effective, adaptive, and flexible organizations is the presence of paradox. He defined paradox as a situation in which contradictory elements are present at the same time. The effectiveness actually results from the *tension* inherent between the simultaneous opposites, a tension in which neither element can dominate over the other.

Physical science's recent profound concern for dealing with uncertainty, ambiguity, and chaos have direct implications for organizational theory and management science (Cameron, 1986; Quinn & Cameron, 1988). Pascarella and Frohman (1989) refer to both the "paradigm shift" (cf. Kuhn, 1970) and the new science of chaos (Gleick, 1987) in the paradox of managing the purposeful system. The case is aptly made that this paradoxical role is as significant in management and organizational change as it is in scientific experiment. It is no longer enough to play the passive observer in system change. The facilitator must be connected tightly with the system while, at the same time, removed enough to see and help the larger enterprise adapt and flex.

This behavior illustrates the more general requirement of "loose and tight" coupling in effective systems, as observed by the authors of the immensely popular management book *In Search of Excellence* (Peters & Waterman, 1982). This need for loose–tight coupling is a prime illustration of organizational paradox. Cameron (1986) introduces this and four other conditions of paradox that describe what is needed to achieve effectiveness. Cameron's five conditions of paradoxes are:

- The organizational need for *loose–tight* coupling
- The need for *high specialization* and *high generality* of work roles
- The need for leadership *continuity* and leadership *change*
- The need for deviation-*amplifying* and deviation-*reducing* processes
- The need for *expanded* information and *inhibitors* to information overload

STS and Paradox.   STS is a *methodology* for managing paradoxes (such as Cameron's list above) through managing in the "void" (cf. Chapter 5). Member competence is developed by the continuous design and improvement of a purposeful system. There are other approaches to coping with paradox, but they are not systemic. "Matrix management," for instance, is a *temporary* approach or response, directed primarily toward one of the conditions of paradox—high specialization and high generality. At the same time that it is addressing paradox, matrix management introduces complicating dilemmas and ironies of its own. Dilemma differs from paradox in that the two opposing factors cannot coexist and one will dominate over the other. An irony differs from paradox in that it is the result of a single event (it doesn't require competing events) that is opposite to that intended. Matrix, as a solution, contains the built-in dilemma of loyalty to the project "boss" versus the functional "boss" (Davis & Lawrence, 1977). In addition, applying matrix management faces one with the irony of building the social "glue" for success of the project team and then ignoring it when it's time to disband (cf. Kidder, 1981).

Matrix "organization" is a formula, or solution, in which members are committed to a project, but not necessarily to the product, to the purpose, or to the other people in the system. STS, however, is a way of attending to the paradox of both the product and the people as a process—solutions resulting from its application are unique to each system.

Total quality management (TQM) was described in Chapter 1 as a U.S. Defense Department program for contractors that has become widespread in much of civilian industry as well. The TQM pattern typically contains two elements, statistical process control (SPC) and employee participation. It is intended to address the organizational paradox of "the cost of quality." For many years, conventional wisdom held that increasing product quality would cost more because of slower processing (to be more careful) and increased inspection staff. Now, of course, managers realize the savings of "doing it right the first time" and the increase in consumer loyalty from high-quality goods. But in this sense, TQM is a one-dimensional approach to organizational improvement—it lays no claim to addressing the sociotechnical design paradox, the paradoxes enumerated by Cameron, or Peters and Waterman, nor is TQM purpose and product focused beyond "high quality."

❦ Nonlinear Technical Processes

Increasing sophistication of technology and complexity of environment presage and require nonlinear transformation processes. Nonlinear knowledge-creating technologies have no fixed starting point, but they do share with more conventional technical processes the characteristic of having concrete outputs. Identifying the paradoxical issues to be resolved, that are instrumental to the pursuit of system mission and philosophy, adds a concrete beginning to the technical process and permits the continued use of the purpose- and throughput-oriented paradigm.

Even though the variance matrix examples in the technical systems model presented in Chapter 4 appear linear, the model is not limited by that constraint. Since the mid-1980's, published reports have presented cases in which a non-linear throughput has been accommodated by the STS technical system analysis (e.g., Taylor, Gustavson & Carter, 1986). The early STS model addressed unidirectional, liquid-flow processes, such as oil refining or papermaking. It was a minor adjustment to adapt this robust methodology to non-linear processes where later events could influence earlier ones and the process could proceed along multiple paths simultaneously.

❦ Information and Knowledge-Processing Systems

Work in North America is already largely *information work*, in which workers and their technology transform data into information or transform information into customer satisfaction or use information processing technology to aid decision making or help guide work. Increasingly, information workers accomplish *knowledge work* in which new information in the form of ideas, impressions, interpretations, notions, or beliefs is created or developed. This new information is useful for understanding or manipulating complex phenomena. Engineers, managers, and consultants are knowledge workers—they form new information from old. But other occupations, such as nurses and nurse's aids, legal assistants, and operators of personal computers are also becoming knowledge workers. In a large urban police department, for instance, detectives found that an interactive computer system designed to help investigations by identifying suspects by certain attributes was not useful to them until they had developed a trustful relationship with the analysts who could (but did not necessarily) monitor the coding and keying quality feeding into the system. The analysts' relationship to their detective co-workers was not unlike secretaries' relationship to managers, except that the "reputation" of the computer system acted initially to discount the analyst's contribution to the detective. Many detectives were suspicious of the analysts (together with the computer system) as untrained in police work, as threats to their own jobs, or as just producing "garbage" (Glasser, 1981). The analysts who overcame these barriers through helpful and competent work literally became knowledge workers along with the detectives they assisted.

As the importance of knowledge work increases in North America, it becomes more urgent to design it for excellence in performance and quality of working life. In knowledge work, the throughput is often accumulated knowledge and persuasive argument. This throughput frequently has no concrete starting point (this is in contrast to other intangible delivery systems, such as service systems, which have "requests" as inputs). Variances are more difficult to identify with throughputs like this because there is no norm or average from which deviations are identified. Nonlinear knowledge technologies, although having no fixed starting point, do share the characteristic of having concrete outputs. They are also typically found to regard their environments as increasingly chaotic. Those environments confront knowledge workers with issues or paradoxes to be resolved before ordinary information processing can begin.

The identification of issues to be resolved which are instrumental to the pursuit of system mission and philosophy adds a concrete input to the throughput and permits the continued use of the purpose- and throughput-oriented paradigm. These issues do not vary—instead, "deliberations" (Pava, 1983) on key issues provide an answer given or position taken on each one, based on the system's values and on chaotic situational conditions. Such deliberations are useful, as well, in dealing with the throughput variances that occur during more routine aspects of the system's work.

The use of a technical analysis matrix to examine the relationship between variances in throughput (as it becomes more tangible toward the output end of the technical system) and "issues" identified can be constructive in identifying the effects of the variances on positions taken on the issues.

EFFECTIVE USE OF NEW TECHNOLOGY

As technologies become more complex and flexible in their application, so must people become more competent and empowered in their response.

The Product-Focused Paradigm. Katz and Kahn's (1966) classic organizational systems text proposed "purpose" of the enterprise as an important aspect of open systems. "Purposeful" systems and the pitfalls of teleological models were thereafter actively debated, and purposeful systems emerged as a practical perspective. An STS change effort undertaken in 1967 at an oil refinery in Great Britain, began with the creation and dissemination of a purpose statement, or "management philosophy" as the first step in the process (Hill, 1971). In management circles, Peter Drucker is widely known for the significance he places on the importance of business purpose (cf. Drucker, 1974). In general, this shift to purpose/product orientation—and the STS emphasis on it—is clearly apparent from the perspective of the 1990s, but it wasn't so clear at that time. Indeed, STS has been applied in many ways in the past 40 years. For simplicity, STS can be grouped (along with other organizational improvement efforts) into three categories:

> *Solving a Problem.* The technology doesn't work the way it should, or personnel turnover is too high, employees aren't accepting direction from supervisors, or expenses are exceeding budget.
>
> *Promoting a Solution.* "Autonomous (or self-managed) work groups" are inaugurated, "pay for knowledge" wage programs are introduced, "quality circles" are implemented, "PC's" (office automation) or "CIM" (computer-integrated manufacturing) are installed, or "MRP-II" (manufacturing resource planning) is proposed as the one best way to succeed.

Pursuing a Purpose. Mission and philosophy guide design (Davis & Sullivan, 1980; Hill, 1971; Taylor & Asadorian, 1985). The British refinery project was among the first STS change efforts in which the technology was consciously examined in terms of what happens *to the product*—and not "what characterizes the machines," or "what tasks the operators perform." Employees were asked to understand how the *product* flowed smoothly—and not just how to *react* when things go badly.

The Central Role of Product Focus in STS. The STS technical system methodology (as described in Chapters 4 and 5) can provide not only a deep and unique understanding of a system's function for its members and outsiders, but it can provide a logical and measured basis for guiding change and incorporating "movements" and solutions (such as TQM).

Technical system methodology, including key variance understanding, has started to become the basis for identifying the primary quality aspects and key performance indicators in TQM programs. When technical system data are compared with the expectations vocalized in the company's statement of mission and purpose, some of the requirements of change are highlighted in bold relief. In addition, technical systems results, as a list of key variances, can be used as the raw material for individual, unit, and system performance data. Such performance data, based on the common denominator of the system—issues successfully resolved and throughput deviation reduced or eliminated—is novel, perhaps even revolutionary. By comparison, the conventional performance indicators are activity oriented. They not only focus attention on the wrong stuff, but measures of production are typically unable to absorb the complexities of technical systems in order to be valid and fair to employees. New performance measures based on key variances become the common language of all people concerned with the product and purpose of the enterprise, and they include the tools (i.e., technical system matrix and variance control table) required for everyone involved to understand the complexity of interrelations among the measures. Key issues and variances are identified before the system is improved and, as such, they can become baselines against which to compare the performance results of the subsequent changes and improvements to the system. In addition to the value of STS technical methodology, the related STS social systems methodology provides deep understanding of the value of human intervention in the identification and control of key issues and variances, as well as in response to nontechnical internal events and to the chaos outside the system.

Like more conventional work, STS treats knowledge work as

throughput focused. A major difference between them, however, is that the throughput in knowledge work typically has no concrete starting point. Technical system "variances" are difficult to use with throughputs like this because there is no norm, modal case, or average from which deviations are identified. As described in the preceding section, key issues (paradoxes that are instrumental to the pursuit of system mission and philosophy) add a concrete origin to the system's cycle. These issues do not vary—instead, "deliberations" on key issues provide an answer given, or position taken, on each one based on the system's values and on chaotic situational conditions.

❦ *Professionalization of the Work Force*

More professionalized employees—those who consider themselves to be competent in their skills, to be of central importance to the enterprise, and who hold a belief and commitment to its purpose—are required for knowledge work. Information, as it becomes knowledge, demands this professionalization. In addition, the production of future manufactured goods will require that more service for (and awareness of) the user be included. This work, therefore, requires more skill, more understanding of the "big picture" by the employees doing the work. Such newly professionalized employees, today and in the future, frequently work beside professionals (as conventionally defined—e.g., engineers, scientists, etc.). To a degree, all conventional professionals are loners by choice and by training, and prefer to work by themselves. More of them, however, are finding that working together with others produces results that would be difficult if not impossible to do alone. In Chapter 7, we discussed professionalization and quality of working life, but the newly professionalized work force, often working together with highly trained and educated conventional professionals, affects successful design much more—it is a major source of exploiting the potential of new information technology.

❦ *Can Work Ever Truly Be Nonroutine?*

In Chapter 5, the notion of "managing in the void" was introduced to show how necessary it was to prepare system members at all levels with the understanding of product and purpose in order to make adjustments for events that had never (in their experience at least) occurred before. This requirement of being prepared for the unexpected is revealed in every organization operating in a complex or chaotic environment. This world of the unexpected causes the authors to state that no work today can be considered completely routine.

Knowledge Work and Nonroutine Operations. Although much knowledge work requires more flexibility from both management and employees, there is probably not much knowledge work (even for professionals) that is truly one-of-a-kind. There is no completely nonroutine work (unless artists are included as "workers"), any more than there is a completely routine work process. The authors have discovered through their own redesign experiences that there is always room for surprises. The work of scientists, engineers, physicians, and other professionals can (and often does) have a nonroutine component, but it also has much routine as well. Thus, the STS methods of future work design will owe a great deal to those of the present as described in this volume. The critical work will be to establish how to understand and deal with the increasing numbers of unpredictable but nonrandom events that will surely occur.

On the Nature of Nonroutine Work

Over the past decade those enterprises that have excelled in their "businesses" have done so because they were prepared to adapt quickly to unpredictable, but "understandable" events. This "managing in the void" is a competence that STS design yields for organizations in virtually every industry.

The cause of success is not (or is rarely) removal of the root cause of problems. Solving organizational or operational problems, although necessary, does not assure success in the day-to-day operations of an enterprise. Conversely, however, designing for the normal, or the ordinary—even when it contains much that is nonroutine—can often also solve the root cause of problems experienced in the industry or experienced in the previous performance of the system.

❧ Organizational Change in Form and Function

STS and Structural Change. Before sociotechnical systems methodology was conceived in the late 1940s, organizational structure in

North America was virtually dictated by the bureaucratic models of the Imperial Roman Army and the pre-Reformation Christian Church (Weber, 1947), together with the mechanistic model of F. W. Taylor's *Scientific Management* (Taylor, 1911). Combined, these dictates became the rigid guidelines for organizations structured by specialized, functional departments (bureaus or offices), with the operational work structure of those departments divided into the smallest, most easily instructed tasks. Organizing an enterprise by product line, by profit center, by environmental complexity, or by social values was unheard of.

Some management consultants developed the practice of decentralizing and transferring responsibility from higher levels to lower ones in the organizational hierarchy with considerable success after World War II. Such restructuring was successful apparently as much by the novelty of the change as by the new alliances; because these same consultants could, later, advise their clients to "centralize" their structure again—and the cycle could evidently be repeated over time.

STS has always addressed the issues of organizational purpose and structural change. Through the years it has been characterized as promoting the "autonomous group" or "self-managed team" (Beekun, 1989; Kelly, 1978). This assertion has been accurate in some specific cases, but the impact of unique structural solutions to system purpose remains the dominant STS theme. Since its beginning, STS has been the source of *unique* and ongoing changes in reporting relationships and functional responsibilities through *informed understanding* of the system.

"It's hard work to make improvements without changing anything"

Mikhail Gorbachev
(address to the Supreme Soviet Congress, February 1986)

Matrix organizations, on the other hand, are largely temporary structures, set up in parallel with the permanent structure, to complete a project. In some organizations, such projects may take years to complete (Pace, Smith, & Mills, 1991), but the luxury of operating in the stable environments which permit this is rare and becoming rarer. Thus, matrix structure is a special and important case of an emerging model, known as the "parallel organization," which is a way of coping with the need for system flexibility—*but within* an existing traditional "machine-type" organization. In a parallel organization a temporary, or at least separate, structure is devised to operate (for as long as it is useful) beside the existing organization. This makes traditional managers happy because they don't have to change. The matrix organization's manifestation of this "parallel" device uses temporary "multifunctional teams" to achieve this flexibility.

TQM and Matrix Organization.   Recent experience with TQM in manufacturing suggests that organizational design prescriptions encompass a broad range between two extremes. At one extreme are "multiskilled groups" (defined as employing all technical and support skills for a complete profit center). At the other extreme are "matrix" groups where specialists (such as engineering, purchasing, materials, production planning, and other staff skills) are attached to a production unit but return to their functional departments when they are "finished."

STS and TQM: Structural Changes.   TQM is normally accomplished through training, leadership, and participation alone. STS requires these factors as well, but its main effect is to promote system understanding that allows managers and employees to make informed choices about changes in structure, technology, physical space, and control of jobs and procedures. There is ample opportunity to use TQM (and other quality-enhancing programs) within the framework of sociotechnical systems methodology. With appropriate changes in sociotechnical system aspects, an enterprise can truly make the most of a seriously supported TQM program.

STS APPLIED TO NEW WORK MODELS AND OPPORTUNITIES

The most successful and lasting sociotechnical systems innovations have resulted from changes that have addressed a whole system. Early in his program of perestroika (restructuring), Mikhail Gorbachev was already beginning to understand what many managers still struggle with in our society—that the structure of one's system (for Gorbachev, the Soviet system) must be changed, not merely improved on or elaborated on. As later events showed, however, Gorbachev was not willing to embrace structural change even though he realized its necessity.

ẇ Case I: Innovative Design in a Financial System

One may argue that a financial function doesn't lend itself to systems thinking. Performing one function of an existing multifunctional structure could be seen as self-perpetuating the current organizational structure. However, if the analysis is done on the whole system and not just the single-function department, one can look at the organization in systems terms. This allows the functional area to look at how it really should fit in, or be structured, in light of the larger system and in fulfillment of the organization's purpose. It is with this understanding that this case is presented.

A finance (controller's) organization, supporting a worldwide business unit (its customer), undertook a sociotechnical system study for redesign. The origins of the project, the direct outgrowth of the strong convictions of the Controller, were threefold—(a) to better use talent and provide growth opportunities for clerical personnel, (b) to implement a new financial computer system that would lay the foundation for improved information accessibility and integrity, and (c) to retain a pool of financial "consultants" that the department had developed internally. The 60-person department contained 20% managers and supervisors, 35% accountants, and 45% administrative and support staff. The environmental state of the system at the time of the redesign included three years of "downsizing," customers asking for help making sound financial decisions, increasing globalization and complexity in the business, increased integration of information systems, and the competitive need to "do more with less."

During the preanalysis steps, management and staff specialists attended STS workshops and then met in an off-site retreat to decide if they wished to undertake the STS approach to change. Once having decided on STS, all members of the finance department were assembled together to be introduced to the process and an intensive question-and-answer session ensued. Shortly thereafter, a steering committee of managers and important system customers was formed. Following the formation of the steering committee, six internal STS workshops were conducted for all finance members and selected customers. From workshop participants an STS design team of volunteers was assembled and the analysis began.

STS Coping with Paradox. Although it was able to operate within one mission, the finance department delivered several paradoxical products and processes. One of these paradoxes was the customers' need for financial *advice* in addition to the delivery of more traditional financial services such as accounts payable and accounts receivable. "Do more with less" was a paradox, as was the desire for close relationships with the department's customer systems. In contrast with the traditional finance department's role as objective, remote, and conservative (the "green eye-shade" folks), this department promoted a philosophy to involve people (customer and finance members alike) and include them in ongoing decisions. Other paradoxes faced by the system included the need for generalists and specialists and the loose–tight controls in a controller's function. Many of these paradoxes were created by a combination of forces emanating from the department's new philosophy statement and from the environment of the enterprise.

Nonlinear Technical Process.   The degree of iteration among steps in the STS scan for this system was increased. Although they discovered that the unit operations for each product were linear and sequential, the STS team soon discovered that their system actually had seven financial outputs or products which together formed a nonlinear flow. The team found that six of these seven were not only related to one another, but were synergistic. Figure 11.1 displays these nonlinear relationships among the system outputs.

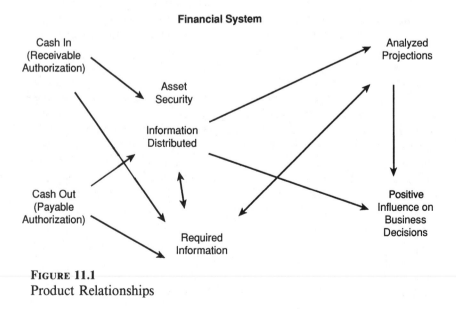

Figure 11.1
Product Relationships

Throughput and Product Focus. The mission of the system was stated as "a positive influence to cause financially sound business decisions." The inputs the STS team identified were "opportunities," which they felt could come from inside the system (from their own fertile minds) or from outside the system. The system's outputs were seen as new and useful knowledge, and innovative and unique solutions to problems that would lead to "actions taken by customers" that reflected the influence of the finance department and its information. For all seven products, the process flow contained five unit operations between input (ambiguous input for some products) and concrete output. The STS team learned that the technical analysis was flexible enough for knowledge work of this complexity.

Knowledge Work and STS Design. As they began the analysis, the STS team learned that for a knowledge work system, although the output is readily identifiable, the input is ambiguous and there is often no recognizable beginning (or object to be transformed). In the case of the finance system, there were ideas, suggestions, or issues needing resolution. These formed the paradoxes to be resolved and they became the starting point for the finance system. Successful knowledge work systems effectively manage paradox. Deliberations among focal roles provide the resolution of the key issues in the initial unit operations. Cooperation and coordination among focal roles contribute to the control of key variances in the remaining unit operations. The throughput is as identifiable as it is in more conventional systems—it is accumulated information and knowledge and persuasive argument, and it is intended to influence the customer. Deliberations among *focal roles* provide the resolution of key issues in the initial unit operations. Cooperation and coordination among focal roles contribute to the control of key variances in the remaining unit operations.

The technical matrix for the finance department is shown in Figure 11.2. Note that the matrix contains both paradoxical issues or opportunities to be resolved, as well as variances to be controlled. It can be seen that the first three unit operations in the matrix have no defined boundaries. That is because the key issues (#3, 4, 13) are largely nonlinear and are managed by decisions of value, not decisions of fact. As the finance technical process moves to later unit operations, the process becomes more routine and the variances in the flow are more predictable and controllable.

Process control in information systems provides several challenges to the variance control analysis described in Chapter 4. For one thing,

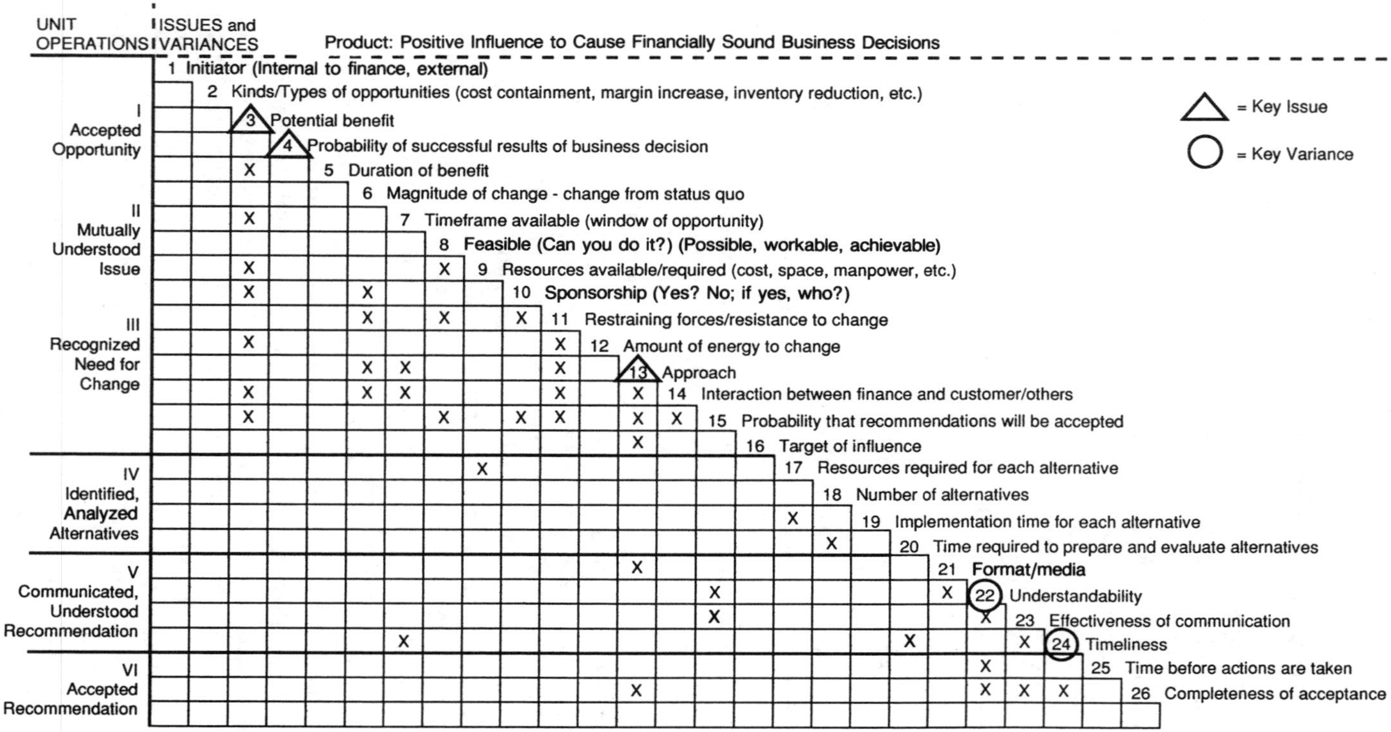

UNIT OPERATIONS | ISSUES and VARIANCES   Product: Positive Influence to Cause Financially Sound Business Decisions

△ = Key Issue
○ = Key Variance

1 Initiator (Internal to finance, external)
2 Kinds/Types of opportunities (cost containment, margin increase, inventory reduction, etc.)
3 Potential benefit
4 Probability of successful results of business decision
5 Duration of benefit
6 Magnitude of change - change from status quo
7 Timeframe available (window of opportunity)
8 Feasible (Can you do it?) (Possible, workable, achievable)
9 Resources available/required (cost, space, manpower, etc.)
10 Sponsorship (Yes? No; if yes, who?)
11 Restraining forces/resistance to change
12 Amount of energy to change
13 Approach
14 Interaction between finance and customer/others
15 Probability that recommendations will be accepted
16 Target of influence
17 Resources required for each alternative
18 Number of alternatives
19 Implementation time for each alternative
20 Time required to prepare and evaluate alternatives
21 Format/media
22 Understandability
23 Effectiveness of communication
24 Timeliness
25 Time before actions are taken
26 Completeness of acceptance

I Accepted Opportunity
II Mutually Understood Issue
III Recognized Need for Change
IV Identified, Analyzed Alternatives
V Communicated, Understood Recommendation
VI Accepted Recommendation

214

FIGURE 11.2
Technical System Matrix

key issues and paradoxes do not vary; they exist until resolved, or if they do vary, it is not around a known standard or norm. Second, the resolution of issues becomes the organization's position based on its values. Third, understanding interrelationships between issues and variances is necessary for managing paradox. Finally, the process is "chaos-in, clarity-out."

The variance control analysis and social analysis that the finance group completed showed that, in this system, key variances and issues were controlled by intuition and analysis rather than by design, that most clerical members did not recognize their role in the transformation, and that managers were most highly involved in variance control. Each of the seven products were currently produced individually with little (and fragmented) learning opportunity. Finally, support systems were not well developed to help deliver any of the products.

Professionalization of the Work Force.   The controller, herself, had indicated that she wanted to better use the talents of all her work force, and in particular to provide growth opportunities for clerical personnel. The STS team also enunciated the need for more skills and competence by adding such statements as: "We are encouraged to grow, advance, and contribute to our fullest potential," and "We feel able to take control of our own destiny" to the system's philosophy declaration.

Nonroutine Work: Designing for the Ordinary in Order to Achieve the Extraordinary.   The environment of the system described here was chaotic. This means that it was not random but not predictable either — it could be understood. It was dynamic and complex, requiring multiple missions or rapid changes in missions and organizational values that remained stable or evolved slowly. In short, in less routine systems, the human values provide the stability and the technical environment is dynamic and unpredictable. Similarities between more traditional systems and the one described here are an identifiable output, a transformed throughput, and a clear, but complex purpose. The nonroutine aspects of this system were the "issues" or paradoxes, described above. These issues were the result of statements in the philosophy (such as "we want to involve our customers in the process") together with pressures from the external environment (such as lack of time to talk to customers). Issues often also arose as a result of external changes and the decisions which had been routine were now uncertain. In this sense, the system lacked concrete input; its environment was chaotic so that initial conditions had a great potential impact on the key issues and on subsequent events.

The design that evolved from the STS team's efforts proposed to change the system from a functional organization (with each of its divisions handling a different accounting specialty) to five customer-oriented organizations (client-service teams) in which the clerical employees and accountants would work together to serve one of the department's five major clients. This team-based "service" would include all accounts payable/receivable work for that client, all reports and financial information that the client required, as well as the financial "consulting" services that the finance department had been developing. Department procurement of their new financial data processing/information managing system had been delayed, so it wasn't available to build into the STS team's provisional design. This design was presented to the department's managers just prior to the installation of a new controller and it remained pending for the next three months, while the new controller became familiar with the operations and the pending changes. In the end, the design was not fully implemented. The managers were unwilling to make the changes necessary to assure real improvement in department performance.

There were several lessons about design and change from the project. The design process for the project went according to the description in Chapter 8, but management support was lacking because the original controller had accepted a lateral transfer out of the department shortly after the completion of the social system analysis. Her replacement was not chosen for three months, and the middle managers in the department had neither the motivation nor the initiative to take the risk necessary to support the STS team's proposals. An important lesson from this example is that opportunity-driven change is more difficult to implement than problem-driven change. The former controller saw the opportunities clearly, but her subordinate managers (and her successor) did not. "If it ain't broke, don't fix it" became the operational response from that group. Although those middle managers might have learned to support the STS team's proposed design, they clearly required even more time than the several months available to them. The new controller wasn't interested in what he saw as change for change's sake and he felt that his new subordinates weren't either. The process of support fell into a vicious cycle. The new controller, when he arrived, didn't sense support for the project from the middle managers who had adopted the "wait for the new boss" attitude. The former controller, on the other hand, quickly understood and accepted responsibility for every step of the approach she had taken — but she was no longer there. The pitfalls of taking the sponsor away from a change before it has been institutionalized has been well documented (Walton, 1975).

⚙ Case II: Innovative Organization in an R&D Function

The subject of this case was the semiconductor (S/C) product design department (known hereafter as component design engineering, or CDE) in a Silicon Valley firm. This case was unique in several ways. To our knowledge, it was the first reported application of the STS analysis and design technique in the computer-assisted design (CAD) technology of circuit layout drafting (Taylor, Gustavson, & Carter, 1986). This case also addressed the organizational issues of professional engineers in the S/C industry.

CDE, the group responsible for the design of the company's integrated circuits, was organized functionally, with fewer than 100 employees. There were seven separate groups of architects, logic and circuit designers, layout designers, and groups for product planning, applications, and documentation. More than 80% of these employees had college degrees. Of those who had degrees, at least two-thirds of them had an advanced degree — Master of Science or a Ph.D. The specialist qualifications of these employees had shaped the functional nature of the CDE organization. This functional division was marked by conflict and friction among the various groups in CDE.

Coping With Paradox.   It was 1980 and times were changing in the S/C industry. On one hand, what had begun as a strictly high-tech industry was fast changing from being "engineering driven" to being "marketing driven." Furthermore, for the company to remain competitive, the products CDE would be designing were much more complicated than those of the past and would require more than individual designers working alone to create them. This paradox of engineering no longer choosing what to design, together with the need to design more complicated S/C products, was a factor in late 1979 and early 1980 when the project in CDE began.

A steering committee of the company's top management people was assembled by the CDE director to make certain that the project was supported. Volunteers for an STS design team composed of CDE employees from each level of the hierarchy and from each functional group were requested by CDE management, who selected 10 people. The STS team's charter was to complete the STS process while meeting periodically with the steering committee to present current progress and what they had learned, and to identify what support they needed in order to continue the process.

Knowledge Work and STS Design. The STS team undertook the process as presented in this book. When they had completed the scan, the STS team discovered that the company's business was really bigger than what they had originally envisioned. They concluded that the output of CDE was not hardware but was information. When they began, many on the STS team viewed the company as being driven by technology and not by markets. The R&D emphasis in this company, they felt, was a response to competition in product development industrywide. On the other hand, the dominant company management view emphasized the importance of markets and of customer preference. CDE originally saw itself, not as part of a marketing company or a manufacturing company, but as a design company. In this view, marketing would go out and try to find a place for products that CDE invented and manufacturing would make them.

As they began the STS analysis, the STS team members learned that although their output was readily identifiable, the inputs were ambiguous and there was often no recognizable beginning (or object to be transformed). They began to understand their process as chaos-in and clarity-out. The issues or paradoxes to be resolved became the starting point for the system. They would learn that successful knowledge work systems effectively manage paradox.

Deliberations among focal roles provided the resolution of the key issues in the initial unit operations. Cooperation and coordination among focal roles would contribute to the control of key variances in the remaining unit operations. CDE throughput in the later unit operations was concrete and identifiable as in more conventional engineering systems — it was data, from a variety of sources, as it became information for a "manufacturable" integrated circuit in a semiconductor medium that satisfied a market need.

Nonlinear Technical Process. The initial stage of the technical systems analysis produced a view of product flow or throughput that satisfied the STS team members' conviction that their work was creative and nonlinear. Figure 11.3 presents the set of "unit operations" and their interrelationships that the STS team developed. Their colleagues in the CDE felt that this descriptive graphic was a most useful contribution to their sociotechnical systems understanding.

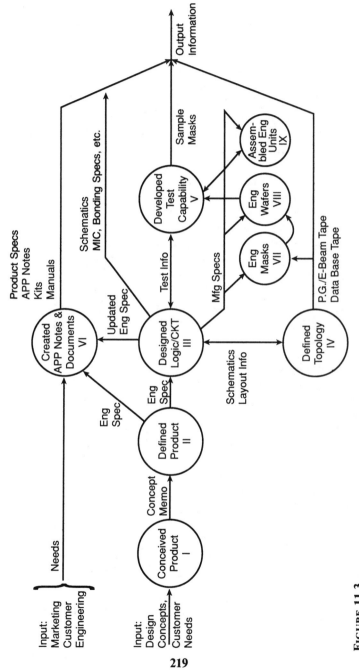

219

FIGURE 11.3
Technical Throughput Flow (Unit Operations)

Throughput and Product Focus. For the engineers on the STS team, the technical system analysis was clearly a valuable part of the analysis phase. They quickly agreed among themselves that their product was "information" to manufacturing and marketing functions, in place of the more conventionally attractive idea that they produced the circuits themselves. Benefits of the STS technical analysis were (a) clarification about the product of the CDE system and its key variances and how those variances were controlled; (b) giving people (both within CDE and between CDE and other functions) a common language — the language of the product — to unify their communication and bridge the gaps among their separate languages of specialization; and (c) access to specialists who could help the STS team become knowledgeable about particular elements with which they were unfamiliar.

In examining the control of their key variances, the STS team concluded that marketing did not provide enough information to them. During this process the STS design team also began to realize the importance of CDE's acceptance by marketing. They became very interested in receiving information from outside of their closed system and in understanding what was going on out in the environment. They decided that CDE really did need to work with marketing people. The operative question for the STS team became, "How do we get market data, and how do we do it now?"

Professionalization of the Work Force. Functional specialization among design workers is, and has been, widespread in Silicon Valley companies. For engineers, this typically creates an elite "caste" of individual "star" performers with predictably high wages. Layout specialists (the people operating the CAD technology) aren't required to have a college degree, but they do possess special, more narrow skills. This specialization of layout designers has promoted high wages for their group as well. This combination of individual engineering "stars" and a clannish underclass of layout designers has not encouraged good organizational commitment or cooperation in the design of integrated circuits. Most of the companies in the Silicon Valley have been organized in this functional way to recognize and support both types of design specialists. It seemed likely that if CDE involved both types of specialists with the "product," greater understanding and empowerment would be promoted.

Nonroutine Work: Designing for the Ordinary in Order to Achieve the Extraordinary. The STS team recommended a new CDE organization in which layout designers and engineers, with most of the skills required to create a manufacturable integrated circuit design, comprised a "product team." After discussions among the company's management, CDE management and the CDE staff, the design was implemented. With this design, the use of the CAD technology was adapted for the purposes of the CDE system, and not merely for the maximized use-hours of the technology itself. In the new design, layout designers and engineers had a closer, more synergistic relationship, which made their adversarial relationship a thing of the past. Layout designers could better understand the whole process, and they could identify with a single product or family of related products. Additionally, engineers were hired to learn computer-assisted, design-based layout techniques, which further improved relations within the product design teams and improved layout effectiveness by further shortening the communication links between circuit design and layout. Design engineers began doing some of their own CAD layout, and in so doing, they inspected their own circuit design work—thereby catching flaws that they, themselves, had built into the product. This new organization was based on the realization that the product of CDE was information—information that manufacturing used to manufacture and test the product, and also information that marketing used to sell the product. A larger role for technical writers was created. This expanded role was more involved during the circuit design/development cycle (rather than merely after it) to obtain information from the engineers and to train new customers in the application of the product.

CDE management undertook an informal assessment of the new product-team organization in June 1983, more than a year after its implementation. Twenty-five percent of the CDE's staff and most of its managers met to review their experience with the new product-team organization. Over three-fourths of this group reported that morale was higher because of increased communication and understanding within the teams. Among the factors mentioned as enhancing team morale were member support for one another, increased "ownership" of decisions made by the team (especially by layout designers), and increased awareness and learning about the total design process and its progress. Half of the respondents also expressed mixed feelings and, in some cases, frustration with some part of the effects of the new structure. Some managers complained, for example, that decision making by consensus removed the ability to simply dictate decisions to subordinates, or that it took too long (in an industry where time is always short), even though it led to the "ownership" mentioned above as a positive aspect. Some engineers questioned the quality of decisions made by a team because the "best" idea may not always be the one accepted. Engineering specialists commented that they had difficulty obtaining layout support from other design teams when they needed it. Meetings that lasted too long, or that did not concern them, were mentioned as drawbacks by some layout designers. A number of managers, engineers, and layout designers commented that the product-team structure interfered with close professional relationships among people with similar skills and formal training, and that attempts to deal with this issue had not worked out as well as they wanted.

A telling comment stated by a manager outside CDE was that despite the fact that the sociotechnical systems analysis and design process required a long time and many man-hours to complete, its usefulness was more essential for the then-current design projects (such as a 32-bit microprocessor), which required a team structure, than for the more simple projects of the past. He continued that the one-man (or "master–slave") organization that worked for earlier generations of products would simply not be appropriate anymore. He concluded that it was unfair to compare the performance of the new organization with its multiperson, multiskilled, product-oriented focus to past arrangements over a time during which the integrated circuit products had changed so much. He rated the new organization "right for the times facing the industry."

CONCLUSION

The future of STS is exciting. More and more organizations are recognizing its potential. STS theorists and practitioners are continuing the search for new and unique applications. The principles will survive and live on, demanding new approaches and applications. Those who truly understand and are willing to go the extra mile, challenging the mechanistic and machine-age paradigms, will discover new horizons—learning new ways to manage and integrate the opposites. The choice is to accept the basic tenets STS has to offer and struggle through the learning that is required to produce new insights, or to accept the accepted systems. To those leaders, pioneers, and "paradigm busters" who choose the former, we, the authors, wish continued success.

REFERENCES

BEEKUN, R. I. "Assessing the Effectiveness of Sociotechnical Interventions: Antidote or Fad?" *Human Relations*, 42, 1989, 877–897.

BELL, D. "Notes on the Post-Industrial Society: I and II." *Public Interest*, 6, 24–35, 7, 102–118, 1967.

CAMERON, K. S. "Effectiveness as Paradox: Consensus and Conflict in Conceptions of Organizational Effectiveness." *Management Science*, 32, 1986, 539–553.

DAVIS, L. E., & C. S. SULLIVAN "A Labour-Management Contract and Quality of Working Life." *Journal of Occupational Behaviour*, 1, 1980, 29–41.

DAVIS, S. M., & P. R. LAWRENCE *Matrix*. Reading, MA: Addison-Wesley, 1977.

DRUCKER, P. *Management: Tasks, Responsibilities, Practices*. New York: Harper and Row, 1974, 1.

DRUCKER, P. *Managing in Turbulent Times*. New York: Harper & Row, 1980.

GLASSER, J. "PATRIC at the LAPD." *Office Automation Digest*, Reston, VA: American Federation of Information Processing Societies, 1981, 335–338.

GLEICK, J. *Chaos: Making a New Science*. New York: Viking Press, 1987.

HILL, P. *Toward a New Philosophy of Management*. London: Gower Press, 1971.

KATZ, D. R., & R. L. KAHN *The Social Psychology of Organizations*. New York: Wiley, 1966.

KELLY, J. E. "A Reappraisal of Sociotechnical Systems Theory." *Human Relations*, 31, 1978, 1069–1099.

KIDDER, J. T. *The Soul of a New Machine*. Boston: Little, Brown, 1981.

KUHN, T. S. *The Structure of Scientific Revolutions*. 2nd ed. Chicago: University of Chicago Press, 1970. (Originally published 1962)

PACE, R. W., P. C. SMITH, & G. E. MILLS *Human Resource Development*. Englewood Cliffs, NJ: Prentice Hall, 1991.

PASCARELLA, P., & M. A. FROHMAN *The Purpose-Driven Organization*. San Francisco: Jossey-Bass, 1989.

PAVA, C. *Managing New Office Technology*. New York: Free Press, 1983.

PETERS, T. J., & R. H. WATERMAN *In Search of Excellence: Lessons from America's Best Run Companies*. New York: Harper & Row, 1982.

QUINN, R. E., & K. CAMERON *Paradox and Transformation: Toward a Framework of Change in Organization and Management*. Cambridge, MA: Ballinger, 1988.

TAYLOR, F. W. *The Principles of Scientific Management*. New York: Harper, 1911.

TAYLOR, J. C., & R. A. ASADORIAN "The Implementation of Excellence: Socio-Technical Management," *Industrial Management*, 27(4) 1985, 5–15.

TAYLOR, J. C., P. W. GUSTAVSON, & W. S. CARTER "Integrating the Social and Technical Systems of Organizations." In D. D. Davis, (ed.), *Managing Technological Innovation*. San Francisco: Jossey-Bass, 1986.

WALTON, R. E. "The Diffusion of New Work Structures: Explaining Why Success Didn't Take." *Organizational Dynamics*, 1975, 3(3), 2–22.

WEBER, M. *The Theory of Social and Economic Organization.* Translated by A. M. Henderson & T. Parsons. New York: Oxford University Press, 1947.

ZUBOFF, S. *In the Age of the Smart Machine: The Future of Work and Power.* New York: Basic Books, 1988.

Name Index

225

Subject Index